Panic
Persecutions

We are living through an intellectual crisis.
The woke ideology is over-whelming our cultural and political
institutions, as well as captivating many of the young minds in our
society. But, in these pages, you will find ordinary people standing
up for what is right. Our society needs individuals like these who
have the courage of conviction and commitment to liberty and
equality for all. Each of the essays enclosed provides a portrait and
defense of liberal values, not just in revisiting the arguments and
principles of a free society, but also in that these individuals are
making the arguments at risk of themselves being canceled, shamed
or punished in various ways. They are willing to pay the price to pass
the banner of freedom onto the next generation. These authors are
living, breathing examples of how to fight for Enlightenment values
and how to do it with dignity and civility.

– AYAAN HIRSI ALI

For those who feel that academia and
journalism are losing their minds, *Quillette*
has offered lungfuls of fresh air – reasoned,
nondogmatic, and often common-sense analyses
that have been banished from the mainstream
outlets. This timely collection showcases
some of the new voices it has discovered, while
spotlighting the repressive and regressive forces
that are imposing orthodoxies on intellectual life.

– STEVEN PINKER

First published in 2020 (hardcover)
This paperback edition 2021
by the Black Spring Press Group
Suite 333, 19-21 Crawford Street
London
United Kingdom

A Quillette Imprint
INTERNATIONAL EDITION

Cover and interior design by Edwin Smet

Set in DTL Fleischmann 11 / 16 pt

ISBN 978-1-913606-72-5

WWW.EYEWEARPUBLISHING.COM

Editorial note
For this edition, given the various English nations represented,
American spelling, punctuation and grammar was used.

Publisher's note
For a publisher, nothing can be of greater importance than the
freedom of all writers to write what they believe they need to express; and for all
publishers to be able to share those works publicly, within reasonable legal limits.
I may not agree with everything in this book, yet I am immensely proud
to have had a hand in publishing it.

Panics and Persecutions

20 Tales
of Excommunication
in the Digital Age

EDITED BY
Claire Lehmann
Colin Wright
Jamie Palmer
Jonathan Kay
Toby Young

Quillette

Table of Contents

Part I: The Mob Mentality

Plus ça change

One of the most famous works of art to emerge from the French Revolution is *The Tennis Court Oath*, Jacques-Louis David's pen-and-ink sketch of the June 20, 1789 meeting where more than 600 deputies of the Estates-General pledged their "unwavering resolution" to create a new constitution for France.

Five historical figures stand out from David's sketch. At the center is the man who'd administered the oath: astronomer, and future Paris mayor, Jean-Sylvain Bailly. To his right is Maximilien Robespierre, the austere teetotaler who would go on to briefly rule France as dictator. Seated before Bailly is the pamphleteer Abbé Emmanuel Joseph Sieyès. Off to Sieyès' left, striking an extravagant pose, is the comte de Mirabeau — who'd become a political lynchpin of the Revolution's short-lived constitutional period — and Antoine-Pierre-Joseph Marie Barnave, a member of the Revolution's ruling triumvirate at the time David created his sketch in 1791.

Within three years of taking their oath, all but one of these five men would be dead. Bailly was guillotined in late 1793. Barnave's head came off two weeks later. Robespierre lost his own the following summer, having already shot away half his jaw in an unsuccessful suicide attempt the day before. Mirabeau, who died of natural causes in 1791, was dug out of a crypt at the Panthéon by a revolutionary mob, and flung into an unmarked pit. Of the quintet, only Sieyès would survive to witness the counterrevolutionary period, having had the good sense to give up politics and lie low. When it came to what we now call "cancel culture," the Jacobins were world-class experts.

The ideological witch-hunts of our own era, whose victims take center stage in the *Quillette* essays reprinted in this volume, do not herald any kind of equivalent bloodbath. The French Revolution took place against a backdrop of apocalyptic war, famine, and devastating economic crises. Life was cheaper then, and it was possible for extremists to justify murder in the name of their beliefs. The victims of modern cancel culture may lose their jobs, their friends, and their reputations. But none will lose their head. Nevertheless, it is useful to look to the French Revolution, as well as similar periods of upheaval, as a means to help us understand today's radicalized cliques. While Twitter mobs certainly do not command the powers of life and death, their social and ideological dynamics carry unsettling historical overtones.

The problem we are experiencing now is not to be confused with literal *censorship* (except as that term may be applied loosely). Unlike Robespierre and his Committee of Public Safety, modern cancel culture enforcers typically do not rely on government edict. Instead, they pursue crowdsourced social-media campaigns aimed at shaming heretics and threatening their professional livelihoods. In this way, such mobs yoke progressive ideology to the inherently conservative social instincts that lead all of us to conform to expectations, and align our ideas with those of our neighbors. Even in the 1940s, George Orwell noted, "the sinister fact about literary censorship in England is that it is largely voluntary." Yes, you could publish unfashionable opinions, he noted, "but to do so was to make sure of being ignored or misrepresented by nearly the whole of the highbrow press. Both publicly and privately you were warned that it was 'not done.'" One suspects that every writer in this volume can relate in some way to these words.

At the time Orwell was writing *Animal Farm* and *Nineteen Eighty-Four,* more than a decade after *New York Times* reporter Walter Duranty spun Soviet lies about the Ukrainian Famine and Stalin's show trials, the bulk of the British intelligentsia was still scathing toward anyone within its ranks who criticized the USSR, or who satirized its leader. Inevitably, as Orwell predicted, these attitudes found their way into mainstream politics and popular media; and therein remained ensconced, at least in part, until the Soviet Union fell apart in 1991. Orwell focused on the intellectual cultism that infected the world of high arts and letters not only because this was the world he knew best, but also because these rarified domains lie upstream from education, media, party politics, and, ultimately, public opinion. That is something we ask readers to keep in mind as they read the essays that follow, many of which describe academic and artistic subcultures that may seem remote from the lives of ordinary people.

* * *

The radicalization of today's progressive left, like the countervailing transformation of the populist right, can't be described as "revolutionary," because it doesn't offer any real alternative to traditional politics. Look beyond the street protests, the vandalized statues, the cancelation campaigns, the exotic theorems of intersectional identity; and one finds that the actual political demands are either ludicrous ("abolish the police"), meaningless ("decolonize our cities"), or simply represent further extrapolations of established progressive policies, such as hiring quotas, affirmative action in education, and enforced equity-training sessions.

This helps explain why modern social justice proponents typically seem dour and artistically lifeless compared to their hippie grandparents: They dwell on the theme of oppression, but have no realistic theory about how to alleviate it. And since their power typically extends only to the representational aspects of life — the hashtags we are allowed to use, the books we are allowed to write, the clothes we are allowed to wear, the acceptable names for buildings and streets, the pronouns people must recite – these are the subject of their most passionately expressed grievances. Unlike the progressive counterculture of the 1960s, which encouraged sexual openness, flamboyant individualism, and euphoric cultural mixing, today's social justice crusades are built around joyless rites of self-interrogation, announced publicly but conducted inwardly.

As many have noted, these rituals bear an unsettling resemblance to ersatz religious ceremonies, complete with rites of devotion, penitence, excommunication, and even martyrdom. This is not a coincidence: Like the religions they displace, political cults offer adherents a totalizing theory of good and evil that conflates ideological correctness with moral worth. Robespierre himself made this connection explicit in his final months, presenting Parisians with an elaborate "Festival of the Supreme Being" (in which he of course presided as high priest). In a speech delivered during this period, he claimed the power to strike down the sinful, defending "terror" as a species of justice that is "prompt, severe and inflexible," and therefore "an emanation of virtue."

But as Orwell noted, political cults diverge from true religions in that their "doctrines are not only unchallengeable but also unstable." In 1789, a Frenchman could lose his head for denying the legitimacy of monarchism. In 1792, he could suffer the same fate for asserting the opposite. By 1793 and 1794, even the slightest deviation from republican orthodoxy drew furious denunciation by one-time friends and colleagues, which in turn generated a climate of paranoia that destroyed longstanding friendships, and empowered the most sociopathic revolutionary elements. This same vicious, dehumanizing dynamic runs through the stories in this book.

One reason the French Revolution comes up often in any discussion of broad political and ideological trends is that it set the template not only for modern classical liberalism, but also for its *rejection*. In its liberal form, the Revolution peaked with the Constitution of 1791, which created a democratic constitutional monarchy. But following the execution of Louis XVI, a new constitution was drafted, one whose provisions were permanently suspended amidst the Reign of Terror. As with communists, religious fundamentalists, Cold War McCarthyites, and autocratic populists, the architects of this terror argued that the Republican project was too urgent to be constrained by the need for due process, free speech, the right of assembly, or other civil liberties. It's a theme one often detects among today's most ardent progressives, who view themselves as vanguard elements in a Manichean battle against racism and fascism. Even the color-blind ideals that informed the Civil Rights revolution of the 1960s – their version of the Constitution of 1791 – is dismissed as a smokescreen for conservative enemies.

Another lesson of the French Revolution is that the same communications technologies that permit political dissent and intellectual pluralism also can be co-opted by tyrants and mobs. The seeds of the revolution were planted in the arcades of the Palais-Royal, then under the control of the liberal-minded Louis Philippe II, Duke of Orléans. It was a sort of proto-Reddit in bricks and mortar, an anything-goes zone where rabblerousers could distribute scandalous anti-royalist pamphlets and newspapers, or harangue one another in cafés with political speeches. And it was this plucky ethos that guided the revolution in its early years, and which inspired the Jacobin Club to throw open its doors to the public, so that anyone could walk in and cheer or jeer at speakers. Over time, however, the speakers began reacting to the mob, instead of vice versa. And newspapers published fatwas against any politician deemed guilty of *modérantisme*.

We often say that *Quillette* is a place where "free speech lives." But we also understand that laws and policies that nominally protect free speech don't guarantee that people can say what they think, or that the marketplace of ideas will remain functional. The current wave of crowdsourced dissent-suppression campaigns provides just one of many historical examples that show how free speech depends as much on a hospitable intellectual culture as on legal codes. And as the essays collected here will attest, education and intellect do not, on their own, protect against ideological autocracy. Just the opposite: Habituated to the respect and deference of *hoi polloi*, the little Robespierres who control university faculties and social-media cliques tend to include some of the most educated members of our society. (*L'Incorruptible* himself, remember, was a scholarship student who derived his grandiose theories on human virtue from the cream of Enlightenment thinkers and the great orators of Ancient Rome.) It is not ignorance that fuels their inquisitions, but hubris and an appetite for power.

One of the problems we face is that intellectual liberty has no dependable constituency, since those who are most in need of it tend to be those who have the least power. Free speech and due process are now often described as conservative values. But not so long ago, they were proudly claimed under the liberal banner. As anyone who remembers the rise of the religious right in the 1980s can attest, the reins of cultural power get tossed back and forth in cyclical fashion. And only by internalizing history's lessons can partisans on each side remain grounded in principles that transcend their own fleeting, parochial self-interest.

* * *

Let us end this introductory text with one particularly important lesson. In 1762, three decades before the French Revolution, a 28-year-old Frenchman named Jean Calas hanged himself in the Toulouse home of his 68-year-old father, a local Protestant merchant. As a subsequent national investigation showed, the death was an obvious act of suicide, likely brought on by gambling debts and professional frustrations. But a rumor went around Toulouse that, shortly before he died, the son had announced his intention to convert to Catholicism, and that the father had conspired with other family members – and even with a faithful Catholic servant who'd raised the boy from infancy – to murder the son in a fit of Protestant fury.

It was a completely preposterous theory. Yet the chief magistrate of Toulouse, seeking to ingratiate himself with the mob, put the whole Calas family in chains, including two daughters, the servant, and a friend visiting from Bordeaux. Jean Calas himself, meanwhile, was hailed as a Catholic martyr, and buried in a local church while local friars put on a lurid theatrical portrayal of his supposed last days, complete with a skeleton holding the pen with which he was supposed to have renounced his Protestant faith.

Eventually, the father was executed and the rest of the family was cast into disgrace and poverty. In his 1763 *Treatise on Tolerance*, wherein the tragedy of the Calas family serves as a centerpiece, Voltaire explained that it was only when the mother "was alone in the world, without bread, without hope," that "certain persons, having soberly examined all the details of this horrible affair, were so struck by it that they urged Madame Calas to emerge from her solitude, go boldly to the feet of the throne, and ask for justice." Amazingly, the widow's case was taken up with great vigor by the Council of State, which (urged on by Voltaire himself) "unanimously ordered the *parlement* of Toulouse to transmit to them the whole account of its proceedings." In time, Louis XV had the sentence against Calas annulled, fired Toulouse's chief magistrate, and paid the family 36,000 livres.

The Calas scandal became a powerful cautionary tale of show-trial justice gone amok. Robespierre (a toddler when Calas hanged himself) and every other member of the Committee of Public Safety would have known about it. Yet such precedents did not detain them as they implemented the Law of 22 Prairial, which prescribed summary execution for anyone caught "impairing the purity and energy of the revolutionary government." Nor, a century later, did Robespierre's own example protect Alfred Dreyfus from unjust imprisonment on false charges of treason. As in many other spheres of human behavior, lessons on mob justice learned by one generation must be relearned, the hard way, by the next.

As journalists, we find that the best way to explore such lessons is by telling the stories of men and women who've been branded, in one way or another, as heretics. In this volume, you will find 20 such reports, all of which originally were published online by *Quillette* between 2018 and 2020. In some cases, the authors have supplied short postscripts. But aside from standardizing the texts to American spelling (the majority of writers being from that side of the Atlantic), they are reproduced here largely unchanged.

Whether or not readers embrace the substance of the heresies described in the essays that follow, we hope their narratives demonstrate why we should not permit ideologues to decide which viewpoints may or may not be expressed. Whether on the hunt for Catholics, Protestants or Jews, royalists or republicans, capitalists or communists, all mobs present themselves as virtue's servants. Let us now hear from victims of that insidious conceit.

By *Quillette* Editorial Staff – September 2020

A Mania for All Seasons
By Samuel McGee-Hall

There are many people for whom hate and rage pay a higher dividend of immediate satisfaction than love. Congenitally aggressive, they soon become adrenalin addicts, deliberately indulging their ugliest passions for the sake of the 'kick'...Knowing that one self-assertion always ends by evoking other and hostile self-assertions, they sedulously cultivate their truculence...Adrenalin addiction is rationalized as Righteous Indignation and finally, like the prophet Jonah, they are convinced, unshakably, that they do well to be angry.

These words first appeared in 1952, in the pages of Aldous Huxley's *The Devils of Loudun*. While many of Huxley's works are better known and more widely read, there may be no text, past or present, more relevant to our turbulent era than this account of a seventeenth-century witch trial.

Huxley composed this passage to shed light on the mind of a thoroughly unlikeable individual by the name and title of Father Urban Grandier, in particular. But he also offered it as a more general analysis of the mindset afflicting those who burned Grandier to death – with the approval of both the Catholic Church and the State of France – for being a sorcerer in 1634. In the context of the entire work, this passage was part of a close inspection of the susceptibility of humanity to moral panics, show trials, and mob justice across the ages.

For, although *The Devils of Loudun* is a book about particular persons at a particular time in a particular place and the atrocities they committed, it is more obviously an inquiry into the reality of demons and their inception. And on these questions, Huxley is emphatic, even to the point of indicting himself – they come from inside each of us:

Looking back and up, from our vantage point on the descending road of modern history, we now see that all the evils of religion can flourish without any belief in the supernatural, that convinced materialists are ready to worship their own jerrybuilt creations as though they were the Absolute, and that self-styled humanists will persecute their adversaries with all the zeal of Inquisitors... Such behavior-patterns antedate and outlive the beliefs which, at any given moment, seem to motivate them...In order to justify their behavior, they turn their theories into dogmas, their bylaws into First Principles, their political bosses into Gods and all those who disagree with them into incarnate devils... And when the current beliefs come, in their turn, to look silly, a new set will be invented, so that the immemorial madness may continue to wear its customary mask of legality, idealism, and true religion.

Huxley's dissection of a seventeenth-century social pandemonium, whipped up in an era of shifting sexual mores, is a timeless indictment of the latent monstrousness within all human beings. And it carries a particular relevance for our fevered political moment, replete with monomaniacal intersectionalists, proselytizers for utopian ethno-states, religious fanatics, Antifa vandals, paranoid anti-Semites, millenarian conspiracists, and virtually anyone else called upon by some Hegelian or Abrahamic doctrine to ceaselessly fusillade public discourse with slurs and bitter invective.

* * *

Assigned to the Diocese of Poitiers as the priest of Saint Croix in the town of Loudun, France in the 1630s, Father Urban Grandier was – by the standards of any age – an insufferable egomaniac and – by the standards of his own day (and, to an extent, our present time) – a sexual deviant and generally morally dissolute individual. Shortly after his arrival, Grandier abused his position of power and influence to flout his vows of celibacy and sleep with, and then discard, a series of widows. In addition, he impregnated a 16-year-old young woman (Phillipe Trincant) placed under his tutelage by his best friend in the town, the Public Prosecutor of Loudun. Discovering Phillipe was pregnant, Grandier dropped her without a qualm. Following the birth of Phillipe's child, she and her family were practically ruined in the eyes of their fellow citizens.

Fueling these cruelties was an infinite capacity on the part of the priest for haughtiness, rumor, and slander that extended well beyond his sexual proclivities. Grandier repeatedly contravened, defied, and openly insulted persons of influence throughout society for the pettiest of reasons. The most notable of these was the man that would soon run France, Cardinal Richelieu – an arrogant act of carelessness that likely sealed Grandier's fate at the stake years later. Huxley reports that Grandier entangled himself in quarrels in which swords were drawn against him as a result of his vicious remarks. On at least one occasion, he instigated a contest of the Dozens with the *lieutenant criminel* of Loudun, which escalated from slander and insult into a feud of such a pitch that the priest had to barricade himself inside the chapel of the city's castle to escape an armed mob. In the few brief years following his arrival in the town, it would hardly be an exaggeration to say, Grandier offended or wronged at least half of Loudun (and a third of the town was protestant, so they already disliked him as a point of sectarian principle), as well as a considerable portion of the Roman Catholic hierarchy in France.

Although there were repeated attempts to bring Grandier to justice for his transgressions and crimes – at least one of which involved a stay in prison – he generally managed to escape punishment. An exceedingly clever and eloquent (if not a precisely moral or forward thinking) man, the priest thereby was saved the trouble of learning anything that might help him mend his ways.

Then, in 1632, an infestation of demons at the Ursuline convent of Loudun – concentrated on the Sisters therein – was attributed to Grandier by the nuns and, subsequently, members of the Roman Catholic hierarchy. Spurred forward by their own hatred of Grandier, and supported by large portions of Loudun's populace wronged and ruined by the priest, within two years of the nuns' possession, Grandier was tortured and burned to death for the crime of sorcery.

During the period leading up to his execution, the town of Loudun was to be turned into a circus of the type that would be immediately recognizable to anyone familiar with today's 24-hour news cycles. As sensational stories of blasphemies, supernatural phenomena, and horrifying public exorcisms raced across Europe, these events created a lucrative, continent-wide tourist industry in the town. In the midst of this grim side-show, it is also a matter of record (principally from the journals of clergy, citizens, and visitors) that several of the nuns, townspeople, and priests bore false witness, later retracted those falsehoods, and altogether exploited these young women to fill the coffers of the town, the Church, and the pockets of a few enterprising individuals selling baubles and false relics while women were being tortured and humiliated before their eyes. Some of the nuns even attempted suicide to assuage the guilt they carried for their lies, until they were prevented by their ecclesiastical superiors and encouraged to redouble their fabrications.

* * *

Throughout *The Devils of Loudun*, Huxley frames the mayhem in the Christian terms with which those in seventeenth-century Europe were equipped to understand it. To provide further insight, he applied the scientific findings and theories of the 1950s (some of which have since been discredited) and analyzed the psychology of the "possessed" and Grandier through the rather unscientific lens of Christian and Eastern mysticism. He also applied theories of parapsychology that most, in our present era, would categorize as outright quackery. It is through this combination of early seventeenth- and mid-twentieth-century intellectual paradigms that he dissects the anatomy of a state-approved murder, and the epidemic of lunacy that instigated it. Despite some of his unconventional methods, his observations are, on the whole, piercing:

> At any given time and place certain thoughts are completely unthinkable. But this radical unthinkableness of certain thoughts is not paralleled by any radical unfeelableness of certain emotions, or any radical undoableness of actions inspired by such emotions. Anything can at all times be felt and acted upon, albeit sometimes with great difficulty and in the teeth of general disapproval. But though individuals can always feel and do whatever their temperament and constitution permit them to feel and do, they cannot think about the experiences except within the frame of reference which, at that particular time and place, has come to seem self-evident...In 1592 sexual behavior was evidently very similar to what it is today. The change has only been in thoughts about that behavior. In early modern times the thoughts of a Havelock Ellis or a Krafft-Ebing would have been unthinkable. But the emotions and actions described by these modern sexologists were just as feelable and doable in an intellectual context of hellfire as they are in the secularist societies of our own time.

Focusing on the shifting sexual mores of the age – the move from Medieval to Renaissance sexual attitudes (what Huxley refers to as the 'gray dawn of respectability') – as well as the horrific backdrop of the 30 Years War and the paradigm-shattering onset of systematic scientific inquiry into virtually every corner of human life, Huxley argues that this tumultuous era generated not only technological and epistemological upheavals, but also a chaotic reconfiguration of sexual attitudes and practices.

Huxley frames Grandier as something of a cad in a cassock. He was a man who, in earlier times, would likely have never been called to account, let alone punished, for his indiscretions and abuses – an egomaniac without the perspicacity to notice he had strolled into a new era where the sanction of even the most powerful institution on earth wouldn't be enough to save him from the unprecedented social upheavals then occurring. To the nuns, Huxley attributes a form of sexual obsession with (and, given that he could get away with that for which the Sisters would be utterly destroyed, potentially sexual resentment *towards*) Grandier. Either the nuns resented Grandier's amoral promiscuity, or they wished that he would seduce them and were furious when he did not. When an exploitive narcissist like Grandier collided with the sexual frustration and panic of women delivered unwillingly into cloistered celibacy by families unable to pay medieval dowries, it was inevitable that something awful would happen.

It was not, however, inevitable (let alone just) that a man innocent of the ancient charge of sorcery in the service of Satan would be burned to death even after he confessed (under torture) to his previous, and very real, transgressions, and practically begged to be killed for what he *had* done. Nor was it inevitable that a group of women, who were almost certainly mentally disturbed to one degree or another, would be manipulated by prominent persons in the town and various members of the Roman Catholic hierarchy in order to destroy a man who had previously given them so much trouble.

And yet, even though there were people who knew the truth of what was being done to Grandier — some of them powerful enough to prevent his horrible fate — that is precisely what happened.

* * *

In our present age, the ugly truths provided by Huxley seem prescient. To read this book is to understand that what the world (and the western world, in particular) is currently experiencing is nothing new. With regard to the more wicked and wretched aspects of human psychology across the ages, the observations and arguments presented in *The Devils of Loudun* cut clear to the bone. Huxley's analysis of human sexuality will be called sexist — and in certain instances, it is — and yet the case he makes for a sexual panic is convincing.

Others will find his arguments about the human propensity for mob justice insulting on the grounds that we, unlike our forebears, know better. But the priesthood and townspeople of Loudun almost certainly felt the same condescending superiority over those who preceded *them*, and so on, down the line into the relative fog of antiquity and the absolute fog of prehistory.

Neither of these criticisms, however, changes the predicament in which society presently finds itself. Sexual abuse; sexual panic; character assassination; the interminable search for evil in every corner of human interaction; the fear to disagree openly or to defend ideas we find noble and people we know are being treated unjustly; the rejection of logic in favor of presupposition; us-versus-them thinking as the source of personal and group identity; the specter of mob justice — all of these are, Huxley argues, abiding human attitudes and actions which produce such a frenzied assault on procedural and proportional justice that they undermine the very foundations of our shared society.

It is fitting, therefore, to allow Huxley the final word on our perennial mania — a diagnosis of our terrified moment:

> The effects which follow too constant and intense a concentration upon evil are always disastrous. Those who crusade, not for God

in themselves, but against the devil in others, never succeed in making the world better, but leave it either as it was, or sometimes even perceptibly worse than it was, before the crusade began. By thinking primarily of evil, we tend, however excellent our intentions, to create occasions for evil to manifest itself...Today it is everywhere self-evident that we are on the side of Light, they on the side of Darkness. And being on the side of Darkness, they deserve to be punished and must be liquidated (since our divinity justifies everything) by the most fiendish means at our disposal... And on a very small stage, this precisely was what the exorcists were doing at Loudun. By idolatrously identifying God with the political interests of their sect, by concentrating their thoughts and their efforts on the powers of evil, they were doing their best to guarantee the triumph (local, fortunately, and temporary) of that Satan, against whom they were supposed to be fighting.

When Censorship Is Crowdsourced

By Jonathan Kay

On the op-ed page of *The New York Times*, former Central Intelligence Agency general counsel Jeffrey Smith recently argued that Donald Trump's decision to revoke the security clearance of former CIA director John Brennan "violated Mr. Brennan's First Amendment right to speak freely." It's an intriguing thesis. And, being a former lawyer who once wrote long law school essays about constitutional freedoms, I read it with keen interest.

But I also felt a twinge of nostalgia as I parsed Smith's lawyerly arguments. Notwithstanding the nature of Mr. Trump's treatment of Mr. Brennan, the gravest threats to free speech in democratic countries now have little to do with government action (which is what Constitutions serve to restrain). And with few exceptions, public officials now sit as bystanders to the fight over who can say what.

Last month, Facebook, Apple and Google deleted gigabytes of video, audio, and text content from Alex Jones' *Infowars* web site – part of a larger speech-pruning process that is applied every day to numerous (less prominent) extremists who, like Jones, combine conspiracism and hatemongering. Twitter, on the other hand, allowed Jones' *Infowars* and personal accounts to remain active – but then abruptly changed course in early September. Why? Who knows. All of these online services make users sign on to terms-of-service agreements that prohibit abusive speech and the advocacy of violence. But the lines are blurry, and there's lots of wriggle room. Even if there weren't, it wouldn't matter anyway, since these are private companies that can pretty much ban anyone they want, so long as they're willing to accept the blowback from remaining users. These companies aren't making *legal* decisions in this sphere. They're effectively taking political positions on what is and isn't beyond the bounds of mainstream discourse.

And since social media is the way we all communicate with one another every day, their power over information flows has become enormous. Taken together, Facebook's Mark Zuckerberg, Twitter's Jack Dorsey, Reddit's Alexis Ohanian, and Google's founding duo of Larry Page and Sergey Brin have far more impact on what we see and hear than any government.

If you are, like me, a middle-aged person who has been concerned about protecting free speech since your college days, these developments will have a profoundly disorienting effect. When I was a university student in the early 1990s, it always was assumed that the primary threat to free speech was government –

especially government in the Big Brother form that George Orwell had taught us to expect and fear.

This model of censorship and counter-censorship persisted into this century. In the years after 9/11, for instance, conservatives in my own country, Canada, became consumed with the question of what could and could not be said about militant Islam under Canadian human-rights codes. In the process, we made folk heroes out of Ezra Levant and Mark Steyn, who were willing to thumb their noses at provincial bureaucrats whose diktats truly did seem aimed at censoring right-wing ideology.

Some of these battles are still being fought in obscure tribunal boardrooms. But for the most part, they're yesterday's drama. Levant and Steyn both published their anti-Islamist manifestos in national print magazines. While one of those magazines still exists, albeit in reduced form, the real to and fro of ideological debate now takes place on borderless electronic fora (such as *Quillette*) whose content is, within some limits, free of any government oversight. Compared to the situation a decade ago, the source of censorship in our lives has been massively decentralized.

In many creative spheres, in fact, censorship hasn't just been decentralized. It's been *crowdsourced*. Which is to say: The very writers, publishers, poets, musicians, comedians, media producers, and artists who once worried about being muzzled by the government are now self-organizing on social media (Twitter, especially) to censor each other. In its mechanics, this phenomenon is so completely alien to top-down Big Brother-style censorship that it often doesn't feel like censorship at all, but more like a self-directed inquisition or Chinese communist struggle session. But the overall effect of preventing the propagation of stigmatized ideas is achieved all the same.

Consider, for instance, the current preoccupation with cultural appropriation – a doctrine that, in my country, now serves to dictate what subjects Canada's novelists and poets are permitted to take on in their work. In some cases, the process by which individual artists assess whether they are or aren't allowed to tell a particular story truly does resemble the bureaucratic application process for a government program – as I showed in my *Quillette* reporting on the bizarre saga of novelist Angie Abdou, who was repeatedly forced to submit her novel to various indigenous authorities before publication (and even then was hounded and attacked because she had dared to voice a young First Nations character). But it's important to remember that no *actual* government censor had any involvement in Abdou's case. The effort to censor her was entirely crowdsourced among other members of the literary community.

Or, to take a fresh example, take the case of Shannon Webb-Campbell, a young Canadian author who recently was slated to release a collection of poetry through a small Toronto-based publisher called

Book*hug. (The publisher's original name was Book-thug, but this was changed in 2017 amid complaints that "thug" was racist — which should tell you all you need to know about the politics of both Book*hug and the art-house Canadian literary community within which it operates.) Indeed, the book already had been printed and readied for shipment when Book*hug abruptly decided to yank the volume from its catalog, pulp all physical copies, and delete Webb-Campbell's page from its site (visitors received a 404 error code). They also published an effusive apology on their main web page, declaring that the book was "causing pain and trauma to members of indigenous communities."

The reason for this, Book*hug went on to disclose, was that Webb-Campbell — who herself is partly indigenous — had written about the death of another indigenous person in a way that "does not follow Indigenous protocol with regard to these matters." The nature of these "protocols" was not explained.

The same day, Webb-Campbell published a lengthy confession on her Facebook page, in which she admitted to various thought crimes, especially her failure to secure permission from family members before presuming to describe the death of an indigenous woman. She also pleaded for mercy on the basis that "as a mixed Mi'kmaq-settler writer, who did not grow up within my culture due to colonialism and the ripple effects of intergenerational trauma, I was unaware around the protocol of material of this nature. I feel very ashamed by my lack of knowledge." Webb-Campbell also pledged to deposit the poem into a sort of memory hole, promising that it would never again be spoken aloud by her own lips.

I am not a poet, nor indigenous, nor a member of the broader Canadian literati. I had never before heard of Webb-Campbell, nor Book*hug. Yet I found myself incensed on Webb-Campbell's behalf. In what world do poets have to ask *permission* to create verse about others? Did Homer run his Patroclus death scene past descendants of Menoetius and Philomela?

Yet, amazingly, not a single prominent member of the Canadian literati was willing to publicly condemn this public shaming of Webb-Campbell by her own publisher. And to the extent the media covered her de-platforming, it was airily portrayed as a teachable moment that showed how artists all needed to be more sensitive about what they wrote. The CBC, in particular, uncritically included the preposterous accusation that "publications like Webb-Campbell's contribute to a narrative that normalizes violence against indigenous women and girls."

Nor, as far as I can determine, did a single Can-Lit heavyweight utter a public complaint when Webb-Campbell was abruptly bounced from April's Ottawa Writers Festival. At that event, Webb-Campbell had been scheduled to share the stage with the former president of a prominent NGO that purports to support the right to free expression. When

I found myself seated beside this august figure at a Toronto dinner party in the days before the festival, I asked whether he intended to raise his voice against Webb-Campbell's treatment. His response was that he planned to run this thorny issue past an indigenous woman he knew — a wise old soul, by his description, who would tell him "exactly what to do" (which, as things apparently turned out, was nothing). Days later, when I made myself a pest by tweeting directly at the literary festival about all of this, the reply came: "Baffled by your need to speak for those who can and do speak so well for themselves — especially those who have not asked for your help or advice. If [Webb-Campbell] said she was silenced or censored, we would have had [her] here even without the book."

While I rarely like to concede defeat in a Twitter smackdown, I had to admit that this festival's social-media people had me dead to rights — for it's absolutely true that Webb-Campbell wasn't censored in any formal sense. None of the events I am describing here involve the government. Nor was Webb-Campbell muzzled in any way by Book*hug, which presumably would have been only too happy to have her publish her book elsewhere. Webb-Campbell could have put the controversial poem on Facebook, or tweeted it out line by line. But she did none of this. Instead, she swallowed her pride, signed the confession that had been placed in front of her, and prayed that she would be readmitted into CanLit's good graces — which, in fact, now seems to be happening, following an elaborate, months-long display of performative contrition on Webb-Campbell's part.

One aspect of *Nineteen Eighty-Four* that does still ring true in the current age of crowdsourced censorship is the reverse classism at work. In Orwell's Oceania, the intellectual class is scrutinized relentlessly for the slightest deviation in thought or speech, while "proles" are free to wallow in astrology, smut and sentimental storytelling:

> There was even a whole sub-section – Pornosec, it was called in Newspeak – engaged in producing the lowest kind of pornography, which was sent out in sealed packets and which no Party member, other than those who worked on it, was permitted to look at.

The same principle applies in broad form today. Canadian tabloids publish material every day that would be deemed offensive to Ottawa Writers Festival types. But with rare exceptions, it gets a pass, because it is seen, in effect, as a sort of ideological Pornosec. The world of Canadian poetry, on the other hand, is a tiny rarefied world run by, and for, a few hundred CanLit party members – all relentlessly scrutinizing one another for ideological heresies through the panopticon of social media. In this environment, Webb-Campbell's status as a reliably leftist, thoroughly woke poet who proclaimed her guiding light to be "decolonial poetics" was not a mark in her favor. Just the opposite: It confirmed her status as a full Party member, thereby making her subject to all applicable ideological strictures. When the scarlet letter is sewn upon such a specimen by one publisher within the tiny and incestuous world of Canadian poetry, it is sewn upon her by all. And while it was once imagined that artists and writers had a special duty to speak out against censorship, dogma, and speech codes, they are now conditioned to believe that their highest duty is toward avoiding offense and "staying in their lane."

This, in capsule form, is how crowdsourced censorship works in the literary field. And analogous stories could be told about academia and other creative métiers. It is up to the government to maintain a free marketplace of ideas. But freedom from government censorship doesn't mean much when the stall-owners in the marketplace of ideas organize their own ideological protection rackets to drive one of their own out of business. Venerable groups that once led the fight for free speech and freedom of conscience, such as PEN and the ACLU, seem completely unequipped to deal with the new threats: Their entire organizational culture always has been directed at pushing back against government monoliths, not decentralized mob subcultures.

But the fact that government has no *direct* role in this new kind of censorship does not mean that public policy can't be part of the solution. For while it's true that government isn't directly engineering these newly emergent forms of crowdsourced speech suppression, the public-funding model on which these subcultures rely can indirectly encourage them.

The reason Book*hug can pulp Shannon Webb-Campbell's book without worrying much about lost readers or earned revenue is that, to a rough order of magnitude, they don't have any readers or earned revenue. Like most small, high-concept book publishers in Canada, Book*hug is overwhelmingly dependent on subsidies, which are what allow it to publish obscure manifestoes and poetry volumes that, outside of copies assigned to review, libraries, friends, and family, might be expected to sell a few hundred copies.

Or fewer. I recently consulted an online index that tracks Canadian book sales. For the latest Book*hug releases, the median number of books sold, per title, seems to be about 60. The tracking service does not claim to capture all book sales, estimating its accuracy at about 85%. (Direct sales at book-launch events, for instance, may escape capture in the data.) So, let us be generous and assume that the median book sells 100 copies, or even double that. It doesn't matter: In commercial terms, this is a non-entity. Which means there really is little or no financial penalty to be suffered if Book*hug publishes, or doesn't publish, Shannon Webb-Campbell instead of some other author. Everyone in this heavily subsidized subculture is playing with house money, as are the niche literary journals run by charitable entities (including one where I briefly served as editor). And the real asset to be husbanded in all these places isn't the affection of readers — since there aren't any — but rather the editors' collective reputation for ideological purity among peers, donors, and Twitter followers.

By way of counterexample: It's notable that when the CanLiterati attacked novelist Joseph Boyden after he was accused of falsely inflating his indigenous bona fides, his publisher, Penguin Random House Canada, stuck by him — perhaps because he is a famous author whose books are actually bought and read. But even at these large publishing houses, where titles are picked to sell in stores instead of to pose with at book launches, the inquisition has its agents. One editor, for instance, told me he'd love to recruit famed novelist Steven Galloway, following the release of information showing that he'd been railroaded on false rape claims at the University of British Columbia. But doing so, he explained, was impossible, at least for now, because he'd catch hell for it on social media. What matters in a witch hunt isn't whether you believe someone is a witch — it's whether your colleagues do (or, at least, pretend to).

None of this is entirely new, of course. There have been other periods in which writers and artists have crowdsourced their own censorship. This included the Red Scare in the United States; and the interwar period in Europe, when Orwell's peers were expected to line up behind the socialist (and then communist) dogmas of the period. Putting aside the crushing effect on morale and social relationships among writers, Orwell noted, this also served to turn an uncountable number of writers into babbling propagandists.

"Few if any Russian novels that it is possible to take seriously have been translated for about fifteen years," Orwell wrote in *The Prevention of Literature*:

> In western Europe and America, large sections of the literary intelligentsia have either passed through the Communist Party or have been warmly sympathetic to it, but this whole leftward movement has produced extraordinarily few books worth reading. Orthodox Catholicism, again, seems to have a crushing effect upon certain literary forms, especially the novel. During a period of three hundred years, how many people have been at once good novelists and good Catholics? The fact is that certain themes cannot be celebrated in words, and tyranny is one of them. No one ever wrote a good book in praise of the Inquisition.

As I have noted before, these lines have aged unusually well. Poetry that required someone else's permission to write isn't poetry worth reading. And more and more, the crowdsourced censorship I see in the creative fields is turning writers, artists, and academics into glassy-eyed automatons. They are perfectly skilled at writing land acknowledgments, speaking the correct pronouns, and retweeting the right hashtags, but increasingly useless at everything else. In another age, these people might have blamed the government for this. Today, on the other hand, they can only blame themselves.

The Public-Humiliation Diet
By Toby Young

Reading about film director James Gunn's defenestration by Disney for having tweeted some off-color jokes 10 years ago, I was reminded of my own ordeal at the beginning of 2018. I'm British, not American, a conservative rather than a liberal, and I didn't have as far to fall as Gunn. I'm a journalist who helped set up one of England's first charter schools, which we call "free schools," and I've sat on the board of various not-for-profits, but I'm not the co-creator of *Guardians of the Galaxy*. In some respects, though, my reversal was even more brutal than Gunn's because I have spent a large part of the past 10 years doing voluntary work intended to help disadvantaged children. It is one thing to lose a high-paying job because of your "offensive attitudes," but to be denied further opportunities to do good hits you deep down in your soul. At least Gunn can now engage in charity work to try and redeem himself, as others in his situation have done. I had to give up all the charity work I was doing as a result of the scandal. In the eyes of my critics, I am beyond redemption.

My trial-by-media began shortly after midnight on January 1, when I started trending on Twitter. The cause was a piece about me in the *Guardian* news-paper, which had just gone live. The headline read: "Toby Young to Help Lead Government's New Universities Regulator." That was a bit misleading. I was one of 15 non-executive directors who'd been appointed to the board of the Office for Students, a new higher-education regulator, not one of its leaders. The reason was because of the four schools I've co-founded, and because I'm one of a handful of conservatives involved in public education. Liberals outnumber conservatives on nearly all public bodies in Britain, and the Office for Students is no exception. Of the 15 non-executive directors announced on January 1, only three were identifiable as right-of-center, myself included. The chair, Sir Michael Barber, is the former head of research for a left-wing teaching union and spent eight years working for Tony Blair in Downing Street.

But I'm also a journalist, and in the course of my 30-year career, I've written some pretty sophomoric pieces, many of them for "lad mags." I spent 48 hours in the Welsh mountains simulating the selection course for the Special Air Service, Britain's elite special forces unit. I went undercover as a patient at a penis-enlargement clinic in London. I even got a professional hair-and-make-up team to transform me into a woman, and then embarked on a tour of New York's gay bars to try and pick up a lipstick lesbian. I wrote a best-selling memoir about these and other misadventures in journalism called *How to Lose Friends & Alienate People* that was turned into a Hollywood movie starring Simon Pegg. In other words, not your typical appointee to the board of a public regulator.

I've also, like James Gunn, made some stupid jokes on social media many moons ago that I wish I could take back. But they're out there, along with everything else I've ever written, and it doesn't take long to find them. The reason I was trending on Twitter is because literally thousands of people were Googling me and coming up with reasons why I wasn't a fit person to be on this board.

I thought the row would blow over within 24 hours, but what began as a Twitter storm turned into a major story (it was a slow news week). Nine days later, when I announced my resignation from the Office for Students, I was leading the BBC news.

How did that happen? Well, it didn't help that I'm pro-Brexit and was a prominent campaigner for the Leave side in the referendum over Britain's membership in the European Union. Many distinguished academics thought that alone was enough to disqualify me from regulating Britain's universities. The British professoriate is passionately pro-EU and believes anyone who doesn't share their view is a racist bigot.

But the main reason I became such a lightning rod is because I had been appointed by the Prime Minister. If it could be shown that I was an unsuitable person to sit on this board, that would embarrass Theresa

May. And boy, did they go at it. Nine days later, I had been tarred with all the vices of a privileged white male – tarred and feathered.

The first wave of attacks took the form of dredging up articles I'd written in the past and mining them for evidence that I held unpalatable views. For instance, someone on Twitter found a 17-year-old piece I'd written for the *Spectator*, where I'm an associate editor, headlined: "Confessions of a Porn Addict."

Notwithstanding the headline, it was actually a fairly serious article defending the British Board of Film Classification's increasingly liberal attitude toward pornography, and pointing out that sexual violence is more prevalent in countries with draconian anti-pornography laws – such as Iran, Saudi Arabia, and Indonesia – than in Holland, Denmark, and Sweden.

In support of the argument that porn doesn't deprave and corrupt, I referenced the poet Philip Larkin's fondness for bizarre erotica, and cited an incident he relayed in a letter to the novelist Kingsley Amis. The most celebrated English poet of the postwar period was loitering outside a sex shop in London's red-light district, too embarrassed to go in, when suddenly the owner stepped outside.

"Was it bondage, Sir?" he politely inquired.

As a matter of fact, it was.

Unfortunately, in the course of relaying this anecdote, I described Larkin as a "fellow porn addict."

Hence the headline at the top of the piece.

It was the sub-editor's idea of a joke – and I thought it was funny, too, until the article was cited as evidence that I wasn't a fit and proper person to serve on a public regulator. It was a good illustration of Kingsley Amis's rule about self-deprecating remarks: "Memo to writers and others: Never make a joke against yourself that some little bastard can turn into a piece of shit and send your way."

A couple of hours after it surfaced on Twitter, the London *Evening Standard* ran a piece headlined: "New Pressure on Theresa May to Sack 'Porn Addict' Toby Young from Watchdog Role."

That was followed up by the *Times* of London the next day: "'Porn addict' Toby Young Fights to Keep Role as Student Watchdog." The story began: "Fresh pressure to remove Toby Young from a new universities watchdog was heaped on Theresa May yesterday when it was revealed he has admitted to being a porn 'addict.'"

Note the use of the word "revealed," as if this unsavory fact had just come to light, rather than been dug up by some online metal-detectorist frantically searching for anything I'd written that could be deemed "offensive." One of the few people to come to my defense was Fraser Nelson, the editor of the *Spectator*, who marveled at the prosecutorial zeal of my enemies: "At one stage, the top 10 articles in our online archive (going back to 1828) were all Toby Young's, as his army of detractors were hard at work."

It goes without saying that no one is actually offended by any of this material, or at least very few people. After all, it would be a bit odd if people spent hours trawling the Internet in the hope of finding opinions or jokes that genuinely upset them – and then broadcast them far and wide in the hope of upsetting lots of other people, too. Rather, they're looking for stuff they can pretend to be shocked by, Captain Renault style.

When Fraser told me about the search activity, I joked that at least a new generation of readers was discovering my work. But, of course, these offense archaeologists are about the least sympathetic readers an author could have. They're just looking for sentences and phrases they can take out of context to cast you in a bad light. The same technique has been used to shame Kevin Williamson, Bari Weiss, Daniella Greenbaum, Sam Harris, Bret Weinstein, Dave Rubin, Jason Riley, Heather Mac Donald, Jordan Peterson, Charles Murray, and countless others. It's cherry-picking – or rather, cherry bomb-picking. As Ben Shapiro, another victim of this tactic, wrote recently: "It's not that these people are hated because they've said terrible things. It's that they're hated, so the hard-Left tries to dig up supposedly terrible things they've said."

The term "offense archaeologists" isn't mine, by the way. It belongs to Freddie deBoer, the essayist and blogger who wrote a brilliant piece about the toxic effect that this climate of intolerance is having on public discourse. "That's what liberalism is, now – the search for baddies doing bad things, like little offense archaeologists," he wrote. (I would link to it, but he later deleted it, presumably because some Witchfinder General sniffed it out and started preparing the ducking stool.)

The most serious of the charges against me is that I'm a "eugenicist." That claim was based on an article I'd written for an Australian magazine in which I discussed the possibility that in the future a couple might be able to fertilize a range of embryos in vitro and, after analyzing their DNA, choose to implant the one likely to be the most intelligent. If that ever does become possible, the first people to take advantage of it will be the rich so they can give their children an even bigger head start. In other words, it will make the problem of growing inequality and flat-lining social mobility across the industrialized world even worse.

My solution, as set out in the article, was that this technology, if it comes on stream, should be banned for everyone except the very poor. I wasn't proposing sterilization or some fiendish form of genetic engineering. Just a type of IVF that would be available for free to the least well off, should they wish to take advantage of it. Not mandatory, just an option.

I called this "progressive eugenics," which in retrospect was clearly a mistake. It was more like the opposite of eugenics – free IVF for the poor – but few people bothered to read the piece. The fact that I'd used the E-word was enough to damn me.

That was exhibit A in the case for the prosecution.

Exhibit B was my attendance at an academic conference at University College London (UCL) in 2017, at which some of the speakers had a history of putting forward contested theories about the genetic basis of intelligence. My reason for going was because I had been asked – as a journalist who has written about genetics – to give a lecture by the International Society of Intelligence Researchers at the University of Montreal later in the year, and I was planning to talk about the risks of venturing into the nature-nurture debate, particularly if your views run afoul of blank-slate orthodoxy. I thought the UCL conference, which was invitation-only, would provide me with some anecdotal material that I could use in Montreal – and it did. I referred to the clandestine gathering in my lecture, comparing these renegade academics to the Czech dissidents who used to meet in Václav Havel's flat in Prague in the 1970s.

So, because I discussed a form of embryo selection in an Australian magazine, and because I attended this conference at UCL, I was the *Spectator*'s answer to Josef Mengele. It doesn't matter that my father-in-law is Jewish, and so under the Nuremberg Laws my children would have been murdered because they have a Jewish grandparent. In the eyes of my critics, I was a Nazi.

According to Green Member of Parliament Caroline Lucas, my "horrific views on eugenics" rendered me "unfit for public office." The left-wing journalist Polly Toynbee wrote a column in the *Guardian* headlined: "With His Views on Eugenics, Why Does Toby Young Still Have a Job in Education?" The Labour politician Dawn Butler, the shadow minister for women and equalities, accused me on *Question Time*, Britain's flagship current affairs program, of "talking about eugenics and weeding out disabled people."

She just made that up, by the way. I have never talked about "weeding out disabled people." I found that particularly distressing because I have a disabled brother and I am a patron of the residential-care home he lives in. I hope he wasn't watching *Question Time* that night.

That's one of the worst aspects of seeing your name dragged through the mud — the fear that people you know and care about are going to believe some of the terrible things people are saying about you, and the feeling that there's nothing you can do about it. You can get out there and defend yourself, of course, but once the calumnies have gathered momentum it's hard to stop them metastasizing. To paraphrase a remark that is often attributed to Mark Twain: A piece of fake news gets all the way round the world and back again, and starts trending on social media, before the truth has put its boots on. (In fact, a researcher at

MIT recently published a paper in the journal *Science* showing that the truth takes six times longer, on average, than a lie to be seen by 1,500 people on Twitter.)

Another example: An essay I wrote in 1988 about the English class system, which included some unflattering descriptions of socially awkward boys at Oxford, was dredged up as evidence that I was opposed to poor kids going to university. A former BBC journalist and self-professed Marxist accused me on Twitter of despising "working class kids who try to make good through education."

Hard to know where to start with that one. As an Oxford undergraduate, I was part of a widening participation program that involved visiting schools in deprived parts of the country to try and persuade the students to apply to the university. I joined the US-UK Fulbright Commission as a Commissioner in 2014, and have supported the Commission's work to secure full scholarships at American universities for British students from disadvantaged backgrounds. At the high school I helped set up, four out of every 10 children are from underprivileged backgrounds and our exam results put us in the top 10 percent of all high schools in England. Eighty-three percent of our graduating class this year got college offers, 63 percent from Russell Group universities, Britain's Ivy League.

How could an essay I wrote 30 years ago – *30 years ago* – be a legitimate basis on which to judge my attitude toward social mobility and not all the work I've done since? As David French wrote in the *National Review* about Ben Shapiro, we should judge people on the sum total of their work, not some isolated tweet or hot take.

In my case, it was as if observing progressive speech codes when talking about certain groups – such as disadvantaged kids – is more important than actually helping them. In today's topsy-turvy world, virtue signaling trumps being virtuous.

The allegations continued. Two of the most hurtful ones against me were that I'm a misogynist and a homophobe. Those claims were based on ill-judged comments I'd made on social media. Like James Gunn, I had deleted them – because they were asinine, ill-conceived attempts to be provocative, usually late at night after several glasses of wine – but the outrage mob thought that made them *more* indicative of what I'm really like, not *less*. In their eyes, these were the moments I had let slip the mask of decency and revealed the hideous gargoyle beneath.

Six years ago, I tweeted something about the cleavage of an MP sitting behind the leader of the Labour Party in the House of Commons, and three years before that I made some similar observations about several female celebrities, including Padma Lakshmi, the Indian cookbook author whom I used to work with on a cooking reality show. That was enough to get me labelled a misogynist.

Those tweets were awful and I wish I hadn't sent them. I'm not convinced that objectifying women is itself a form of harm, but it dehumanizes them, turns them into something "other," and that can be a way for men to give themselves permission to cause harm. But does sending those tweets make me a misogynist? Someone who hates all women, including my wife, whom I've been happily married to for 17 years and our 14-year-old daughter? That verdict has a horrible finality about it, as if I will forever be defined by a few lapses of judgment, and nothing else I have done — *could do* — will assuage the guilt.

To rub the point in, numerous people expressing outrage about this on Twitter added the hashtags #MeToo or #TimesUp, as if I am morally indistinguishable from Harvey Weinstein. For the record, I've run several medium-sized organizations in my career, and employed hundreds of people, and I've never been accused of sexual harassment or discrimination or anything remotely like that. On the contrary, I've always been supportive of my female colleagues. If you write off all men who've engaged in locker-room banter as misogynists, don't be surprised when that term stops eliciting the moral outrage you expect. It's the feminist equivalent of playing the race card.

Eight years ago — again on Twitter — I described George Clooney as being "as queer as a coot." That made me a homophobe. Again, stupid thing to say, but the dictionary definition of a homophobe is "a person with an extreme and irrational aversion to homosexuality and homosexual people." I wanted to protest that I had taken on Nigel Farage, then the leader of the right-wing United Kingdom Independence Party, in a public debate about gay marriage. That in the secondary school I helped set up, I had worked hard to create a welcoming environment for LGBTQ staff and students. That some of my best friends are...

But I knew I'd just be howling into the void. Trial by media is like being in the dock at a Soviet show trial – no due process. Guilty as charged. Next stop: social Siberia, as Canadian novelist Steven Galloway discovered. But unlike Galloway, who was falsely accused of rape, I was *sort of* guilty. Whenever I lapse into self-pity in the company of my friends and claim I was the victim of a witch hunt, they gently point out that I wasn't entirely innocent. The women accused of being in league with the devil in 17th-century Salem weren't actually witches, whereas I *had* written the offending articles and tweets. I was a self-described "porn addict," even if I hadn't meant that line to be taken literally.

My counterargument is that some of those accused of devil worship were, in fact, guilty of other offenses, such as adultery, but that didn't make them witches. Like Massachusetts Bay Colony deputy governor Thomas Danforth, those sitting in judgement upon me claimed to be able to peer into my soul and see the festering corruption within. I wasn't just being accused of having thought and said some inappropriate things. Rather, those were evidence of a diseased mind.

My most egregious sin was a tasteless, off-color remark I made while tweeting about a BBC telethon to raise money for starving Africans in 2009. That was reproduced on the front page of the *Mail on Sunday*, Britain's second-biggest-selling Sunday newspaper. The headline ran: "PM's Disgust at Student Tsar's Sordid Tweets." I'd now been promoted from "helping to lead" the new universities regulator to "student tsar" in order to fuel the outrage machine.

At this point, the cry for my scalp had reached fever pitch. An online petition calling for me to be sacked from the Office for Students had attracted 220,000 signatures. My daughter was refusing to go to school. My wife said that if one more person came up to her and said, "Are you okay?" she was going to hit them. I felt I had no choice but to issue a public apology and stand down.

In one respect, that was a mistake. I had been warned that abasing oneself at the feet of the outrage mob and apologizing would just embolden them. They will take it as a blanket admission of guilt and demand that you be removed from all your remaining positions until you've lost your livelihood — and so it proved to be.

In the weeks that followed, I was forced to resign from the Fulbright Commission, stripped of my Honorary Fellowship by Buckingham University, and I had to give up my nine-to-five job as head of an education charity – the one that paid the mortgage and enabled me to put food on the table and clothe my children. But I don't regret apologizing, not entirely, because it was heartfelt. When I saw my puerile tweet on the front page of the *Mail on Sunday*, I was filled with a burning, all-consuming sense of shame. I wanted to crawl into a cupboard and hide. My first thought was: "Thank God my father's not still alive."

My dad, Michael Young, was involved in education, too. He helped set up the Open University, Europe's largest higher-education institution, and was elevated to the House of Lords by James Callaghan, a Labour Prime Minister. Several pieces appeared after I resigned saying I had disgraced his name, including one by a journalist who'd known my father and whom I've always liked and respected. This same man had written a relatively sympathetic profile of me for the *Guardian* seven years earlier. That's one of the most disheartening things about being shunned and cast out by your colleagues – the people you hoped would stick up for you join the lynch mob along with everyone else. It was as if he was taking me aside into a dark room, handing me a glass of whisky and a revolver and telling me to do the decent thing.

Being publicly shamed is a brutal, shocking experience that strips you of your dignity, and I'll always look back on it as one of the low points of my life.

But, thankfully, my thoughts never turned to suicide. Others haven't been so fortunate. Earlier in 2018, Jill Messick, a Hollywood producer, became the subject of an online witch hunt when she was falsely accused by Rose McGowan of covering up for Harvey Weinstein. She decided not to challenge McGowan's account because she didn't want to make it harder for other victims of sexual harassment to come forward. But the gap between the person she knew herself to be and the anti-feminist villain she was being portrayed as on social media became too much, and on February 7, she took her own life.

It's that gap that causes the pain. Quinn Norton, who was hired and then fired by *The New York Times* in the space of eight hours following an online mobbing earlier this year, wrote a good article for *The Atlantic* about her ordeal. She said her detractors created a "bizarro-world" version of her, an online doppelgänger. It was the usual show trial in which people dug up things she'd said on social media in the distant past, deliberately turned a deaf ear to nuance, irony, and context, and transformed her into a pantomime villain. You know in your heart of hearts that that's not who you are, but the willingness of others to believe the worst can lead to self-doubt. *If so many people think I'm a bad person, maybe I really am.*

This is a form of cognitive dissonance, I think. Surveying the burning wreck of my career, I was initially consumed by a terrible sense of injustice. *Why me? What have I done to deserve this?* I hadn't realized it before my life unraveled, but I had been laboring under the illusion that we live in a fair universe – the just-world fallacy. I thought that if I was, on balance, a good person, the universe would somehow take that into account when deciding my fate. I'm not religious – I don't even believe in karma. At least, I didn't think I did until events conspired to make it crystal clear that karma is a big fat stinking lie. Then, to my astonishment, I found myself in a state of shock. *It's all so unfair!* But like many people whose worldview is upended by reality, instead of abandoning my just-world hypothesis, I doubled down on it. Not consciously, but semi-consciously – involuntarily. Cognitive dissonance. So I began to think, "Maybe I deserve all this public ignominy and shame."

That triggered a few depressive episodes, but what saved me from spiraling down into the full-blown, clinical depression that often follows an experience like this was exercise. During those nine days in January when I became the most reviled man in Britain, I lost half a stone (seven pounds). I joked to my wife that I was on "the public-humiliation diet." Like many middle-aged men, I've often dreamed about losing weight and getting into shape, but haven't had the time to do anything about it. Now, unexpectedly, I did. I decided to bank that half a stone, lose some more weight and do some exercise – finally get rid of that spare tire. So I've been doing 15 minutes of high intensity interval training (HIIT) every day, often followed by five minutes of stomach crunches, then a run or a swim. I'm now two stone lighter than I was on January 1, and, while I can't claim to have a six pack, I do have the faint outline of one. (I can see it, even if my kids fall about with laughter whenever I tense my stomach muscles and say, "Look, look!")

It's been wonderfully therapeutic. In part, that's because it has enabled me to regain control over some small aspect of my life. Okay, I may not be able to battle the outrage mob, and my enemies may have succeeded in destroying my career and ruining my reputation. But, hey, at least I can control my own body weight! Small potatoes in the grand scheme of things, but it means I don't feel like a complete victim.

Then there's the self-flagellatory dimension. Exercising hard, particularly HIIT, hurts. (The clue is in the name.) The part of me that blames myself for what's happened, and thinks I deserved everything I got, gets a lot of satisfaction from punishing the miscreant responsible. I've become a hair-shirt conservative.

Finally, there's the serotonin. After I'd suffered my reversal of fortune, I sought consolation in Jordan Peterson's *12 Rules For Life*. But it had the opposite effect. I read the infamous chapter about lobsters, and discovered that crustaceans who've been bested in a fight suffer from reduced levels of serotonin, and as a result become "a defeated looking, scrunched up, inhibited, drooping, skulking sort of lobster, very likely to hang around street corners and vanish at the first sign of trouble." As with lobsters, so with humans, Peterson argues, which immediately made me think that I was going to start behaving like a pathetic loser in the lobster-dominance hierarchy. But, thankfully, I didn't. And the reason, I think, is because of the exercise, which boosts serotonin. My sudden, vertiginous loss of status – like something out of a Tom Wolfe novel – undoubtedly depleted my serotonin levels. But the daily, intense physical exercise seems to have made up for it. This lobster will live to fight another day.

Six months have passed since I experienced my time in the stocks, and I'm still trying to process what happened (as you can probably tell). I keep circling back to the same question: Why were some people prepared to cast judgment based on such meager evidence? Why did certain words I'd used in the past count for so much more than my actions?

I think the answer must have something to do with the rise of identity politics. In the Oppression Olympics, I'm not about to win any medals. As a white, heterosexual, cis-gendered male, I'm an apex predator in the identitarian food chain, and, as such, responsible for all the injustices suffered by the oppressed, including historic injustices dating back hundreds of years – colonialism, slavery, sexual exploitation, you name it.

That's the context in which I was labelled a "homophobe" and a "misogynist," not to mention a "porn addict," a "eugenicist," and someone who "despises working-class students." As far as the hashtag activists are concerned, *all* white, heterosexual, cis-gendered males are guilty of those sins – and that goes double for Brexit-supporting, middle-aged Tories. They assume we must hold all these toxic beliefs because how else could we justify the "structural inequality" that preserves our privileged status? It simply doesn't occur to them that there's an intellectually respectable case for free-market capitalism, or that there could be a moral basis for opposing end-state equality – 100 million plus killed by communism, etc. – or that those of us who don't share their philosophy are equally concerned about justice. The conservative tradition is entirely unknown to them.

Even if your social-media history is squeaky clean, you're going to have difficulty persuading the intersectional Left that you have a useful role to play in public life if you tick all the wrong demographic boxes, as I do. The best thing you can do is "check your privilege" and stand aside. This is how Suzanna Danuta Walters, professor of sociology and director of the Women's, Gender, and Sexuality Studies Program at Northeastern University, put it in a recent comment piece for the *Washington Post* titled, "Why can't we hate men?":

So men, if you really are #WithUs and would like us to not hate you for all the millennia of woe you have produced and benefited from, start with this... Don't run for office. Don't be in charge of anything. Step away from the power. We got this. And please know that your crocodile tears won't be wiped away by us anymore. We have every right to hate you. You have done us wrong.

Maybe I'm kidding myself. After all, some of the other people appointed to the board of the new regulator were men — even white, heteronormative men — and no one objected to them. But it was a disheartening episode for someone who's been involved in politics all his life and was looking forward to contributing more. As a non-executive director of the Office for Students, I was hoping to address some of the problems afflicting Britain's universities — soaring tuition fees, grade inflation, the growing intolerance for unorthodox ideas — by sitting round the table with people of different views and having a lively debate. The person who replaced me is a liberal, which means the number of "out" conservatives on the 15-person board has been reduced to two. As New York University professor Jonathan Haidt has pointed out many times, our society prizes every kind of diversity except the one that matters most of all — viewpoint diversity. We're not going to come up with democratic, workable solutions to difficult problems if we stay within our echo chambers and refuse to engage seriously with our opponents.

Which is why it pains me to see fellow conservatives mimicking the mobbing tactics of the identitarian Left, whether it's going after Al Franken, Joy Reid, or James Gunn. We should not embrace the witch-hunter's credo that says people are defined by their worst moments, that if you've said something crass or insensitive about a victim group, particularly if you're "privileged," then you suffer from a form of original sin so deeply imprinted on your soul that no amount of good works can expunge it. The outrage mob seem to be in thrall to a particularly unforgiving religious cult. Nietzsche said that the west's tragedy in the 20th-century was that we would be afflicted by the same puritanical abhorrence of out-group behavior as our Christian forebears, but because we could no longer bring ourselves to believe in God there would be no way to save these malefactors – guilt without the possibility of redemption. Good theory, wrong century.

Will I get a second chance?

I'm still writing for the *Spectator*, which has never wavered in its support, doing editing for *Quillette* (thanks, Claire!), and working on a book about the neo-Marxist, postmodernist Left. None of this pays the mortgage, but it keeps me busy. My wife Caroline, a lawyer who gave up her job to care for our children, has re-entered the work force, so our household income should recover.

In March, I stepped down from the board of the charity I co-founded that looks after my schools – the fifth position I've had to give up since my public shaming. That was the biggest blow of all. I've written an international best-seller, starred in a one-man show in London's West End, and co-produced a Hollywood movie. But getting involved in education and trying to give others the opportunities I've had is easily the most rewarding thing I've ever done. I hope that one day, when this period of liberal McCarthyism has passed, I'll be allowed to resume that work.

AUTHOR'S POSTSCRIPT – SEPTEMBER 2020

Psychologically, I've made a full recovery from my cancellation. Career-wise, it hasn't affected my ability to make a living as a journalist, which is a relief, but it has made it impossible for me to set up any more schools: No education charity wants someone with my baggage on their board. That's a source of ongoing sadness, but I've found other outlets for my institution-building energy. I've set up an organization called the Free Speech Union (FSU) – a non-partisan, mass-membership, public-interest body that stands up for the speech rights of its members. So far, most of our activity has been confined to the UK, but we accept international members, and I hope to set up branches in other countries soon, starting with the United States. Part of the reason for setting it up was to provide a support network for other people who find themselves in the position I found myself in at the beginning of 2018. The worst part about it was the feeling of being isolated and alone, with no one to intercede between me and the mob baying for my blood. I hope the FSU can help in that respect.

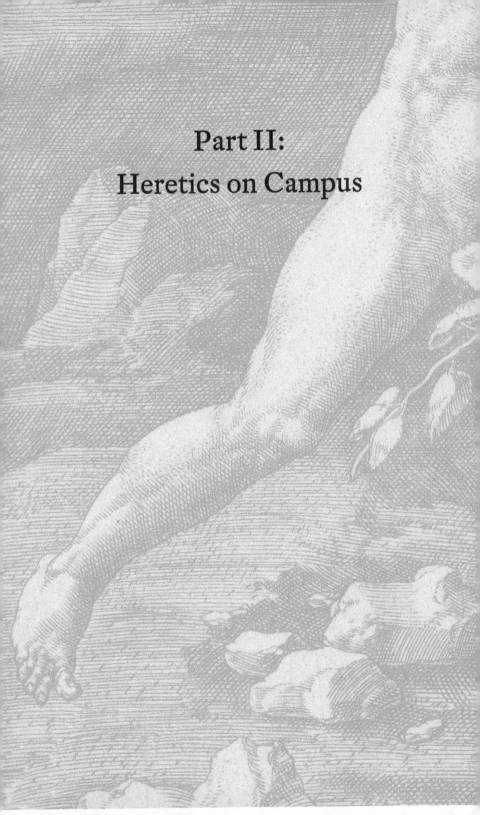

Part II:
Heretics on Campus

Steven Galloway's Tale:
A Literary Inquisition
By Brad Cran

On August 8, 2015, a day after the University of British Columbia (UBC) announced the sudden resignation of its president, Arvind Gupta, UBC's Jennifer Berdahl, professor in Leadership Studies in Gender and Diversity, published a blog post in which she opined that "Gupta lost the masculinity contest among the leadership at UBC, as most women and minorities do at institutions dominated by white men."

Berdahl held the Montalbano Professorship, a position financed with a $2-million (all figures Canadian) donation from Board Of Governors Chair John Montalbano, specifically focused on "the advancement of women and diversity in business leadership."

Montalbano called Berdahl directly and accused her of making him look like a hypocrite. He also told her that he had contacted her dean about the issue. Berdahl shot back with a second blog post that accused Montalbano of trying to silence her. "I have a right to academic freedom and expression," she wrote, "free of intimidation and harassment."

On August 18, the UBC board of governors convened a meeting to deal with the controversy. As

Montalbano came out of the room, a reporter confronted him, followed him down the hall and out of the building to his car, while telling him he was incompetent and that it was unacceptable that he had nothing to say.

The next day, August 19, UBC's Faculty Association published a letter, demanding that Montalbano resign. The university then appointed former B.C. Supreme Court Justice Lynn Smith to investigate the claims of infringement on Berdahl's academic freedom. All of this was front-page news: UBC sits at the heart of intellectual life in Vancouver, and is considered the finest university in western Canada.

In the meantime, Montalbano personally contacted former UBC President Martha Piper, who agreed to step in as Interim President in order to lead UBC through the crisis until a new president could be appointed. Piper had led UBC from 1997 to 2006, and was no stranger to controversy, having begun her original term dealing with the fallout from a 1997 conference at which police pepper-sprayed student protestors on campus. Within academic circles, Piper is widely seen as a respected university administrator, with 17 honorary degrees to her name. She served in her interim role till June 2016, when she was succeeded by Santa J. Ono, who remains the school's President and Vice-Chancellor.

On October 16, 2015, a month after Piper stepped in as Interim President, Madam Justice Smith released her report on Berdahl's claim that her academic freedom had been compromised. Although no single person was to blame for what had happened, she concluded, the school as a whole hadn't done enough to protect Berdahl.

"Sometimes," Smith wrote, "several relatively small mistakes can lead to a failure of the larger system." Montalbano resigned from the UBC Board of Governors the same day.

None of these events relate directly to famed Canadian novelist Steven Galloway, who was suspended from his position as chair of UBC's Creative Writing program a month later, following the airing of thinly evidenced sexual-assault allegations. But for reasons described below, they are crucial to understanding how and why UBC reacted in the disastrous way it did when the claims against Galloway emerged.

In normal times, UBC would have investigated and dismissed the claims against Galloway – as an independent investigator eventually did – while obeying something that at least approximated the norms of due process. But these were not normal times.

Thanks to the Gupta resignation, and the Berdahl-Montalbano meltdown, this had now become what was arguably the most tumultuous period at UBC since the university's founding in the late nineteenth century, with the two top positions at the institution being vacated in just over three months. In addition, three Vice-Presidents had previously vacated positions under Gupta, including the Provost.

But Piper also had some good news to announce, if only she could prevent it from being overshadowed by scandal. A recently completed fundraising campaign, seven years in the making, would, by UBC's claims, propel the university into the prestigious global ranks of Harvard and Princeton. The campaign raised $1.62-billion, exceeding the $1.5-billion goal declared a decade earlier.

Piper was set to make the announcement at the Vancouver Board of Trade on the morning of November 18. But as that date drew closer, two fresh scandals appeared.

* * *

First, CBC Television's prominent investigative show, *The Fifth Estate*, announced that it would be airing an exposé called *School of Secrets*, which contained accusations that UBC had not acted on allegations of sexual assault leveled against a UBC history department PhD candidate from Russia. The segment was scheduled to air during the same week as the fundraising announcement.

Then, on November 13, the Friday before the scheduled Board of Trade announcement, Chelsea Rooney, formerly a student in UBC's Creative Writing Department, came forward with the shocking claim that Galloway, who had served as the UBC Creative Writing Chair since 2013, had violently raped an unnamed student four years earlier. Rooney would also make the stunning claim that she was able to bring forth no fewer than 19 other former or current UBC students who also alleged abusive behavior at Galloway's hands.

From this point onward, Rooney would become the face of the allegations against Galloway. The woman he stood accused of raping, a former professor in her 40s, would become identified in the media only as "MC" (or Main Complainant, a term used internally at UBC).

Rooney made a voicemail available to Creative Writing Faculty that, according to the accusation, featured Galloway apologizing for raping MC. (In a subsequent investigation, it was determined that, in fact, he was apologizing for his part in their lengthy consensual affair.) In the message, Galloway stated that he was a changed man. He also requested that he be the one to break the news of his behavior – which he recognized as improper – to his mentor, former Creative Writing Department Chair Keith Maillard.

"I think actually what I'm asking for is maybe a chance, if you wish it, for me to turn myself in," Galloway said on the voicemail. "Keith's opinion of me matters a great deal to me, and I'm pretty ashamed of the way I used to be and act. I can assure you that I am no longer that way."

This voicemail was presented as evidence to support MC's claims. But it should also have served to arouse skepticism, even at this very early stage in the scandal. Under Canadian law, sexual assault is properly treated as a serious crime that can be punished with a life sentence. Would a university official such as Galloway confess to this crime over voicemail, while also asking permission to confess the same crime to his mentor, because he was worried about how the news might affect his reputation?

Few figures in the UBC community wanted to ask such questions at the time. Students and staff were horrified by the claims, and were understandably eager to express support for any woman who had suffered. In retrospect, other questions should have been asked. No police report had been filed in regard to the alleged assault on MC. Nor had there been a police complaint in regard to unlawful confinement, or administering a noxious substance – both of which, as we shall see, could have followed from the claimed narrative.

Since 2015, MC has changed her story several times, including changing the date of the alleged assaults from 2012, when she was an MFA student in the UBC Creative Writing program, to 2011, when she wasn't. She also originally alleged one assault, but later claimed there had been three. As for those other 19 victims of Galloway whom Rooney claimed she could bring forward, it turns out there is no evidence that they exist.

But it would be many months before Canadians would know any of this. And in the media, reports focused on Galloway's suspension from UBC amid serious allegations. Rooney received sympathetic treatment from reporters, who presented her as a whistleblower with a tragic back story. "I had a rage-filled, alcoholic father who beat and raped our mother in front of us," she said in an interview. "We spent several nights in women's shelters, in fear of our lives."

In this same interview, tagged to the launch of her 2014 book *Pedal*, Rooney candidly admitted that the act of writing had "forced two revelations on me: how narcissistic I am, and how much shame I carry because of my abuse...For me, narcissism describes a tendency to imagine myself at the center. To imagine that the people in my life are doing things to me, and events are occurring because of me...It's a terrible way to live. I still scan for threats, but more and more I catch myself doing it."

It's impossible to say whether this narcissistic tendency to "imagine herself at the center" of things is what caused Rooney to become MC's most zealous champion, notwithstanding early signs that the underlying claims were unfounded. (Rooney did not respond to interview requests.) But largely as a result of her campaign on MC's behalf, UBC officials would make a move that altered the lives of many people – all for the worse: For what is believed to be the first time in its history, UBC would publicly announce a disciplinary action against a faculty member before any investigation had occurred.

"What I've always been mystified by," says Andreas Schroeder, who taught in UBC's Creative Writing program from 1994 to 2017, "was that faculty were assured [that] *nineteen* other women were coming forward with allegations – but it never happened." Schroeder remembers that during these events in November 2015, no concrete information was presented to departmental staff. Instead, he says, the flow of information was conducted through gossip and second-hand claims that seemed to evaporate when you tried to track down the alleged source. The UBC Creative Writing Department became a tense place. Schroeder said that there were rumors circulating that faculty emails were being monitored. A culture of fear set in.

Things had been set in motion within the department on Sunday, November 15, when an emergency meeting of Creative Writing staff was held at the home of professor Linda Svendsen. Only select faculty were chosen to attend. One of the agenda items listed on the minutes was *"Fifth Estate."* The Galloway voicemail was played to the room, and a decision was made to request that the dean suspend Galloway and remove him as department Chair. Less than one business day had passed from the time that an unproven four-year-old allegation had been brought forward by Rooney on behalf of MC, yet Galloway's fate was essentially decided in that room.

"I saw Steven called a rapist," said a Creative Writing instructor who still works within the department, and who spoke to me on condition that they remain anonymous. "I saw anyone who dared defend him called a rape apologist. I've watched the department go from a vibrant, welcoming place to a place full of cautiousness and fear and closed doors."

* * *

At this point, it's worth pausing to describe just how large Galloway loomed, as both a figure at UBC and in Canadian arts and letters more generally. He is one of the few first-tier novelists that his country has ever produced. Galloway's 2008 novel, *The Cellist of Sarajevo*, was an international bestseller, listed for numerous literary prizes. When he became acting chair of the UBC Creative Writing program in 2013, he made his impact felt immediately, taking steps to improve morale and increase public exposure for the school and its students.

As his first act as Chair, Galloway installed a large brass marine bell outside his office, for students to ring when they handed in their thesis, thereby completing their graduation. Prior to that, a student would submit his or her bound work to the departmental secretary, which felt like an anticlimax. Once Galloway's thesis bell was installed, ringing it became a major event, with the secretary going down the halls knocking on doors to let everyone in the department know someone was about to have their moment. Students and faculty came out into the hall to clap and cheer for the graduating student, who stood under the bell and rang it.

Following the claims against Galloway, however, signs of his presence were removed from the department. The university sent the bell to Galloway's house in a plain brown box.

On the day after the meeting at Svendsen's house, November 16, Galloway was informed of his suspension by email a few minutes before he was to speak at Wright State University in Dayton, Ohio. In a panic, he phoned Annabel Lyon, a novelist who taught in his department. He told her he'd been suspended pending an investigation, at which point, he recalls, she hung up on him. Hours later, she texted him, asking him to call her again. When he did, she put him on speakerphone with another professor, Nancy Lee, and the program administrator.

As in a novel by Kafka, Galloway had no idea of the specific allegations against him – although he guessed they were related in some way to MC. Galloway still felt remorse for his affair with MC, which had ended in early 2013. Although he was not department chair at the time of their intimate relationship, nor did he supervise MC's thesis, Galloway knew that sex between teachers and students was frowned upon

— even if it was not explicitly forbidden by UBC rules.

He told Lyon and Lee about the affair, and apologized profusely. In effect, he was delivering a version of the confession that he had delivered in his voicemail to MC. (At the time, Galloway didn't know that Lyon and Lee had already heard the recording the day before.) By his account, the trio on the other end of the line then told him that they did not know anything about what was going on. At one point, Galloway remembers, Annabel reassured him that they had been friends for 15 years (which was true), and that everything would be okay (which was not).

The trio repeatedly asked him if he was suicidal. Galloway told them he was not, joking that he was way too much of a coward to kill himself. His focus was on catching a plane in a few hours and meeting his partner in Toronto. While he was speaking to them, one of the three people on the other end of the call phoned the police in Ohio. Someone from UBC would also contact MC to tell her to not sleep at home in case Galloway turned up in Toronto to kill her.

Two officers showed up at Galloway's hotel room in Ohio. After interviewing him, one attending officer contacted Lyon, who (according to the police report) told him Galloway was suicidal, manipulative, and would tell them anything to get what he wanted. The responding officer removed Galloway from his hotel in handcuffs, seated him in the back of a squad car and transported him to the psychiatric ward of

Miami Valley Hospital where he was strip searched and incarcerated on a 72-hour involuntary psychiatric remand known as a pink slip.

The next morning, while Galloway was still incarcerated, Martha Piper took to the podium at the Vancouver Board of Trade to announce UBC's $1.6-billion in new funding.

Back on UBC campus, administrators and faculty were preparing to publicly announce Galloway's suspension. Lyon and Svendsen convened an emergency meeting to tell all faculty and adjunct teachers that they were taking over as acting co-chairs, effective immediately. They also informed faculty that Galloway had been suspended over "serious allegations," and that precautions were being taken to protect students and provide them with counseling. Whether intended or not, the word "protect" suggested that Galloway was associated with crimes so serious that his mere presence on campus might subject students to emotional trauma, or even physical danger.

The following day, UBC issued a press release using similarly ominous language. It announced that Galloway had been suspended, and that steps were being taken to protect the "safety, health and well-being of all members of our community." Dean of Arts Gage Averill then gave multiple media interviews. "We're in a position right now where we're dealing with allegations," he said. "Nothing has been determined in regard to Professor Galloway, certainly not any finding of fault. So we want to protect his rights, understand the allegations, and respond to them."

Alas, that train had already left the station.

Following the predictably emotional reaction within the Creative Writing department, Lyon spoke of her own sense of shock — striking the tone of a neighbor who tells news reporters about how the notorious criminal living next door seemed like a regular guy who said hello and stopped by for coffee. According to one UBC instructor who witnessed these events, Lyon told colleagues that the allegations were "upsetting for me, too. I mean, he used to change my kids' diapers for god's sake." (Lee, Lyon, and Svendsen were invited, by email, to describe their own recollections of the events described in this article. None provided any comment for attribution.)

Even by this time, none of the allegations against Galloway had been spelled out. All that was known — even internally — emerged from the series of lurid accusations from MC that were filtered through Rooney, and then again through an inner circle of faculty members who, conveniently, had just taken leadership of the department.

"I sat at dinner parties and heard people [who did not know Galloway] outlining the horrid rumors they'd heard like they were the truth," said the above-quoted UBC instructor who asked to remain anonymous. "A friend, who'd been at [another] dinner party with someone from UBC's own equity department, told [another] friend that '16 other women are coming forward.' The strange leaks from people working at the university were particularly alarming and, as we later [learned], utterly false."

This instructor reported to me that many faculty members were afraid to speak out. But a group of adjuncts who felt they had little to lose met with representatives of the dean's office. When they asked why UBC released such an innuendo-heavy press release, one of the dean's representatives reportedly replied: "We can't be held responsible for what happens on social media."

This was a presumed reference to the *Fifth Estate*'s Ronna Syed, who'd produced *School of Secrets*, and broke the Galloway suspension announcement on Twitter. Within minutes of Syed's tweet, several women who had appeared in *School of Secrets* were following up on Syed's post by attacking Galloway and suggesting he was a rapist. *The Fifth Estate* announced they would be postponing the airing of *School of Secrets* till the following week — presumably with an eye toward updating the episode with material about Galloway. Piper released an official apology to the women victimized in the original scandal, and *The Fifth Estate* published it on their web page as the lead-in to the segment, offering UBC a small but precious PR victory amid the tumult. (In the end, the allegations against Galloway never made it onto the aired version of *School of Secrets*.)

Galloway remained silent during this period, following the recommendations of the UBC Faculty Association, whose President, Mark MacLean, released a statement criticizing UBC for going public with Galloway's suspension and the unspecified allegations. There were some other people supporting Galloway, too. Random House Canada said it was "proud" to be Galloway's publisher, and that it "looks forward" to publishing more of his work. Fellow B.C. author Angie Abdou told a reporter that Galloway "is whip smart and absolutely hilarious," as well as "kind and generous." But these were lonely voices, quickly targeted by a growing mob within the world of Canadian literature, which sought to create a united front against Galloway.

Rooney accused MacLean of silencing women. "They will now feel afraid to share information, which is exactly how silence becomes abusive and damaging," she told CBC. "If we want to talk about the truth, if we want to talk about these types of events that happen every day within every kind of institution, then we have to actually talk about it."

Her reaction to the Faculty Association statement would set the tone for the two-pronged media strategy adopted by Galloway's accusers over the next two and a half years. First, Galloway's guilt was to be assumed as a matter of fundamental truth. And second, demands for fair play and due process were to be interpreted as efforts to "silence" victims of sex abuse and emotionally injure Galloway's supposed victims.

However spurious these claims proved to be as a matter of law, they were successful in tarring Galloway and his defenders on social media. Even as of this writing, with the claims against Galloway now having been undermined on multiple fronts, Galloway's most aggressive critics continue to apply the same tactics. In Toronto's *Globe & Mail*, for instance, writer Alicia Elliott – who helped lead the Twitter campaign both against Galloway and anyone seeking to ensure that he received due process – wrote a recent article entitled "We must value a woman's pain above a man's reputation."

Moreover, since no one was releasing information showing just how flimsy the case against Galloway really was, the media naturally went hard on the narrative of a supposed workplace sex tyrant leading one of Canada's elite academic programs. As with the above-described relationship that developed between UBC and the CBC in late 2015, the bond between Galloway's accusers and certain reporters would become close. Both parties had their own interests in presenting the story as a shocking case of abuse.

Rooney, in particular, continued to be presented as a hero of what later would be called the #MeToo movement. An op-ed about sexual assault policy that she published in the *Vancouver Sun* listed her as "one of several people who came forward to expose flaws of process by UBC in its treatment of students and faculty reporting misconduct by Steven Galloway."

* * *

As the third week of November 2015 unfolded, it became clear that almost all of Galloway's closest friends and colleagues at UBC were now set to bolt and run. Not only did most refuse to support Galloway, but, taking their cue from Lyon, many became active members of the anti-Galloway mob.

It is hard to know how many of these people actually believed MC's claims, and how many were simply trying to align themselves with the new power structure within the department that already seemed to be purging some of Galloway's hires. But everyone saw where things were headed: To defend a heretic is to invite suspicion that you are also a heretic.

Things got worse on Friday, November 20, when Associate Vice-President of UBC's Office of Equity and Inclusion said her team would take a "leadership role" on Galloway. At the time, British Columbia's provincial government was bringing in legislation requiring post-secondary institutions to implement standalone sexual-assault policies. With the airing of the *Fifth Estate* episode imminent, university officials were under intense pressure to offer a demonstration of their commitment to addressing the issue. Someone in power at UBC seems to have panicked. For nothing else can properly explain the disastrous series of decisions that then took place.

In a stunning breach of protocol and fairness, the

Office of Equity and Inclusion conscripted Rooney — MC's own spokesperson — to gather additional evidence of complaints against Galloway. UBC even provided Rooney — who was an ex-student with no official standing at the university — with a letter on Office of Equity and Inclusion letterhead, stating to Rooney's recipients: "You are receiving this letter from me because the person delivering it to you thinks you may have a complaint against Professor Steven Galloway. As you are likely aware, the University is investigating a complaint against Professor Galloway."

Beyond mandating a university-approved fishing expedition for accusations against Galloway — conducted by a complete amateur, with no apparent experience or expertise in the field of investigations, who already had announced her unwavering belief in MC's accusations — the letter went further, actually encouraging recipients to take action on their own initiative: "Counseling Services can also provide information on options for filing a complaint and can facilitate the process should you choose to make a complaint."

Readers may be excused for having to read that sentence twice before realizing that the university's "counseling services" were effectively being offered as a conduit to prosecution.

The Office of Equity and Inclusion even included a down payment of flattery for anyone kind enough to assist with the campaign: "We understand how challenging this may be for you to come forward. We honor your strength and will do our utmost to support you in this process." Indeed, the language seemed to go so far as to suggest that *failing* to come forward with some complaint or other might be interpreted as a sign of weakness, or even cowardice, in the battle for social justice.

In her 2013 book, *Mobbed!: What to Do When They Really Are Out to Get You*, Dr. Janice Harper writes, "Most work places are staffed by people who rarely have training in investigative methods. More often than not, they ask leading questions in an accusatory or overly sympathetic tone. They record notes in a manner [that] uses the information they obtain selectively. They do not ask follow-up questions to vague statements unless doing so would support their foregone conclusion." Based on what I have learned from those involved in Rooney's campaign, it was a textbook example of the procedural bias Dr. Harper describes. "If you're receiving this email, it's because you've either experienced or witnessed incidents that can speak directly to [Galloway's] character," Rooney wrote to individuals who, she believed, might have the kind of stories she wanted. "The range of abuses I've heard over the last week are multiple and sad... They have left me feeling terrible and worried... Right now, it is just one woman against an institution. Forgive my optimism, but I believe in this moment we have the power to disrupt traditional narratives."

"I strongly encourage you to anonymously reach out to Laura Kane, a reporter with the BC bureau of the Canadian Press," Rooney added. "I just spoke with her, and she [is] great. A very safe person to talk to. Warm and empathetic and well-versed in these issues...You can remain anonymous and your story will still have an impact on what happens in the Creative Writing department."

Only after one interaction went badly did Rooney seem to realize that she had gone too far. "I am writing to apologize for asking you to contact the reporter," she wrote in a November 24, 2015 email to one recipient. "It was poor judgment...I'm sorry. It was a bad day. I had heard so many stories at that point." In keeping with Rooney's own self-assessment, she put herself at the center of the narrative – a victim who has been traumatized by her exposure to terrible truths, but who was now fighting back. Rooney also cast MC's struggle in heroic terms, as "one woman against an institution" – which is ironic, given how isolated Galloway had become, and how both the institutional power structures of UBC and the disembodied mob power of Twitter had been stacked against him.

Rooney functioned as a one-woman team. She was officially regarded as a complainant by the university; she was voicing MC by proxy, including as a media point person; and she was serving the university as *de facto* investigator. As one UBC Creative Writing Faculty Member told me, "She took it [Steve's destruction] up like a full-time job."

She'd promised to bring forward 19 assault complainants against Galloway. Instead she brought forward herself and seven of her friends. And even in these cases, the complaints were mostly frivolous – the sort of stories one might see on RateMyProfessors.com. All of the allegations made by these eight "Ancillary Complainants" (as they became known) were eventually dismissed. More importantly, so was the central rape allegation made by MC.

* * *

UBC, to its credit, eventually realized that some form of professional fact-finding was required. For this task, the school commissioned Madam Justice Mary Ellen Boyd – a retired B.C. Supreme Court justice who actually knew how to interview people in a neutral way and follow up on inconsistencies in their stories. While Boyd would not be subjecting complainants to rigorous cross-examination in an adversarial manner, she would be conducting her questioning with an appropriate degree of skepticism. As of December 2015, Rooney's free-for-all was over.

Of the eight Ancillary Complainants interviewed by Boyd, the one whose story seemed most damaging was a UBC creative writing student named Anna Maxymiw, who describes herself on social media as a rough-and-tumble "bro" journalist. (Only complainants who have publicly identified themselves as such are named in this article.)

Maxymiw told Boyd that she and Galloway were often physically playful with each other – sometimes aggressively so. She would regularly punch him in the arm, she said, and she once put a snowball down the back of his shirt. She did not dispute Galloway's assertion that she had told him that he was "a shitty writer."

At her most brazen, Maxymiw once slapped Galloway in the face. In response, Galloway joked that after she graduated, he would slap her back. Maxymiw told Madam Justice Boyd that she and Galloway "razzed" each other about the slap and that it became a running joke between them. She said she had been a "pig-headed loudmouth."

In 2012, Galloway went out for drinks with a number of students, including Maxymiw, to celebrate their graduation. Galloway joked with Maxymiw around the table and then, in the presence of multiple witnesses, said, "it's time." He then slapped Maxymiw lightly, in the spirit of the long running joke, and without intent to harm. All of this is in Boyd's report.

A few months after the slap, Maxymiw had published an article about "walking a carrot" and sent Galloway a direct message through Facebook that said: "i think slap therapy is actually less weird than taking a carrot for walkies. wouldn't you agree? besides, you bought me a 3-dollar beer after, and that made me happy. (I'm a simple woman)." Prior to the airing of MC's allegations in November 2012, the slap was still very much a joke between them, and one that Maxymiw herself seemed to remember fondly.

In assessing whether any of this constituted misconduct, Boyd determined that:

> Given what each of them actually experienced, knew or understood about each other in this situation – namely that the slap was the culmination of their own longstanding 'joke' – it is difficult to conclude that the slap was an act of harassment or abuse. The matter was out of mind for the next 3½ years before [Mayxmiw] was reminded of what had occurred, and in light of the recent allegations regarding MC, reconsidered the matter and decided (in the context of allegations of choking and rape) that the slap was objectionable…Bizarre as the incident was, I am unable to find that it amounts to a single incident of personal harassment.

Some have seized on the fact that Galloway would sometimes go out drinking with students – an informal ritual at the local Legion Hall, on Thursday evenings. Boyd heard from many students about this, but eventually concluded as follows:

I entirely dismiss the general complaints that [Galloway] intentionally created a culture where students felt pressure to participate in drinking sessions, whether on or off campus, that he plied students with alcohol or otherwise went about deliberately creating a sexualized environment. I also dismiss the complaints that the Respondent expected students to participate in drinking sessions and befriend him, understanding that they could not otherwise enjoy the benefits of a system of favoritism.

Erin Flegg, a former UBC student whose Ancillary Complaint Boyd dismissed because it did not contain even a *prima facie* allegation of improper behavior, told Boyd that "I acknowledge that [Galloway] never behaved in a disrespectful manner toward me," and "I did not feel either threatened, or unsafe, or vulnerable vis-à-vis Galloway." (She did, however, object to Galloway hiring Hal Wake, artistic director of the Vancouver Writers Festival, to teach a class on conducting literary readings and interviews. She felt her friend should have been hired for the job instead.)

Ancillary Complainant Krissy Darch came forward with a complaint that Galloway had made her feel ill at ease vicariously. In a writing workshop, Darch explained, Chelsea Rooney was feeling uncomfortable receiving criticism about her work, so Galloway suggested that, as a coping mechanism, she pretend she was a block of butter and that a puppy was licking her. This was a direct reference to a scene from a story that Rooney herself had just submitted. But Darch testified that she was nevertheless "grossed out," since she knew Chelsea was a survivor of sexual abuse.

Darch also told Boyd that when she met with Galloway about her thesis, she asked him to close the door, which he did. As he did so, he said, according to her recollection, "Don't worry, I'm not going to assault you."

Boyd considered the context in which this comment was made: A week before, a man who was angry that he didn't get into the UBC MFA program had stormed into Galloway's office, slammed the door behind him, and threatened to burn the building down with Galloway in it. Police were called. Darch had stood in the hallway listening to the incident unfold. (Darch's thesis was in part about human trafficking. She further complained that Galloway had asked her how she knew so much about the subject, which upset her.)

A male Ancillary Complainant, whose book Galloway blurbed, made two claims that Boyd also ruled could not even be categorized as complaints. The complainant reported that at some indeterminate time in the past, Galloway had participated in a joke about breasts made by an unnamed woman about a man she had been seeing. He also stated he'd heard about the "slap" incident, though did not witness it. Boyd wrote:

"He makes no suggestion that, at the time, [Galloway's] actions caused a 'hostile or intimidating environment.'" The Ancillary Complainant suggested that he'd been motivated to come forward by his support for the #believewomen movement. It was a telling admission, though perhaps not for the reason the complainant imagined.

* * *

At this point, let me pause to offer my own #believewomen caveat: It's not crazy to think that a successful, respectable-seeming novelist who leads an academic department might be a rapist. We hear of stories like this in many industries.

In general, I *do* give women accusing men of rape the benefit of the doubt, since statistics show that most accusations of this type are truthful, and the stigma attached to rape serves to discourage false accusations. When I heard the vague allegations against Galloway, I assumed — as many people did — that he really had committed some form of horrendous indiscretion, perhaps even a crime. And I only began to suspect otherwise after I was attacked on social media by the complainants simply for seeking basic facts about these alleged acts.

When it became clear that Boyd's investigation wasn't going to rubber-stamp the case against Galloway, his critics and accusers — who by now had become a well-organized force on social media – simply bypassed official channels, and continued to prosecute Galloway on Twitter and Facebook. They also collectively attacked anyone who refused to accept the black-and-white narrative of MC as truth-telling sexual-abuse survivor, and Galloway as sadistic villain. Even Boyd was accused of colluding with UBC to uphold the power structures of patriarchy.

What seems closer to the truth is that the ancillary complainants, having been prepared, by Rooney, to be treated as heroes, weren't ready for even a baseline level of scrutiny from a competent and independent legal mind.

Rooney herself was so shaken by Boyd's questioning that she wrote to Dean Averill to ask that UBC hire a sexual assault expert to consult with Boyd. "Her line of questioning left me very concerned about the direction of her investigation," Rooney wrote. On Twitter, Rooney rebuked one of her doubters with the admonition, "Oh, you're an 'I believe the [Boyd] report' kinda person. Okay. Let me guess, you also think victims of sexual assault should go to police?"

The implication here is that Boyd acted as a stand-in for how our legal system fails women when it comes to sexual abuse. And, to be fair to Rooney, the phenomenon she describes can be very real. As *Globe & Mail* reporter Robyn Doolittle authoritatively showed in her 2017 series, *Unfounded*, Canadian police officers dismiss about 20 percent of sexual-assault claims as baseless.

But Boyd makes for a strange target. She is one of the most accomplished female jurists in B.C. history. And in cases where judges must be educated on the intersection of law and sex, Boyd would seem more likely to give lessons than receive them. In one 2001 B.C. Supreme Court case, *Dr. Dutton v. B.C. Human Rights Tribunal et al.*, Boyd upheld a tribunal's findings that a psychology professor at UBC had created a sexualized environment and discriminated against a student on the basis of sexual harassment. Boyd also presided over the trial of Barry Thomas Niedermier, who was convicted of viciously assaulting society's most vulnerable and oft-ignored women, drug-addicted sex workers. (Niedermier's brutality was so severe that police once suspected him of murders now known to have been committed by infamous serial killer Robert Pickton.) Niedermier's victims deserved justice and they found it in Madam Justice Boyd's court.

In her report, Boyd was scathing of Rooney:

> I have spent some time reviewing AC5's [Rooney's] specific complaints, since she is the one complainant who has most vigorously participated in this investigation, conferring with MC, speaking to [Creative Writing] program faculty prior to the November 15 meeting [at the home of Linda Svendson], and then spearheading the gathering of evidence...She

was and is clearly defensive about her role in this matter. After she provided her statement of evidence at my initial interview, I arranged to meet her a second time to ask further questions largely related to her dealings with MC and her subsequent identification of and contact with the Ancillary Complainants. When her Supplementary Statement of evidence was returned to her for editing, she refused to either confirm it or edit it, and instead returned a memorandum in which she disavowed her earlier recollections. Suffice it to say that I found AC5 [Rooney] a biased witness, who has perceived every minor incident here through her own tainted lens. I am unable to place much, if any, weight on her evidence.

Rooney has criticized both the content of Boyd's report, and the procedures surrounding its creation. But as already noted, she declined my request for further comment. MC did not respond to a similar solicitation.

* * *

One odd aspect of the way that the Galloway story has been treated by journalists is that there has been much reporting about the slaps and slights that are the subject of the Ancillary Complaints, but little scrutiny of the actual merits of MC's main rape allegation.

For over two and a half years, Galloway has been vilified, threatened, and driven to the edge of both bankruptcy and suicide. Yet scan through the tens of thousands of social-media posts condemning Galloway, and you will have trouble finding anything that sets out, even in skeletal form, the explosive claims that started this entire debacle. In fact, it took me over a year of research, including interviews with former students and faculty, before I finally heard the claims spelled out in a coherent fashion.

MC claimed that she never had an affair with Galloway; that he had tried to rape her on numerous occasions – including on his boat; and that he finally succeeded in raping her after he drugged her in his office, on a weekday, during normal business hours. MC claimed this happened right before a public reading at UBC by the writer Miriam Toews.

As in many cases that fall apart, it is the small details that are telling. The day of the Toews reading, Boyd noted, made for an improbable timeline – since Galloway had told multiple students by email to come by his office before the reading to pick up reference letters they'd requested from him. Galloway and MC also attended the Toews reading with nearly the entire department in attendance, which – even in light of all that we know about the different ways that people respond to sexual trauma – was not consistent with someone who had been drugged unconscious and then raped shortly before arriving.

MC is five years Galloway's senior, and had arrived at UBC with a master's degree from another institution and two previous tenure-track positions at U.S. universities. (She continues to teach at one of these universities today.) She cannot credibly be cast as a starry-eyed ingénue beguiled by Galloway's reputation. In fact, at the time of their affair, Galloway held no tenure, or any administrative role in the Creating Writing department, but rather was a mere sessional instructor working on a year-to-year contract.

When Galloway and MC called their affair off, they were both married. Both deleted the messages they had sent to one another to avoid having their affair discovered. Fortunately for Galloway, these messages were subsequently retrieved from the cloud. These include over 250 pages of messages between them proving an affair, the existence of which MC had denied to Boyd. They also serve to cast doubt on her allegations of assault on Galloway's boat.

To cite just one example: MC texted Galloway in June 2012, over a year after the date on which, she later alleged, he assaulted her at sea: "Can I write on your boat for a few hours this afternoon. Around 3:00. It's not safe to be at my house." Not only was MC not afraid of Galloway, she apparently considered his boat a refuge from some (unspecified) domestic threat. Galloway's detractors would explain this as a coping mechanism, by which an abused woman might seek to make peace with her tormentor. But given the totality of all the inconsistencies in MC's story, that does not seem plausible — especially since a small boat seems one of the most unsafe places imaginable for a woman to be with a man who supposedly had assaulted her previously.

The messages also include another sexual-assault allegation that MC reported to Galloway — relating to an alleged incident involving another man that, according to her narrative, took place after the time when Galloway supposedly drugged, confined, and raped her in his office.

This was 2013, after their affair had ended. UBC was seeking to fill two tenure-track positions. A writer who was a favorite to get one of the spots had completed his interview, at which point MC joined him at a hotel bar for an evening of drinks that lasted until they shut the bar down. MC alleges this writer then sexually assaulted her when she visited him again the next morning. The writer in question vehemently denies the allegation.

MC texted Galloway to report the alleged assault. She asked him not to expose the writer publicly, but to make sure he didn't get the job for which he applied. Galloway went straight to the then-department chair to disclose what happened. The chair decided to include the Graduate Advisor, and it was decided that the evaluations of the applicant would be adjusted. The candidate did not get the job, and instead the position was given to the aforementioned Nancy Lee, who at the time held a year-to-year position, and who is now a tenure-track faulty member and a staunch supporter of the complainants. (MC was Lee's teaching assistant at the time.)

It's important to keep in mind that the alleged hotel-bar incident involving MC supposedly happened two years *after* the claimed drugging and raping in Galloway's office. This was evidence that Boyd rightly considered – for it raises the question: Would a rape victim report a subsequent sexual assault by a third party to a man who had himself drugged and raped her in his office? Why, one is made to wonder, would she not report it to the department chair, who was also the program equity officer and her thesis advisor, and to whom she eventually reported her allegation against Galloway? Or to the dean? Or to the police? Or, indeed, to *anyone* except the man who'd supposedly raped her?

In a November 2016 exchange, famed Canadian novelist Margaret Atwood – who has stood by her original call for UBC to respect Galloway's right to due process – tweeted that "no one can be asked to believe or not believe a package of unknown things." To which Rooney replied, "I…strongly disagree. We can be asked to *believe* a person who reports sexual assault. And we can *believe* her. And we do."

At the time, this seemed like a she-said/she-said argument about an accusation, the truth of which could never be authoritatively established or denied. Now, it looks like something very different: a debate between a writer who follows the evidence, and another who makes ignoring it a point of principle.

* * *

On April 20, 2016, Martha Piper held an impromptu meeting with the B.C. bureau of *The Globe and Mail*, in which she stated that she was considering banning romantic relationships between UBC faculty and students: "In a power situation where somebody has power over your career, your advancement, your grades, you may say you consent because of the power situation."

By coincidence, just five days later, on April 25, 2016, Madam Justice Boyd officially delivered her final report to Dean Gage Averill. Boyd found that all of the sexual assault allegations in 2011 against Galloway were not proven, based on a balance-of-probabilities standard; and that "for the next two years, from the Spring of 2011 until the Spring of 2013, the parties were involved in an extramarital affair, in which there is no allegation of harassment or assault."

Amazingly, the only thing Galloway had done wrong – have a consensual affair with MC – was the one important thing that MC herself had tried to deny.

But this was not the result the mob wanted. And so even after Boyd submitted her report, UBC would once again look to one of the complainants to find more dirt on Galloway – this time tapping AC4, Sierra Skye Gemma, to investigate Galloway's financial dealings during his time as department head. (On her CV, Gemma is listed as serving as "Financial Processing Specialist, UBC Department of Creative Writing, 2014-2016.")

The Globe and Mail later interviewed Gemma, who stated that she was asked to review requisitions by Galloway, and that "I believe that UBC was very thoroughly investigating all his actions as chair of the program."

Andreas Schroeder saw it differently: "I got the impression that when [Boyd] exonerated Steve, the dean and the program co-chairs realized they'd lost their justification for firing him, but meanwhile they'd gotten everyone so cranked up with their reckless accusations that now everyone expected a firing – so then they started digging into his administrative work, to see if they could cook up some more charges."

But as things turned out, the actual content of the Boyd report didn't really percolate into much of the media coverage – because the report was never officially released, and the propaganda campaign against Galloway on social media and on campus had already served to destroy his reputation.

On June 22, 2016, UBC announced that they were firing Galloway under the conveniently vague rationale of "breach of trust." This result was celebrated on social media by the complainants and their many allies, and used as evidence to support their claims that Galloway was a violent sexual predator. Even though Boyd hadn't backed up MC, or substantiated any of the ancillary accusations, and even though Gemma failed to turn up any financial wrongdoing, it still was possible to ride the public narrative that Galloway was a toxic male who misused his power to have sex with at least one woman. It wasn't true. For hash-tag purposes, however, it was sufficiently truthy.

But of course, people don't live in social media. They live in the real world of human beings. And in that real world, Galloway would slip into a suicidal depression that would require his friends and family to keep him on round-the-clock watch. Anyone who has spent time with the man over the last two-and-a-half years can see not only the mental toll this has taken on him, but also the physical toll. And he would continue slogging through an arbitration process with the university, the ground rules of which required that he say nothing – even as thousands of people told lies about him.

* * *

Following Galloway's bout with suicidal depression, I was asked to publish a letter in defense of his right to due process. I originally declined to do this, but changed my mind in direct response to over-the-top comments by writer Jane Eaton Hamilton, who wrote on Facebook, "I don't know what the allegations here are specifically, but even actions that fall short of rape (harassment, unsafe environments etc.) have long-term impacts on their victims and a true financial cost. If there are multiple reports, even if unprovable in court, or 'unsubstantiated,' you can bet there were multiple 'inappropriate actions' or whatever the allegations are. Smoke really does mean fire." This wasn't just about Galloway, I decided. In a world where suspicion always indicates guilt, due process is dead.

The public letter was published on November 15, 2016, two days from the anniversary of Galloway's suspension and incarceration in Ohio. I did not write the letter, but I did publish it and provide its name, "UBC Accountable." Over 90 Canadian writers would sign it, though many would end up removing their names after being attacked publicly as "rape apologists."

The first person to respond to the letter was UBC President Santa Ono, who messaged me via Twitter, about half an hour after the site went live. This was before any public criticism had been leveled at me or the letter, in what would later become a sort of civil war that separated the Canadian literary community into the modern equivalent of pro- and anti-Dreyfus factions.

At this point, I was still hopeful that UBC would

learn from its mistakes, and belatedly take a leadership role in ensuring due process for Galloway. I wrote back to the new UBC President: "I can't imagine this being a fair thing to inherit at all. Part of the great tragedy is that it has hurt Steven, his family, the complainants, the Creative Writing Department, the writing community, the faculty and the students."

He told me in return that he hoped everyone realized that all of this happened long before he arrived at UBC — a comment that I hoped signaled his desire to treat Galloway, and others, fairly. As it turns out, I was wrong.

When I asked UBC for comment from Piper about any role she may have had in abetting Galloway's railroading, I was provided with a statement from Philip Steenkamp, Vice-President of External Relations, on behalf of the university. It was a boilerplate response, essentially identical to one that the university released in June 2018, following the announcement that it had reached a financial settlement with Galloway, described below, over his claims for reputational damage and infringement of privacy.

Ironically, UBC's communications department sent me Steenkamp's statement just hours after his own resignation was announced. As UBC's student newspaper reports: "Steenkamp is the fifth member of UBC's administration to leave in the past year and the third to do so in the past two months."

* * *

This is not just a story about one novelist whose reputation was destroyed — at least, temporarily — by allegations that did not stand up to fair and unbiased examination. It is also a cautionary tale that shows why due process and the presumption of innocence are pillars of any just society.

That is especially true when someone's guilt becomes the subject of a cult-like obsession. As a Vancouver-based writer, I can attest that it now has become difficult to convince Galloway's detractors to examine any of the actual evidence. It feels like trying to convince a devout Christian evangelist to imagine a world in which there is no such thing as the devil.

Indeed, the language used to describe Galloway truly does evoke demonic themes, as if the man were a font of almost supernatural malignancy. In 2017, for instance, Dalhousie English Department professor Erin Wunker presented an academic paper at the Congress of the Humanities and Social Sciences, in which she reportedly said: "We will never know the scope of Galloway's violence, and can never fully account for it."

But what kind of devil gets paid by his former employer for destroying his image? It was announced that UBC has paid Galloway $167,000 for violating his privacy rights and damaging his reputation — a result highly inconsistent with the idea that he is guilty of anything resembling the "serious allegations" announced in November, 2015.

If UBC were a normal place, and the allegations against Galloway were treated in a normal way, one would think that this development would help lead some of Galloway's detractors to rethink their views. Instead, they have again taken to social media to call him a rapist, mock his suicidal depression, and even threaten him with violence. This includes writer Susan MacRae, who wrote on Twitter that "this past week two actually talented and more successful individuals [Anthony Bourdain and Kate Spade] did commit suicide without alerting the media first – they were even more successful at suicide than Steven Galloway."

As has already been noted on this site, the vicious prosecution of the Galloway hate cult has swallowed up other victims. After the UBC Accountable letter was published, Sierra Skye Gemma took to Twitter to defend herself by means of attacking Margaret Atwood, one of the few novelists in Canada who is even more accomplished than Galloway. In a 74-tweet rant, Gemma contextualizes her attacks with graphic accounts of sex abuse she reports as having endured during childhood.

In October 2017, Gemma shared a post on her Facebook wall that solicited anonymous allegations against men in Canadian publishing on behalf of a Buzzfeed reporter. Rooney's husband Taylor

Brown-Evans, who is an adjunct instructor in UBC's Creative Writing Department (hired by Galloway), also shared this post.

Echoing statements made during the attacks on Galloway, the tone suggests that failure to produce accusations might be seen as tantamount to cowardice in the war against sexual abuse: "If you would like to anonymously name your abuser/harasser (in the Canadian publishing industry), you can share this information with me and I will pass it on, anonymously, to another woman who is collecting abusers' names to pass them on to Buzzfeed's new anonymous tip line... This is what *I* am doing to support survivors. What are *you* going to do to support survivors?"

A few months later, a small Canadian publisher, Coach House Books, announced they were cancelling their poetry program.

In an article for *Buzzfeed*, Scaachi Koul reported details of the decision by Coach House's Alana Wilcox to fire poetry editor Jeramy Dodds, based on anonymous allegations emerging from an email account listed as representing a group called CanLit Janitors. The allegations were, and remain, completely unproven. And as Dodds wrote in an impassioned blog post, he never even had a chance to understand them, let alone properly respond to them, before his reputation and livelihood were destroyed at a stroke. (Online trolls didn't confine their attacks to Dodds, but also targeted his fiancée, calling her "fat," and a "fake feminist.")

Dodds' pleas for fair treatment fell on deaf ears. The railroading of Galloway had shown the Canadian literary world that sentencing comes first, the trial comes later (if at all); and that anyone who raises his or her voice on behalf of the presumption of innocence does so at their own peril.

As for Galloway, he effectively became a blank slate in November 2015. It's as if his soul were dipped in bleach, so that thousands of writers, academics, and social justice activists could then project their worst fears, vices, sins, frustrations, jealousies, and academic theories onto him. He became a stand-in for rape, for "toxic masculinity," and even for the patriarchy itself. On the other hand, MC became a sort of #MeToo Joan of Arc to people who still don't know her real name, nor what she had accused Galloway of doing, nor the reasons why Boyd concluded that those events had never happened. As one of MC's online supporters wrote on Twitter, "MC is my hero. I do not know her, but someday I would like to shake her hand. She did the incredibly difficult thing of coming forward."

* * *

Earlier this year, Atwood summed up her thoughts on the Galloway affair with an essay entitled "Am I A Bad Feminist?"

"I believe that in order to have civil and human rights for women there have to be civil and human rights, period, including the right to fundamental justice, just as for women to have the vote, there has to be a vote," she wrote. In regard to the specifics of Galloway's case, she added, "a fair-minded person would now withhold judgment as to guilt until the report and the evidence are available for us to see. We are grownups: We can make up our own minds, one way or the other."

Atwood wrote that back in January, before Galloway was awarded his $167,000, and before many of the most important details of the Boyd report had leaked out. Objective observers now have the tools they need to act like "grownups" and make up their minds.

Boyd doesn't use the term "liar" to describe MC. And, indeed, it is still possible to imagine that, in her own mind, MC actually does still believe her claims to be true. But even according to the loose balance-of-probabilities test applied by Boyd (far less stringent than the beyond-reasonable-doubt standard employed in criminal proceedings), MC's story didn't add up. By any fair measure, Steven Galloway must be regarded as innocent, and the most important inquiry now isn't into his behavior, but into the university that allowed his reputation to be trashed by a mob.

Which brings us back to Madam Justice Smith, who wrote in her report about Berdahl's academic freedom, that "sometimes several relatively small mistakes can lead to a failure of the larger system." I believe the same general principle applies to UBC's treatment of Galloway. There was no institutional conspiracy against the man — just a series of bad, hurried, self-serving decisions aimed at protecting the university from bad press in the short-term, while causing it to thoroughly disgrace itself in the long run.

* * *

Andreas Schroeder was one of the most beloved instructors in UBC's Creative Writing program for a quarter century. He helped found the League of Canadian Poets and The Writers Union of Canada, where he was a primary force behind Canada establishing Public Lending Rights, through which about 17,000 Canadian authors receive $10-million a year — about $300-million in the pockets of Canadian writers since its inception.

There's arguably no one in Canada who has done more for Canadian writers than Andreas Schroeder. But when you come down on the wrong side of an inquisition, your legacy means nothing. All that matters are your views on heretics.

"For 25 years I was considered a member of the tenured faculty, but all of a sudden I was excised," Schroeder said.

In his final semester of teaching, Schroeder was

the subject of a complaint. In one of several hit pieces on Galloway, UBC's student newspaper would describe an interview with a student, identified only as Erin, who wrote: "Having to be in that class with [Schroeder] a day or two days after I had found out that he had signed that letter [seeking due process for Galloway] was a tough class...It was just this elephant in the room that wasn't being addressed – like everyone just looked pretty visibly upset. Especially the women and queer students."

As an educator, Galloway's legacy was to instill pride and enthusiasm in hundreds of students who passed through the UBC Creative Writing program. The legacy of Galloway's inquisitors, on the other hand, is to convince students that due process, a concept that sits at the foundation of any democratic system of government, is a sinister force that wounds the soul and harms women.

I have known and admired Schroeder since I completed a single year in UBC's MFA program in 2001. I knew Galloway as I knew other people in the literary community whom I would see at large events from time to time, but we were never close. The first time I would have talked to Galloway one-on-one was nearly two years ago, in 2016, when a friend suggested I begin trying to piece together what UBC had done to him. I had no preconceptions. If anything, my credentials as a member of the leftist literati would have pushed me into the accusers' camp. It was the facts that persuaded me, not the man or his literary reputation.

UBC invited me to Schroeder's retirement party, which was held on campus. Co-chairs Lyon and Svendsen didn't show up. And, as if in a scene from *Curb Your Enthusiasm*, UBC put the wrong name (Rhea, the name of another retiring faculty member) on Schroeder's retirement cake. But he was determined to have a good time anyway.

I had the honor of bringing Schroeder a retirement gift. It was a present from Steven Galloway — the large brass marine bell that he had installed in the hall of the Creative Writing department as his first act as Chair. Galloway had planned to keep the bell until after his arbitration, at which time he intended to throw it in the Pacific Ocean. But when he heard about Schroeder's retirement party, he changed his mind.

UBC was once Galloway's family. As much as they would like to now forget he ever darkened their halls, he was, in fact, widely seen as a rising star — a local Vancouver boy who had come up through their undergrad program to become an international bestselling author.

In 2000, *The Vancouver Sun* ran a profile piece on up-and-coming writers called "The 10 Most Vaunted." Nine of the ten writers featured were UBC grads, including Galloway, who described himself as the university's "least likely to succeed." He described a "painfully normal" childhood growing up in Kamloops, B.C., where he worked at MacDon-ald's, never did "anything interesting, ever," and was a total "wuss." To round out the interview Galloway described himself as "an awful writer, just hideous." Seventeen years later, his lit-nerd profile now stands out as the strongest of the 10 featured writers.

After the article ran, Galloway's publisher insist-ed he enroll himself in media training. But Galloway knew what he was doing, and was already on his way to turning compulsive self-deprecation into part of his brand. But while he loved being personally lam-pooned for his awkwardness, he became a tireless defender of UBC Creative Writing and would rise against any public criticism of the department.

What Annabel Lyon said about Galloway chang-ing her child's diapers was true. For many years, he had Christmas dinner with fellow faculty member Nancy Lee and her extended family. Once, on Fa-ther's Day, when Galloway's mentor Keith Maillard was missing his own children, who happened to be out of town, Galloway took him to dinner. On the Ac-knowledgments page of her 2014 novel *Pedal*, Chelsea Rooney thanks "Steven Galloway, who encouraged me to commit to writing at a very important time in my life." (Galloway had actively mentored Rooney, and had helped her shop the book to publishers. He even blurbed *Pedal*, which was published just a year before the accusations against him were aired in late 2015: "*Pedal* is a brave and captivating book, written with an unflinching eye and a deep understanding of the torment that is the human condition. Chelsea Rooney is a major talent.")

The thesis bell symbolized how Galloway felt about his department and its students — before the institution effectively destroyed him because of allegations that ultimately didn't withstand serious scrutiny. I brought the bell back to the UBC campus in the same brown box the University had used to rid themselves of the object.

Any of the many dozens of former Creative Writing students at UBC who rang it would still recognize that bell instantly if they saw it. Only one small detail has changed since the days when it hung outside Galloway's office — a text engraving that Galloway added in tribute to the person who had fought in vain to have it put back up: *Andreas Schroeder, UBC 1993-2017, Never Stop Ringing The Bell.*

AUTHOR'S POSTSCRIPT – SEPTEMBER 2020
Shortly after this essay was published, I spoke to Steven Galloway, who said that a former publishing associate reached out to ask for his forgiveness. He had assumed Galloway's guilt after hearing multiple salacious allegations, but now that he knew the truth he was ashamed for having not stood by him. While this apology was not meant for me, I consider it to be one of the finest compliments I have received as a writer.

The public reaction was likewise positive, with the exception being a self-described Canadian "media critic" named Jesse Brown, who took to Twitter to demand corrections and attack me personally in an attempt to discredit my reporting. Brown had himself followed the story, and consistently reported a one-sided version informed mostly by the same people who falsely accused Galloway in the first place. Brown relied especially on the claims of Chelsea Rooney, despite the fact that her claims were called out as singularly unreliable by the former B.C. Supreme Court justice who investigated the case. Brown thereby re-aired debunked allegations, while also exposing Rooney herself to further criticism and even ridicule.

I'm proud to say that the true facts of this story are exactly as they first appeared in Quillette. The editors checked Brown's claims and found them to be without merit. While Brown couldn't poke any holes in the story, his attitude did help convince Galloway that the only way to truly clear his name would be in a court of law. In October 2018, four months after this article appeared, Galloway filed a defamation suit in a B.C. court, which now is awaiting trial. As Galloway put it to me, "hearing Brown's podcast, calling into question the provable facts in this essay — that was the deciding factor in my decision to commence litigation. The truth is not subjective." Brown is not one of the defendants. But like many media figures who swallowed the false claims against Galloway, he bears responsibility for the injustice that occurred.

It took a long time for Chagnon to acclimatize to the deep interior of the Amazon Rainforest and its unique threats. The insects continued to plague him — not just the flying stinging ones, but termites that claimed unguarded shoes as nests, and spiders and scorpions drawn to warm clothes in the middle of the night. He would later find himself face to face with an anaconda. "I laid my double-barrel twelve-gauge shotgun on the bank next to me," he recalled. Moments later, "the water *exploded* in front of me: a very large anaconda head shot out of the water and whizzed just inches from my face. I immediately went into a rage: This son-of-a-bitch of a snake was trying to kill me!" Chagnon began firing rounds into the snake, which violently twisted and turned as he reloaded, fired, and reloaded. But Chagnon was more worried about jaguars, which were known to kill groups of men in a single attack. From time to time, Chagnon and his companions would find themselves stalked by these predators, sometimes for hours on end. They could be heard at night, prowling around the makeshift camps he slept in as he travelled between villages. One night, he awoke to find a jaguar baring its teeth at him as he lay in his hammock. But the mosquito net and the yelling of villagers confused the animal, which darted back into the bush.

In 1966, Chagnon began working with the geneticist James Neel, who had managed to convince the Atomic Energy Commission to fund a genetic study of an isolated population and was able to pay Chagnon a salary to assist his research there. Neel's team took blood samples from the Yanomamö, and began administering the Edmonston B vaccine when they discovered that the Yanomamö had no antibodies to the measles. In some ways, the Yanomamö sounded like something out of any anthropology textbook – they were patrilineal and polygamous (polygyny); like other cultures around the world, they carved a position for the levirate – a man who married his dead brother's wife; they had ceremonial roles and practiced ritual confinement with taboos on food and sex. But sometimes this exotic veneer would be punctured by their shared humanity, particularly their mischievous sense of humor. Early in Chagnon's research, the Yanomamö pranked the anthropologist by providing him with vulgarities when he asked their names. He did not realize this until he began bragging to a group of Yanomamö about how well he now understood their genealogies. As he began, the Yanomamö erupted into laughter, tears streaming from their faces. They begged him to continue and, oblivious, Chagnon went on: "Hairy Cunt was married to the headman, Long Dong, their youngest son was Asshole, and so on." When he discovered he'd been tricked, Chagnon was embarrassed and furious that five months of patient name gathering had yielded nothing but a litany of insults. From that day forward, he would cross-check all information between individual Yanomamö informants and villages.

But for all the jocularity, Chagnon found that up to 30 percent of all Yanomamö males died a violent death. Warfare and violence were common, and dueling was a ritual practice, in which two men would take turns flogging each other over the head with a club, until one of the combatants succumbed. Chagnon was adamant that the primary causes of violence among the Yanomamö were revenge killings and women. The latter may not seem surprising to anyone aware of the ubiquity of ruthless male sexual competition in the animal kingdom, but anthropologists generally believed that human violence found its genesis in more immediate matters, such as disputes over resources. When Chagnon asked the Yanomamö shaman Dedeheiwa to explain the cause of violence, he replied, "Don't ask such stupid questions! Women! Women! Women! Women! Women!" Such fights erupted over sexual jealousy, sexual impropriety, rape, and attempts at seduction, kidnap and failure to deliver a promised girl.

Internecine raids and attacks often involved attempts by a man or group to abduct another's women. "The victim is grabbed by her abductors by one arm, and her protectors grab the other arm. Then both groups pull in opposite directions," Chagnon learned. In one instance, a woman's arms were reportedly pulled out of their sockets: "The victim invariably screams in agony, and the struggle can last several long minutes until one group takes control of her."

Although one in five Yanomamö women Chagnon interviewed had been kidnapped from another village, some of these women were grateful to find that their new husbands were less cruel than their former ones. The treatment of Yanomamö women could be particularly gruesome, and Chagnon had to wrestle with the ethical dilemmas that confront anthropologists under such circumstances – should he intervene or remain an observer? Men frequently beat their wives, mainly out of sexual jealousy, shot arrows into them, or even held burning sticks between their legs to discourage the possibility of infidelity. On one occasion, a man bludgeoned his wife in the head with firewood and in front of an impassive audience. "Her head bounced off the ground with each ruthless blow, as if he were pounding a soccer ball with a baseball bat. The head-man and I intervened at that point – he was killing her." Chagnon stitched her head back up. The woman recovered but she subsequently dropped her infant into a fire as she slept, and was later killed by a venomous snake. Life in the Amazon could be nasty, brutish, and short.

Chagnon would make more than 20 fieldwork visits to the Amazon, and in 1968 he published *Yanomamö: The Fierce People*, which became an instant international bestseller. The book immediately ignited controversy within the field of anthropology. Although it commanded immense respect and became the most commonly taught book in introductory anthropology courses, the very subtitle of the book annoyed those anthropologists who preferred to give their monographs titles like *The Gentle Tasaday, The Gentle People, The Harmless People, The Peaceful People, Never in Anger,* and *The Semai: A Nonviolent People of Malaya.* The stubborn tendency within the discipline was to paint an unrealistic façade over such cultures – although 61 percent of Waorani men met a violent death, an anthropologist nevertheless described this Amazonian people as a "tribe where harmony rules," on account of an "ethos that emphasized peacefulness."[1] Anthropologists who considered such a society harmonious were unlikely to be impressed by Chagnon's description of the Yanomamö as "The Fierce People," where "only" 30 percent of males died by violence. The same anthropologist who had ascribed a prevailing ethos of peace to the Waoroni later accused Chagnon, in the gobbledygook of anthropological jargon, of the "projection of traditional preconceptions of the Western construction of Otherness."[2]

These anthropologists were made more squeamish still by Chagnon's discovery that the *unokai* of the Yanomamö – men who had killed and assumed a ceremonial title – had about three times more children than others, owing to having twice as many wives. Drawing on this observation in his 1988 *Science* article "Life Histories, Blood Revenge, and Warfare in a Tribal Population," Chagnon suggested that men who had demonstrated success at a cultural phenomenon, the military prowess of revenge killings, were held in higher esteem and considered more attractive mates. In some quarters outside of anthropology, Chagnon's theory came as no surprise, but its implication for anthropology could be profound. In *The Better Angels of Our Nature*, Steven Pinker points out that if violent men turn out to be more evolutionarily fit, "this arithmetic, if it persisted over many generations, would favor a genetic tendency to be willing and able to kill."

The question of whether or not higher fitness for violent males is a universal phenomenon common to all humanity in prehistory remains contested. But Chagnon appears to have thought so: "Conflicts over the means of reproduction – women – dominated the political machinations of men during the vast span of human history and shaped human male psychology." Chagnon's detractors were appalled. Not only was he accusing a pristine Amazon society of rewarding its most violent males with reproductive success, he was also inferring that mankind itself was stained with the blood of our ancestors. This hypothesis threatened to force an entirely new way of thinking about human behavior, and promote a new paradigm of human behavioral ecology. Chagnon had tottered onto the unforgiving battlefield of the science wars, and anthropologists lined up to shower him with criticism and derision. The contempt for Chagnon became so petty that some anthropologists refused to use his transliteration "Yanomamö," opting for "Yanomami" instead. If they couldn't agree on the name of the people, what else could they hope to agree about?

Chagnon considered his most formidable critic to be the eminent anthropologist Marvin Harris. Harris had been crowned the unofficial historian of the field following the publication of his all-encompassing work *The Rise of Anthropological Theory.* He was the founder of the highly influential materialist school of anthropology, and argued that ethnographers should first seek material explanations for human behavior before considering alternatives, as "human social life is a response to the practical problems of earthly existence."[3] Harris held that the structure and "superstructure" of a society are largely epiphenomena of its "infrastructure," meaning that the economic and social organization, beliefs, values, ideology, and symbolism of a culture evolve as a result of changes in the material circumstances of a particular society, and that apparently quaint cultural practices tend to reflect man's relationship to his environment. For instance, prohibition on beef consumption among Hindus in India is *not* primarily due to religious injunctions. These religious beliefs are themselves epiphenomena to the *real* reasons: that cows are more valuable for pulling plows and producing fertilizers and dung for burning. Cultural materialism places an emphasis on "-etic" over "-emic" explanations, ignoring the opinions of people within a society and trying to uncover the hidden reality behind those opinions.

Naturally, when the Yanomamö explained that warfare and fights were caused by women and blood feuds, Harris sought a material explanation that would draw upon immediate survival concerns. Chagnon's data clearly confirmed that the larger a village, the more likely fighting, violence, and warfare were to occur. In his book *Good to Eat: Riddles of Food and Culture*, Harris argued that fighting occurs more often in larger Yanomamö villages because these villages deplete the local game levels in the rainforest faster than smaller villages, leaving the men no option but to fight with each other or to attack outside groups for meat to fulfil their protein macronutrient needs. When Chagnon put Harris's materialist theory to the Yanomamö, they laughed and replied, "Even though we like meat, we like women a whole lot more."[4] Chagnon believed that smaller villages avoided violence because they were composed of tighter kin groups – those communities had just two or three extended families and had developed more stable systems of borrowing wives from each other.

Despite the Yanomamö's rebuke, it is evident from his popular book *Cows, Pigs, War and Witches* and his technical book *Cultural Materialism: The Struggle for A Science of Culture* that Harris saw himself as the world's foremost anthropological theoretician. His mission was to take anthropology to new heights of knowledge by uncovering the material logic behind the world's belief systems and social behavior. Harris threw down a challenge to Chagnon that would shape his Amazon research in 1975: prove that the Yanomamö get more daily protein than what is in a Big Mac and Harris would eat his own hat. While Chagnon and another anthropologist Raymond Hames did indeed find this to be the case in 1975, another anthropologist Kenneth Good found daily protein consumption to be just under that of a Big Mac, leaving the debate in limbo.[5] Nonetheless, these findings probably left Harris uncomfortable, and his opposition to human behavioral ecology and sociobiology continued to escalate.

One evening, Chagnon attended a debate about sociobiology between Edward Wilson and Harris at the Smithsonian Institute. At one point, Harris began describing the dangers of sociobiology, and then paused. "Did you know," he asked, "that there is a certain anthropologist, a man who has become famous for his long-term studies of Amazon Indians, who claims, ladies and gentleman, that this tribe not only has a gene for warfare, but he claims they also have genes for infanticide!" This was such a caricature of Chagnon's actual view that he challenged Harris to defend it during the Q&A that followed the debate. Questions were handed from the audience to the debaters written on cards, and Chagnon demanded that Harris "Identify the anthropologist who claimed that the people he studied had genes for warfare and infanticide." Throughout the question time period Harris kept shuffling Chagnon's question to the back of the pile until the moderator brought the event to a close and thanked everyone for their attendance. Unwilling to let Harris off the hook, Chagnon rose from his seat in the audience and again demanded that Harris identify this famous anthropologist who had spoken of genes for warfare and infanticide. The audience immediately recognized Chagnon from his documentaries and began shouting, "Let him speak! Let him speak!" Momentarily taken aback, Harris confessed that if he had misunderstood Chagnon that he was welcome to return to anthropology, to which Chagnon replied that he had never left anthropology.

While Harris and other anthropologists in the United States continued to criticize Chagnon, his standing began to deteriorate on another front. From the moment he arrived in the Amazon, Chagnon maintained cordial relations with a missionary priest of the Salesians of Don Bosco. In fact, Chagnon and the priest became such good friends that the priest asked Chagnon to kill one of his fellow missionaries for him, a man who had broken his vows of celibacy by sleeping with a Yanomamö woman. The priest worried that this could bring shame to the Salesian order. Of course, Chagnon refused, and his refusal strained their relationship. Their relationship worsened when Chagnon discovered that the missionaries had been distributing shotguns to the natives and that these were being used in warfare. Furthermore, all of

Chagnon's recommendations for preventing measles outbreaks were ignored by the Salesians, who built missions and tried to have the Yanomamö concentrate around them, which helped the disease to spread rapidly. Their relationship finally collapsed altogether after Chagnon cooperated with a documentary that painted the Salesians in a less than flattering light. By the early 1990s, the missionaries were increasingly worried about Chagnon's presence in the Amazon, especially when it came to light that the BBC and *Nova* would be producing a new documentary in the rainforest about his dispute with Marvin Harris. By the early 1990s, the Salesians were attempting to block his lifetime of fieldwork in the Amazon, and they successfully lobbied Maria Luisa Allais, the head of the Venezuelan Indian Commission, to refuse him a permit he required for re-entry.

Then, in 1993, tragedy struck in the Amazon when gold miners crossed the border from Brazil and slaughtered a number of Yanomamö, including women and children. The explorer Charles Brewer-Carías was chosen to head a presidential commission into the massacre, and he wanted Chagnon on the commission as one of the few anthropologists in the world who spoke Yanomamö. When President Carlos Perez of Venezuela learned that Chagnon had been denied an entry permit, he telephoned the Ministry of Education and ordered them to issue Chagnon with one at once. A visibly nervous Maria Luisa Allais offered

Chagnon his papers. That Chagnon went above the head of the Indian Commission and was now installed on the presidential commission investigating the massacre only infuriated the Salesians further. They believed that they ought to be the ones conducting the investigation. On the very first day of their investigation at the site of the massacre, a helicopter arrived bearing men armed with machine guns and a Salesian bishop, who ordered Brewer-Carías and Chagnon to leave. With the government on the brink of a coup and unwilling to enforce law and order in the deep interior of the Amazon, the commission to investigate the massacre quickly fell apart. Chagnon was left with lifelong regrets that there had been no justice for the dead.

Notwithstanding his bitter intellectual rivalry with Chagnon, Marvin Harris would play no role in the sensational accusations that Chagnon had behaved unethically while conducting his research in the Amazon. These would be made by a coalition of less prominent anthropologists, some with official functions in activist organizations, which had been formed to oppose Chagnon in any way possible. David Maybury-Lewis, the head of the organization Cultural Survival, was an early critic of Chagnon, and one of the first anthropologists to complain about the subtitle of *Yanomamö: The Fierce People*. Maybury-Lewis's student Terence Turner, president of Survival International USA, was an even more outspoken critic of Chagnon. Survival International, an organization that has more recently attacked Steven Pinker for *The Better Angels of Our Nature*, has long promoted the Rousseauvian image of a traditional people who need to be preserved in all their natural wonder from the ravages of the modern world. Survival International does not welcome anthropological findings that complicate this harmonious picture, and Chagnon had wandered straight into their line of fire. Their web site still features a petition denouncing Chagnon's characterization of the Yanomamö, signed by a handful of his critics: "We absolutely disagree with Napoleon Chagnon's public characterization of the Yanomami as fierce, violent, and archaic people."

For years, Survival International's Terence Turner had been assisting a self-described journalist, Patrick Tierney, as the latter investigated Chagnon for his book, *Darkness in El Dorado: How Scientists and Journalists Devastated the Amazon*. In 2000, as Tierney's book was being readied for publication, Turner and his colleague Leslie Sponsel wrote to the president of the American Anthropological Association (AAA) and informed her that an unprecedented crisis was about to engulf the field of anthropology. This, they warned, would be a scandal that, "in its scale, ramifications, and sheer criminality and corruption, is unparalleled in the history of Anthropology." Tierney alleged that Chagnon and Neel had spread measles among the Yanomamö in 1968 by using compromised vaccines, and that Chagnon's documentaries depicting Yanomamö violence were faked by using Yanomamö to act out dangerous scenes, in which further lives were lost. Chagnon was blamed, *inter alia*, for inciting violence among the Yanomamö, cooking his data, starting wars, and aiding corrupt politicians. Neel was also accused of withholding vaccines from certain populations of natives as part of an experiment. The media were not slow to pick up on Tierney's allegations, and the *Guardian* ran an article under an inflammatory headline accusing Neel and Chagnon of eugenics: "Scientists 'killed Amazon Indians to test race theory.'" Turner claimed that Neel believed in a gene for "leadership" and that the human genetic stock could be upgraded by wiping out mediocre people. "The political implication of this fascistic eugenics," Turner told the *Guardian*, "is clearly that society should be reorganized into small breeding isolates in which genetically superior males could emerge into dominance, eliminating or subordinating the male losers."

By the end of 2000, the American Anthropological Association announced a hearing on Tierney's book. This was not entirely reassuring news to Chagnon, given their history with anthropologists who failed to toe the party line. During the Freeman-Mead controversy, in which New Zealand anthropologist Derek Freeman had critiqued Margaret Mead's book *Coming of Age in Samoa*, the American Association for the Advancement of Science's magazine *Science* had praised Freeman's critique at the same time the American Anthropological Association had denounced it. Thereafter, the AAA denounced *Science* and the American Association for the Advancement of Science for *not* denouncing Freeman. Now, an Academies of Sciences investigation concluded that Tierney's claims in *Darkness in El Dorado* were "demonstrably false," and that his book represented "a grave disservice...to science itself." The American Anthropological Association, on the other hand, stated that, *"Darkness in El Dorado* has contributed a valuable service to our discipline." A task force was formally set up after this, not to "investigate" Chagnon, which would have violated the AAA's Code of Ethics, but to "inquire" about Tierney's allegations.

Behind the closed doors of that inquiry, tensions developed. "The book is just a piece of sleaze, that's all there is to it," the head of the AAA's task force, Jane Hill, wrote to another anthropologist about Tierney's book. "But I think the AAA had to do something," Hill added, "because I really think that the future of work by anthropologists with indigenous peoples in Latin America – with a high potential to do good – was put seriously at risk by its accusations."[6] Tormented to learn that the anthropological community was actually taking the accusations in *Darkness in El Dorado* seriously, Chagnon was hospitalized after he collapsed suffering from stress. Suspecting that the task force had been constituted to find Chagnon guilty of at least some of Tierney's accusations, the anthropologist Raymond Hame resigned from the panel. In 2002, the AAA accepted the task force's report. Although the task force was not an "investigation" concerned with any particular person, for all intents and purposes, it blamed Chagnon for portraying the Yanomamö in a way that was harmful and held him responsible for prioritizing his research over their interests.

Nonetheless, the most serious claims Tierney made in *Darkness in El Dorado* collapsed like a house of cards. Elected Yanomamö leaders issued a statement in 2000 stating that Chagnon had arrived after the measles epidemic and saved lives: "Dr. Chagnon – known to us as Shaki – came into our communities with some physicians and he vaccinated us against the epidemic disease which was killing us. Thanks to this, hundreds of us survived and we are very thankful to Dr. Chagnon and his collaborators for help."[7] Investigations by the American Society of Human Genetics and the International Genetic Epidemiology Society both found Tierney's claims regarding the measles outbreak to be unfounded. The Society of Visual Anthropology reviewed the so-called faked documentaries, and determined that these allegations were also false. Then an independent preliminary report released by a team of anthropologists dissected Tierney's book claim by claim, concluding that all of

Tierney's most important assertions were either deliberately fraudulent or, at the very least, misleading. The University of Michigan reached the same conclusion. "We are satisfied," its Provost stated, "that Dr. Neel and Dr. Chagnon, both among the most distinguished scientists in their respective fields, acted with integrity in conducting their research...The serious factual errors we have found call into question the accuracy of the entire book [*Darkness in El Dorado*] as well as the interpretations of its author."[8] Academic journal articles began to proliferate, detailing the mis-inquiry and flawed conclusions of the 2002 task force. By 2005, only three years later, the American Anthropological Association voted to withdraw the 2002 task force report, re-exonerating Chagnon.

A statement by the leaders of the Yanomamö and their Ye'kwana neighbors called for Tierney's head: "We demand that our national government investigate the false statements of Tierney, which taint the humanitarian mission carried out by Shaki [Chagnon] with much tenderness and respect for our communities."[9] The investigation never occurred, but Tierney's public image lay in ruins and would suffer even more at the hands of historian of science Alice Dreger, who interviewed dozens of people involved in the controversy. Although Tierney had thanked a Venezuelan anthropologist for providing him with a dossier of information on Chagnon for his book, the anthropologist told Dreger that Tierney had actually written the dossier himself and then misrepresented it as an independent source of information.[10]

By 2012, Tierney had disappeared. He would not write or appear in public again. Chagnon, on the other hand, was elected to the National Academy of Sciences, the most prestigious accolade that can befall a scientist after the Nobel Prize. Chagnon considered this a vindication, but to this day, some anthropologists cling to Tierney's allegations, or some revised version of them. Turner abandoned many of Tierney's claims but spent years looking for further evidence against Chagnon. In 2013, the anthropologist David Price wrote an article for the radical left-wing outlet *CounterPunch* castigating the National Academy of Sciences for electing Chagnon to such a prestigious position, and cited Tierney's book without bothering to mention that the author and argument had since been discredited. Anthropologist Marshall Sahlins, who had also praised Tierney's book in earlier times, resigned from the National Academy of Sciences to protest Chagnon's election. Sahlin's protégé, David Graeber, explained that, "Sahlins is a man of genuine principle... He's never had a lot of patience for shirtless macho Americans who descend into jungles, declaring their inhabitants to be violent savages, and then use that as an excuse to start behaving like violent savages themselves." The row between Chagnon's detractors and supporters continues to this day, in spite of the available evidence. As Alice Dreger told Graeber on social media in 2013, "If Sahlins can't face the facts about what Chagnon didn't do, then maybe he shouldn't be in the Nat Acad of Sci anyway."

Scientific American has described the controversy as "Anthropology's Darkest Hour," and it raises troubling questions about the entire field. In 2013, Chagnon published his final book, *Noble Savages: My Life Among Two Dangerous Tribes — The Yanomamö and the Anthropologists*. Chagnon had long felt that anthropology was experiencing a schism more significant than any difference between research paradigms or schools of ethnography — a schism between those dedicated to the very science of mankind, anthropologists in the *true* sense of the word, and those opposed to science; either postmodernists vaguely defined, or activists disguised as scientists who seek to place indigenous advocacy above the pursuit of objective truth. Chagnon identified Nancy Scheper-Hughes as a leader in the activist faction of anthropologists, citing her statement that we "need not entail a philosophical commitment to Enlightenment notions of reason and truth."[11]

Whatever the rights and wrongs of Chagnon's debates with Marvin Harris across three decades, Harris's materialist paradigm was a *scientifically* debatable hypothesis, which caused Chagnon to realize that he and his old rival shared more in common than they did with the activist forces emerging in the field: "Ironically, Harris and I both argued for a *scientific view* of human behavior at a time when increasing numbers of anthropologists were becoming skeptical of the scientific approach." When Nancy Scheper-Hughes wrote that "if we cannot begin to think about social institutions and practices in moral or ethical terms, then anthropology strikes me as quite weak and useless,"[12] Marvin Harris added that "if we cannot begin to think about social institutions and practices in scientific-objective terms, then anthropology will be even weaker and more useless."[13]

Both Chagnon and Harris agreed that anthropology's move away from being a scientific enterprise was dangerous. And both believed that anthropologists, not to mention thinkers in other fields of social sciences, were disguising their increasingly anti-scientific activism as research by using obscurantist postmodern gibberish. Observers have remarked at how abstruse humanities research has become. And even a world famous linguist like Noam Chomsky admits, "It seems to me to be some exercise by intellectuals who talk to each other in very obscure ways, and I can't follow it, and I don't think anybody else can." Chagnon resigned his membership of the American Anthropological Association in the 1980s, stating that he no longer understood the "unintelligible mumbo jumbo of postmodern jargon" taught in the field.[14] In his last book, *Theories of Culture in Postmodern Times*, Harris virtually agreed with Chagnon. "Postmodernists," he wrote, "have achieved the ability to write about their thoughts in a uniquely *impenetrable* manner. Their neo-baroque prose style with its inner clauses, bracketed syllables, metaphors and metonyms, verbal pirouettes, curlicues and figures is not a mere epiphenomenon; rather, it is a mocking rejoinder to anyone who would try to write simple intelligible sentences in the modernist tradition."

Harris was generally recognized as the most prolific and influential theorist of anthropology in recent decades. Chagnon was one of anthropology's last great ethnographers in the vein of Mead and Malinowski. And, in their later years, both men watched as the field became unrecognizable under the spell of, as Harris put it, the "mantra of Foucault," with its consequent suspicion of objective knowledge independent of the subjective person. By 2004, the cultural materialists who had long disputed Chagnon's behavioral ecological views, but who shunned postmodernism, were among his greatest supporters. Writing in *American Anthropologist*, Daniel R. Gross, Marvin Harris's former student and research collaborator on the protein-warfare theory, came to Chagnon's defense by pointing out numerous instances where the American Anthropological Association had over-relied on the validity of subjective points of view in its task force report. Gross argued that the turn toward postmodernism in the field had irrevocably altered not only the content of anthropological research, but how the American Anthropological Association as a professional body chooses to conduct investigations and handles allegations of misconduct. The AAA's suspiciousness of the authenticity of objective evidence, Gross wrote, "reflects a philosophical stance of postmodern scholarship, in which objective truth may be seen as unattainable and contingent." It was Daniel R. Gross, along with Thomas A. Gregor, who forced the American Anthropological Association to the vote to rescind the 2002 report of the task force.

The quest for knowledge of mankind has in many respects become unrecognizable in the field that now calls itself anthropology. According to Chagnon, we've entered a period of "darkness in cultural anthropology." With his passing, anthropology has become darker still.

AUTHOR'S POSTSCRIPT – SEPTEMBER 2020

On returning from the Amazon, Napoleon Chagnon was once asked to give a talk about Amazonian society to fellow anthropologist Norma Diamond's anthropology class, which included a discussion of Amazonian warfare. Males, it turns out, may fight over women as other animals do under the right conditions. After the lecture, Diamond pulled him aside and professed, "We shouldn't say that native people have warfare and kill each other. People will get the wrong impression." This was a forewarning to Chagnon, a branch extended to him to *self-censor* what both anthropologists knew to be true before external pressure would need to be brought to bear against him.

The history of Chagnon's career shows that cancel culture is not always motivated by a desire to further the truth, but emerges from a complex mixture of motivations. Winston Churchill once observed, "There's no telling what a crazed maniac will do with his back against the wall." Some years later, Leon Festinger found that when people's preconceived ideas are challenged by credible evidence, and their backs are well and truly against the wall, they are *more* likely to fervently promote their beliefs in a desperate attempt to have them socially validated. The reverse applies, too: The source of information creating the dissonance must be socially invalidated. Not challenged but *invalidated*, or better put, cancelled. In the case of Chagnon, the anthropologists tried to use Tierney's slanderous catalogue of accusations, quite removed from the substance of Chagnon's fieldwork, to invalidate his life's research.

Alice Dreger, the historian of science who further exposed Tierney's fraudulent claims, writes about Chagnon's case in her 2015 book *Galileo's Middle Finger*. The book title is a cheeky reference to the ascension of Galileo's public standing after his death and the eventual discrediting of the inquisition that had placed him under house arrest for promoting the heliocentric model of the solar system. Censorship is merely transitory; it is difficult to suppress scientific truths indefinitely. Even if the majority of anthropologists in the field had quietly acquiesced in the cancelling of Chagnon in 2002, the steadfastness of those reputable scholars who bucked the tide and exposed Tierney's fraudulent claims was enough in the end to change sentiment within the field and to spectacularly discredit those who had blindly accepted Tierney's slander. In the murk of our current cancel culture, all might seem dark and lost, but so long as there are some who keep the flame of honest inquiry alight, the efforts of censors and cancellers are always on the edge of collapse.

References

[1,2] Albert, Bruce. "Yanomami" Violence": Inclusive Fitness or Ethnographer's Representation?." (1989): 637-640.

[3] Harris, Marvin. *Cultural materialism: The struggle for a science of culture.* AltaMira Press, 2001.

[4] Kappeler, Peter M., and Joan B. Silk. *Mind the gap.* New York, NY: Springer, 2010.

[5] Chagnon, Napoleon A., and Raymond B. Hames. "Protein deficiency and tribal warfare in Amazonia: New data." *Science* 203.4383 (1979): 910-913.

[6] Dreger, Alice. "Darkness's descent on the American Anthropological Association." *Human Nature* 22.3 (2011): 225-246.

[7] Gregor, Thomas A., and Daniel R. Gross. "Guilt by association: The culture of accusation and the American Anthropological Association's investigation of Darkness in El Dorado." *American anthropologist* 106.4 (2004): 687-698.

[8] Cantor, Nancy. The University of Michigan Statement on 'Darkness in El Dorado.' 2000. Available at: http://ns.umich.edu/Releases/2000/Nov00/r111300a.html

9   Gregor, Thomas A., and Daniel R. Gross. "Guilt by association: The culture of accusation and the American Anthropological Association's investigation of Darkness in El Dorado." *American anthropologist* 106.4 (2004): 687-698.

10   Dreger, Alice. *Galileo's middle finger: Heretics, activists, and one scholar's search for justice.* Penguin Books, 2016.

11, 12   Williams, Gareth. *The other side of the popular: Neoliberalism and subalternity in Latin America.* Duke University Press, 2002.

13   Harris, Marvin. *Theories of culture in postmodern times.* Rowman Altamira, 1998.

14   Chagnon, Napoleon A. *Noble Savages: My Life Among Two Dangerous Tribes–the Yanomamo and the Anthropologists.* Simon and Schuster, 2013.

Women in STEM: The Perils of Honest Discussion
By Stuart Reges

Is It Sexual Harassment to Discuss This Article? — November 17, 2018

Jordan Peterson recently tweeted that, "The STEM fields are next on the SJW hitlist. Beware, engineers." I'm convinced that Peterson is correct, and I feel that my ongoing case has allowed me to see a likely avenue of attack from those who support the equity agenda. They will characterize any discussion of sex differences, no matter how calm and rational, as a form of gender harassment, which in turn constitutes sexual harassment. In other words, if you dare to discuss the science of sex differences — even at a university — there's a good chance that you'll be accused of violating U.S. law.

But I'm getting ahead of myself, so let me back up and explain in more detail.

For me, it started when Google fired engineer James Damore for daring to suggest that men and women are different, and that those differences can explain much of the gender gap in tech. I was disturbed by Google's unwillingness to explore these ideas, and spent nearly a year discussing gender differences at the Paul G. Allen School of Computer Science & Engineering at the University of Washington, where I work. Then I wrote an article for *Quillette* entitled, "Why Women Don't Code," in which I repeated many of the same ideas that got Damore into trouble.

My article initially generated a great deal of interest. Many news organizations wrote about it, including *Inside Higher Ed*, *The Seattle Times*, *The Stranger*, *GeekWire*, and *Campus Reform*. I was invited to appear on podcasts and a segment on our local news. A half dozen people put signs outside their office doors meant to counter my article with slogans such as, "I look like a computer scientist. So do my colleagues of every gender." Nearly 50 messages were sent to a school-wide mailing list in just two days. But the intensity of this backlash did not last.

And then the news came. On October 24, a group of graduate students announced that, "More will be done to address gender harassment at the Allen School." At the University of Washington, graduate student employees are unionized, and this group of graduate students had filed a grievance with their union. They complained that, "the school leadership's past silence in response to gender harassment (see a timeline of incidents here) contributed to a hostile work environment." The timeline they provide related to my *Quillette* article.

I haven't checked every date and detail, but the

timeline seems to be accurate. What I find most surprising is that the students feel that this narrative of events constitutes "gender harassment." Consider, for example, this paragraph that they include, without explanation, in building their case:

> SR [me] replies-all with a "thought experiment" asking "how to make someone like James Damore feel welcome in CSE [Computer Science & Engineering]," quoting Damore's memo and calling Damore's position a "defensible position."

As this process has unfolded, I have come to realize that the mere mention of James Damore awakens a tribal response from supporters of the equity agenda. Saying anything positive about Damore is considered a form of harassment.

The grievance has been settled, and the University of Washington does not discuss the details of such settlements. But the graduate students report that, "We are happy to report that the University has agreed to several of our grievance demands." They list three specific areas:

- The school will offer new "intersectional diversity and sexual harassment training" for student employees and their supervisors.
- A new student advisory group will be set up

that will help the school "make progress" on equity issues.

- A group of mostly senior faculty will review the introductory programming courses "to ensure that they are inclusive of students from all backgrounds."

The third concession hits closest to home because I designed the introductory programming courses, and my primary work responsibility is teaching and managing the courses. Why my courses should be investigated is not entirely clear, but I have heard it suggested that students might be reluctant to take a course from me because of my *Quillette* article.

I encourage people to read the timeline compiled by the graduate students, and I have collected all eight of the emails I sent to mailing lists during the 2017-18 academic year so that people can read those as well. You can judge for yourself, but my intent was to sincerely discuss this issue with others in the school. I pointed them to Steven Pinker's *The Blank Slate*, Gad Saad's invited talk at Google, Heterodox Academy's excellent summary of research on both sides of James Damore's memo, information about the Chicago Principles, and the discussion on gender that Pinker had with cognitive psychologist Elizabeth Spelke at Harvard, which I described as "an example of a true class act with scholars disagreeing without being disagreeable."

How can this be considered "harassment"? Claire Lehmann provided the answer in a recent *Quillette* article entitled "Redefining Sexual Harassment," in which she explores a report released earlier in 2018 by NASEM (the National Academy of Sciences, Engineering, and Medicine) about sexual harassment in STEM fields. Lehmann explained that the report cited alarmingly high percentages of women who were harassed – but with the most common form of harassment reported being gender harassment, which can be something like saying that "women don't make good supervisors."

My only complaint about Lehmann's article is that she made it sound like this is a new interpretation. The task force members who wrote the report did not make this up, although their suggestion that we seriously address it (Recommendation 2) is new. Consider, for example, this section from the primary web page on sexual harassment hosted by the EEOC (the U.S. Equal Employment Opportunity Commission):

> Harassment does not have to be of a sexual nature, however, and can include offensive remarks about a person's sex. For example, it is illegal to harass a woman by making offensive comments about women in general.

This wording has remained unchanged since at least 2009 according to the Wayback Machine. But Lehmann is correct when she says that most people are not aware of this. The NASEM report mentions that:

> Women who experience the gender harassment type of sexual harassment are more than 7 times less likely to label their experiences as "sexual harassment" than women who experience unwanted sexual attention or sexual coercion...This illustrates what other research has shown: that in both the law and the lay public, the dominant understandings of sexual harassment overemphasize two forms of sexual harassment, sexual coercion and unwanted sexual attention, while downplaying the third (most common) type – gender harassment.

Unfortunately, this leaves us with a great deal of ambiguity about what constitutes sexual harassment. The report defines the gender harassment form as "verbal and nonverbal behaviors that convey hostility, objectification, exclusion, or second-class status about members of one gender." Courts will ultimately decide whether such a broad definition is appropriate, but the implications are disturbing.

As an example, consider the Greater Male Variability Hypothesis, which posits that, although men and women may have the same *average* ability in many areas, men tend to have a higher variance, leading to more outliers at the extremes (the tails of the distribution). The theory is often summarized as "more idiots and more geniuses" among men versus women. *Quillette* readers will recall that a peer-reviewed article on the subject that had been accepted for publication was withdrawn because of the controversy it generated.

This raises an important question. Is discussing this theory a form of gender harassment and, thus, a form of sexual harassment? When Larry Summers mentioned it in a public discussion of gender imbalances in STEM, many called for him to resign as President of Harvard, which he did soon after.

James Damore also discussed this idea in his ten-page memo on gender differences. And the National Labor Relations Board released their opinion that his discussion of this theory did in fact constitute sexual harassment:

> Statements about immutable traits linked to sex — such as women's heightened neuroticism and men's prevalence at the top of the IQ distribution — were discriminatory and constituted sexual harassment, notwithstanding effort to cloak comments with "scientific" references and analysis, and notwithstanding "not all women" disclaimers.

I find it amusing that they put the word "scientific" in quotes, as if they aren't quite sure whether this is real science. And the waters are even more muddied by yet another ambiguity: While discussion of sex differences is considered sexual harassment, it does not necessarily constitute *illegal* sexual harassment. From the EEOC web page:

> Although the law doesn't prohibit simple teasing, offhand comments, or isolated incidents that are not very serious, harassment is illegal when it is so frequent or severe that it creates a hostile or offensive work environment or when it results in an adverse employment decision (such as the victim being fired or demoted).

This increases the likelihood that individuals who cross the line by discussing sex differences will be warned not to repeat the behavior, and will probably be okay as long as they comply. Only stubborn individuals who continue to express themselves are likely to be accused of breaking the law. Recall that my school's graduate students claimed that my repeated discussion of this topic had created a hostile work environment.

Count me among the stubborn, and you will understand why this settlement of the grievance put forward by our graduate students is disappointing to me. I'm unhappy that my courses are being investigated. But in some ways, the new forms of monitoring and the new training workshops are more disturbing because they represent an ongoing attempt to pressure me into silence.

I am also disappointed with the University of Washington for settling the case without resolving the central question of whether my discussion of these issues constituted gender harassment. It leaves me and others like me with no clarity about where our free-speech rights end and where illegal sexual harassment begins. It also means that we have failed to properly educate those graduate students. We could have rejected their claim of harassment and championed the idea that universities need to preserve the tradition of open discussion of all ideas, encouraging them to become the kind of anti-fragile scientists and engineers our society needs. Instead, we left them with the impression that they were right to see themselves as victims. and to encourage them to continue to try to silence ideas that leave them with hurt feelings.

I expect to see more of this going forward as the #MeToo movement broadens out. Recommendation 3 from the NASEM report urges us to "move beyond legal compliance to address culture and climate." The next phase of the culture war will include attempts to silence any discussion of sex differences within the STEM disciplines. As Jordan Peterson said, "Beware, engineers."

Demoted and Placed on Probation — January 11, 2020

It all started in June 2018, when *Quillette* published my article, "Why Women Don't Code," and things picked up steam when Jordan Peterson shared a link to the article on his Twitter account. A burst of outrage and press coverage followed, which I discussed in a follow-up piece. The original article was one of the ten most read pieces published by *Quillette* in 2018, and continues to generate interest. A recent YouTube video about it has been viewed over 120,000 times, as of this writing.

In his tweet promoting my article, Peterson took issue with one of my claims. I had written that I thought I could survive at the University of Washington's Paul G. Allen School of Computer Science and Engineering, where I work. Peterson disagreed: "Make no mistake about it: the Damore incident has already established a precedent. Watch what you say. Or else."

As it turns out, Peterson was right. My position is not tenured. And when my current three-year appointment came up for review in December, I was stripped of my primary teaching duties and given a highly unusual one-year probationary appointment. The administration insists this decision had nothing to do with the controversy generated by my article. But as I will explain, that seems highly unlikely. As one faculty colleague put it, an "angry mob" has been after me ever since my article came out.

The Intro Classes

In 2005, the University of Washington hired me to redesign their two introductory computer-science classes. I developed two highly successful courses that have over 4,500 enrollments combined per year and are among the most highly rated 100-level courses at the University of Washington. In a recent internal survey, over 80 percent of the students agreed that the assignments increased their interest in computing and showed them how useful such knowledge can be. Teaching at this scale is a massive undertaking. And for the last 15 years, I have been responsible for overall management of the staff, instructors, and TAs who provide this service.

In response to my *Quillette* article, a group of graduate students in the Allen School filed a grievance against me with their union. The university agreed to several of their demands, including that, "A group of (mostly senior) faculty will review the introductory programming courses to ensure that they are inclusive of students from all backgrounds." A working group was formed and it produced a set of recommendations. These included:

· A relaxation of grading on coding style.
· Allowing students to work together in a group for part of their grade instead of requiring them to complete all graded work individually.
· Training for TAs in inclusion and implicit bias.

- Review of all course materials for inclusiveness. In regard to a lecture that involves calculating body mass index (BMI) using guidelines from the National Institutes of Health, the report noted that it "seems insensitive to present students with a program that would print out that some of them are 'obese' while others are 'normal.'"
- A reduction in the amount of effort expended pursuing cheating cases by 50 percent, even though there has been no recent reduction in cheating cases.

The report also recommends that courses incorporate inclusiveness best practices as outlined in an Allen School document. These include:

- The addition of an indigenous land acknowledgement to the syllabus.
- The use of gender-neutral names such as Alex and Jun instead of Alice and Bob.
- The use of names that reflect a variety of cultural backgrounds: Xin, Sergey, Naveena, Tuan, Esteban, Sasha.
- An avoidance of references that depend on cultural knowledge of sports, pop culture, theater, literature, or games.
- The replacement of phrases such as "you guys" with "folks" or "y'all."

- A declaration of instructors' pronouns and a request for students' pronoun preferences.

Most of these suggestions seem to rely on the notion that undergraduates are delicate. While I agree that we must be careful to ensure that all students feel welcome and respected, we should be helping our students to become anti-fragile. So I will continue to use the BMI example, I will maintain high standards for grading, and I will continue to pursue cheating cases vigorously. I will continue to say, "you guys." and to make occasional cultural references. In the case of pronouns, I have always made an effort to accommodate requests from transgender students, but I refuse to use words that are not part of the English language.

It is the prerogative of the faculty to change the intro classes if they so choose. I understand that inclusive teaching is popular now, so it makes sense that others would want to move them in that direction. Even though this review was precipitated by my *Quillette* article, it is not in itself evidence that I am being treated differently on account of my political beliefs.

My Probation
What I find difficult to accept is that I was reappointed for just one year. The Allen School often hires adjunct and temporary lecturers for only one year, but that isn't how it routinely treats lecturers with a regular appointment. In the 15 years I have been part of the

school, I am the first regular lecturer to be offered less than a three-year extension.

Administration officials claim that my one-year reappointment is part of a more general change in the management of the intro classes, but that doesn't make sense. They are perfectly within their rights to take management of intro away from me, and even to forbid me from teaching intro classes. So why are they threatening my job security as well? I am able to teach a wide range of classes. I have mostly been teaching in intro recently because there have not been enough teaching cycles available for me to teach other subjects. But I have taught five different courses outside of intro. For each of the last seven years, the Allen School has been unable to hire enough lecturers to meet our needs, despite undertaking a nationwide search.

The one-year reappointment is also odd given my faculty rank. I was the first lecturer in the College of Engineering at UW to be promoted to the rank of principal lecturer. The faculty code indicates that the normal period for reappointment for a principal lecturer should be at least three years. The administration had to obtain special permission from the provost to make such a short appointment. It is also perhaps worth noting that I am the only current member of the faculty in the Allen School who has won the Distinguished Teaching Award, which is the highest award given for teaching at UW.

A faculty colleague told me he believes I am in the process of being fired for my political beliefs. He said it became clear during the meeting at which my reappointment was discussed that quite a few people wanted me to be summarily dismissed. Others said it was unacceptable to fire me outright. In the vote that was taken, faculty were asked to choose one of three options: no reappointment, a one-year reappointment, or a three-year reappointment. So the one-year appointment was the middle ground that allowed faculty to punish me without taking the most drastic available step just yet. I have the impression I am expected to feel grateful.

The students weighed in on the decision as well. A poster was plastered throughout the undergraduate labs and the student union encouraging students to visit a web address if they wished to express concern about my possible reappointment. Critical student testimonies were collected in a letter to the dean urging her not to reappoint me.

Heterodox Teaching Is Off Topic
My teaching evaluations haven't slipped in recent years. I am, however, spending more time thinking about how to encourage viewpoint diversity. I have joined the non-profit advocacy group Heterodox Academy, and have met with some of its local members. I attended the 2019 Heterodox Academy Conference and the 2018 faculty conference for the Foun-

dation for Individual Rights in Education (FIRE). As part of my reappointment process, I was asked to describe what I've done and where I see myself going. I mentioned that I would like to expand my work on heterodox teaching.

The faculty members who reviewed my reappointment materials reported that they were "surprised" that I would mention my work in this area. They said that I have a right as a citizen to do this, but they also pointed out that the Allen School leadership had felt the need to respond publicly to my *Quillette* article (presumably a negative). They announced that my work in this area was not related to my professional responsibilities and should therefore be considered "off topic" and irrelevant to a review of my work performance and my consideration for reappointment.

This was particularly disappointing because I am doing some of my best teaching in this area. In the Fall of 2018, I assigned Jonathan Haidt and Greg Lukianoff's 2018 book, *The Coddling of the American Mind*, as part of a seminar for honors students. I received my highest scores ever for this seminar (an average of 5.0 on a 5-point scale). Here are two representative comments from the student evaluations:

> We were asked to share our personal opinions and the reasoning behind them, without any fear of being shamed or irrationally responded to. This allowed for meaningful discussions

to develop, and a level of vulnerability in answering questions and discussing various topics that I have experienced nowhere else in the university setting.

This class really made me think about the way we have learned to perceive the world, especially in regard to tolerance [of] conflicting viewpoints. It made me realize that although we sometimes advocate for diverse opinions, we often shut down a certain group of opinions, which is hypocritical and very dangerous. I think that in order to learn and grow, we have to hear viewpoints that we disagree with, which is unfortunately not something that happens often enough in our society.

The Affirmative-Action Bake Sale

An event in the spring of 2019 provides an illustrative example of the mob mentality that has developed at my university. The state legislature was considering an initiative to reinstate affirmative action in education. In response, the UW College Republicans organized an affirmative action bake sale, at which cookies were sold to Asians for $1.50, to whites for $1, and to African Americans and Hispanics for 50 cents. Cookies were free to Native Americans. This kind of stunt has a long history on college campuses. It drew an angry response from students, and police had a difficult time keeping the peace. One protestor threw a tray of cookies to the ground, but otherwise there was no violence.

I attended the event to see how it was received, and ended up having an hour-long conversation with a young woman about race relations on campus. When I was able to speak to her directly, we were able to understand our different perspectives and how we came to different conclusions about the value of affirmative action. But she was also playing to a gathering crowd, inviting them to join her in condemning me. One young man said to me, "How did *you* get tenure?" When I said that I didn't have tenure, he said, "Good! Because you're not going to get it."

A local publication, *The Stranger*, published an article about the event, which included photographs of my interactions with the young woman. I was quoted as saying, "I don't see racism on campus," and the article's authors reported that the crowd laughed when a student retorted that this is because I'm white. But, as footage of our exchange captured by a local news team later confirmed, what I actually said was "I don't see *rampant* racism on campus" – a small but important difference between a denial of ongoing racism and a disagreement about its prevalence.

A local conservative talk show host named Jason Rantz was at the bake sale, and made his own recordings. In two articles about the event, Rantz posted a five-minute audio excerpt of my exchange with the young woman, during which we debated whether group identity is more important than judging people as individuals. Anyone interested in assessing the attitude I bring to these conversations can listen to that exchange and judge me accordingly. Nevertheless, the day after the article in *The Stranger* appeared, I received a message from the director of the Allen School which included this commentary:

> In my opinion, this is not about freedom of speech, and it's also not about affirmative action, on which there are obviously multiple views that could legitimately be debated and discussed. This is about your lack of sensitivity to minority students and your continued (and almost gleeful) denial of their experiences, which I find extremely regrettable and disappointing coming from somebody of your stature and experience.

He later told me that his judgment was based entirely on the misreported quote. He didn't ask me what had happened. He didn't ask if the quote was accurate. He simply concluded that I was insensitive to minority students. How he decided that I was "almost gleeful" is beyond me, but it indicates a reflexive disapproval among some of my colleagues since the publication of my *Quillette* essay.

A few days later, a blogger identified as "Anonymous Husky" called for me to be fired in a *Medium* post entitled, "Why the UW Computer Science Department Can Do Better than Stuart Reges." The article mentioned the bake sale, my *Quillette* article, and my protest against the war on drugs, which led me to be fired from Stanford in 1991. It was emailed to every member of the computer science faculty and many of the undergraduate TAs I work with.

The New Closet

I spent New Year's Eve of my senior year of high school in a hospital because I almost succeeded in taking my own life with a bottle of rat poison. I was a young gay person who couldn't face telling people I was a member of that hated group known as "homosexuals." Although it was a dark period, that experience provided me with a source of strength later in life. If I was so unacceptable that I thought it was better to be dead than alive, then what was to be lost by telling people what I really think? By the time I got to Stanford as a graduate student in 1979, I was openly gay. Not many people were at the time. When I started teaching at the university, I found that many gay people wanted to talk to me, but almost always in private. They would tell me that they couldn't afford to be as open as I was.

But even I felt the pressure to conform. In 1982, I applied for my dream job. The Stanford Computer Science Department was hiring someone to manage the intro courses. I was doing the job on a temporary basis, but they were looking to appoint a permanent staff member. Unfortunately, their search concluded just after the *Stanford Daily* published a full-page article I had written entitled, "On Being Gay: Feelings and Perceptions." The chair of the department told me that they wanted to offer me the job, but that they had been embarrassed by my article. They wanted me to promise never to publish such an article again. I had an opportunity to be brave and refuse his request, but I didn't. I said that I couldn't make that promise, but that I didn't feel the need to publish any more articles any time soon. That was enough to get me hired. And I didn't write any articles for the next three years until we got a new chair who told me I could publish whatever I wanted.

Over the course of my life, it has been astonishing to watch anti-gay sentiment reverse. Today, the people on campus who need to worry about expressing their ideas are conservatives and religious people. Now it is gay students doing the punishing of anyone who opposes gay marriage, gay adoption, hate-speech codes, and civil-rights protection for gay individuals. Everything old is new again. I'm once again having private conversations behind closed doors in my office with closeted individuals, but this time they are students, faculty, staff, and alumni who oppose the equity agenda. They are deeply concerned about the university's direction, but they are also afraid of jeopardizing their current or future job prospects. They also worry about losing friendships and professional relationships.

Stanley Fish describes this situation well in his recent book *The First*:

> These students, often a minority, but a minority with a loud voice, tend to be wholly persuaded of the rightness of their views; they don't see why they should be forced to listen to, or even be in the presence of, views they know to be false. They wish to institute what I would call a "virtue regime," where people who say the right kind of thing get to speak or teach and those who are on the wrong side of history (as they see it) don't.

As a result, I can't bring myself to look down on the closeted individuals who offer me support behind closed doors. The threat is real, just as it was when I compromised my principles to get a job nearly 40 years ago.

I am concerned that some people believe free speech now is improving on college campuses, when in fact things are getting worse. Yes, we have fewer overt examples of speakers being shouted down and disinvited, but now the censorship is going underground. Those who talk to me behind closed doors censor themselves because they know the consequences of speaking up. As the economist Timur Kuran has explained, this preference for falsification is extremely dangerous because it prevents us from having the meaningful conversations necessary to find practical solutions to problems.

So I understand why many people will choose to stay silent. I did it myself, aged 23, when I stopped writing articles about being gay, so that I could be hired into my dream job. But I'm older now. And although I don't have what people call "fuck-you money," I have enough saved that I can afford to speak my mind. For the rest of you, remember Jordan Peterson's admonition: "Watch what you say. Or else."

AUTHOR'S POSTSCRIPT – SEPTEMBER 2020

In my ninth-grade civics class I came across an odd quote from Alexis de Tocqueville saying that, "I know no country in which, speaking generally, there is less independence of mind and true freedom of discussion than in America." In many ways I have spent my life exploring that idea and coming to realize that De Tocqueville was on to something. I was marginalized in the 1980s for being openly gay before it was fashionable to do so. Then I was fired from Stanford in 1991 for challenging the war on drugs. And now I am being punished for resisting what I have called "the equity agenda." I haven't been fired yet, but it is happening slowly. I'm on probation now and am unlikely to be reappointed. But even worse, I live in a professional limbo where I am no longer invited to participate in the activities around me. De Tocqueville predicted this outcome, writing that those who step outside the bounds of acceptable thought will be told, "You are free not to think as I do; you can keep your life and property and all; but from this day you are a stranger among us." Where I used to look forward to participating in new educational initiatives and outreach projects, I now sit alone in my office and stare at the awards on my wall that were given to me in happier times. And when I find myself in danger of feeling sorry for myself, I start working on a new article to reach out to those who still have eyes to see and ears to hear.

A Biologist's 'Lived Experience' with Cancel Culture

By Colin Wright

Given the moral authority that many progressives assign to the lessons of "lived experience," it seems counterintuitive that they are the ones now strenuously downplaying the scourge of cancel culture. No less a progressive icon than Alexandria Ocasio-Cortez brushed off the phenomenon as just a bunch of entitled people being "challenged" and "held accountable" for their problematic views. *New York Times* columnist Charles Blow believes cancel culture doesn't even exist, except to the extent it's simply a desirable by-product of grass-roots activism. "Once more: THERE IS NO SUCH THING AS CANCEL CULTURE," he tweeted. "There is free speech. You can say and do as you pls, and others can choose never to deal this you, your company or your products EVER."

A common theme is that the *faux*-victims complaining about cancel culture are high-profile cynics, playing the martyr for the benefit of clicks and fans. Ocasio-Cortez describes the complainants as people who "get their thoughts published and amplified in major outlets," while Blow tells us that "the rich and powerful are just upset that the masses can now organize their dissent." It's hard not to see this as a rhetorical shell game. If canceled individuals fade into obscurity, we never hear their stories. But if they *do* manage to get their story out to the media, they're dismissed as pampered pundits. By means of this damned-if-you-do/damned-if-you-don't logic, cancel culture Truthers can pretend away the existence of thousands of victims.

Of course, it's absolutely true that wealthy cancel culture targets such as JK Rowling get enormous attention. But that's not just because of their wealth and fame: It's because their stories act as a stand-in for the many other, more obscure, figures who've been mobbed in the press, on campuses, on social-media forums, and in arts and literary subcultures. The vast majority of cancel culture's victims are people you've never heard of, who don't have the means to fight back, or who have learned to keep quiet so they don't lose whatever reputation or job security they still have.

I know, because I was once one of them.

* * *

This isn't the first time I've alluded publicly to my ordeal. I've spoken about it on Twitter and various podcasts. But the ongoing effort to deny cancel culture's existence has convinced me that I need to lay out my own experience in a more systematic way.

In 2008, I decided to pursue a career as an academic biologist. Science in general, and evolutionary biology in particular, had been a passion from a young age. Even as an undergraduate, I maintained a blog that I used to debunk pseudoscience, and critique creationism and Intelligent Design. I was outspoken, and sometimes launched headlong into debates with Christian conservatives. Creationists and IDers frequently told me I was wrong or stupid, but my critics never called me a bigot.

This changed, however, when I started graduate school in 2013. This was an environment in which I didn't have to worry about right-wing creationists. Rather, the pseudoscience I observed was coming from the other side of the political spectrum – especially in the form of "Blank Slate" proponents, who argued (falsely) that sex differences in human personality, preferences, and behavior are entirely the result of socialization.

It was also during this time that I started to take an interest in what many now call "gender ideology." This ideology not only invites compassionate treatment for trans individuals (which I support), but also promotes the scientifically inaccurate claims that biological sex exists on a continuous "spectrum," that notions of male and female may be mere social constructs, and that one's sex may be determined by self-declared "identity." When I pushed back against these claims, I was smeared as a transphobe. Fearing professional harm, I stopped engaging, ceding the field to those who champion fashionable fictions.

I graduated with a PhD in evolutionary biology from UC Santa Barbara in 2018, and took a postdoctoral position at Penn State. I'd just joined Twitter, and observed that the pseudoscience I'd seen on campus had by now metastasized to the wider world and become the stuff of everyday hashtags. Even scientists whom I knew personally and respected were parroting this nonsense as scientific fact. But I dared not say a word. I would soon be applying to tenure-track assistant-professor jobs; I could not be seen publicly arguing down the claim that internally felt gender feelings trumped biology.

In October 2018, the Grievance Studies scandal gained popular attention, bringing renewed focus on the intellectual degradation within academic fields focused on gender and sex. A few weeks later, one of the world's most prestigious scientific journals, *Nature*, published an editorial claiming that classifying an individual's sex using any combination of anatomy and genetics "has no basis in science." These events, happening in such close succession, pushed me beyond my threshold for restraint. Despite my academic mentors' warnings that speaking up could ruin my career, I let my bottled-up frustrations out in an essay I sent to *Quillette*. It was published under the headline, *The New Evolution Deniers*.

The essay went viral. And while I received my fair share of praise for it, I also knew I'd provided critics with a bona fide gotcha moment. ("I did not train to be a scientist for over a decade just to sit quietly while science in general, and my field in particular, comes under attack from activists who subvert truth to ideology and narrative," I wrote.) Blank-Slate feminists and trans activists alike publicly accused me of wrongthink.

What's worse, my heresies were multiplying, as I had taken to Twitter to defend my views and confront my critics. I also eventually co-authored another *Quillette* essay, with endocrinologist Dr. William Malone and author Julia Robertson, titled *No One Is Born in 'The Wrong Body'*, arguing that children are put at risk of long-term harm if they are indoctrinated with ideologically torqued misinformation about their bodies and behavior.

In October 2019, following the publication of that second article, I received word that someone had posted a new listing in EcoEvoJobs, the largest job board in my field, that read, "Colin Wright Is a Transphobe Who Supports Race Science." This was during the height of the academic-recruitment season. The post was eventually removed by the board operator. But there was no telling how long it was up or how many of my colleagues had seen it. (I expressed concern to the operator, and urged that they vet listings before they go live, but was told this wasn't possible. Luckily, a tech-savvy friend volunteered to run a script that scanned the board for my name on a minute-by-minute basis, and sent me a text message when it got a hit.) At the time, I had nearly a hundred job applications being reviewed by search committees. I locked my Twitter and resolved, once again, to lay low.

But of course, I fell off the wagon. If you're looking for common characteristics among those of us who get targeted for cancelation, it isn't money or privilege. Rather, many of us simply have an inability to mumble slogans we know aren't true. Over time, we become exasperated with dishonest propaganda that masquerades as social justice, and we speak out. It's a habit rooted in the truth-telling, whistle-blowing impulse that, not so long ago, progressives applauded.

I broke my Twitter silence on Valentine's Day, 2020, when *The Wall Street Journal* published an essay I'd co-authored with developmental biologist Dr. Emma Hilton, titled *The Dangerous Denial of Sex*. Although constrained by the space limitations of the op-ed format, Dr. Hilton and I were able to briefly outline the science of biological sex, and detail how its denial harms vulnerable groups, including women, gay men, lesbians, and, especially, gender non-conforming children. Even more than other pieces I'd bylined, this one unleashed a tidal wave of online hate – perhaps because we'd pricked the precious conceit that gender ideology saves children instead of harming them. Several Penn State professors publicly denounced the essay as transphobic. Students and faculty complained to my department's diversity committee that I'd launched "a personal attack on individuals with non-binary gender identity," and that my presence at PSU "made them feel less comfortable."

"In for a penny, in for a pound," as the expression goes. A week later, I tweeted out a *Guardian* article titled, "Teenage transgender row splits Sweden as dysphoria diagnoses soar by 1,500%," accompanied by my own two-word commentary: "social contagion." My tweet would have made sense to those familiar with the work of Brown University academic Lisa Littman, and particularly her scientific paper hypothesizing links between "rapid onset gender dysphoria" (ROGD) and peer contagion within cliques of teenage girls. However, activists were able to contort my comment in a way that suggested I was targeting the children themselves, or that I was comparing gender dysphoria to a virus. Knowing I was on the job market, a Michigan State University graduate student (and president of the Graduate Employees Union) named Kevin Bird accused me of "spreading disgusting transphobic pseudoscience." Unlike other critics, Bird didn't even pretend to be motivated by anything other than a desire to deny me employment in my field: "Colin is now spreading disgusting transphobic pseudoscience. He's on the job market. I hope The EEB [evolution, ecology and behavior] community is paying attention. This isn't how you @DiversifyEEB."

Bird himself offers an interesting case study, because his example illustrates how even a single ideologically radicalized troll can present the appearance of a grass-roots effort. If Bird's name sounds familiar, it's because he is the same activist who led a campaign against his own university's senior vice president of research and innovation, theoretical physicist Stephen Hsu. Bird has no particular distinction in his academic field, has tweeted support for burning banks, and is on record stating that he has no "interest in attaining or discovering truth" when he does science. But he also has worked tirelessly to build up his online stature as a cancel culture enforcer and a warrior "against fascism." As such, he has been able to mobilize flash mobs of online trolls to aid in his deplatforming efforts – which is why Hsu was forced to resign his VP position despite the spurious nature of Bird's racism accusations.

It was around this time that I was contacted by a biology-department chair at a private liberal arts college in the Midwest. He commended me for my writings, and told me that he'd even used my *New Evolution Deniers* essay as a basis for discussion in his own classes. But while he and his fellow biology-department faculty would likely support my hiring, he said, the school's own human-resources department would almost certainly block me as "too risky." These experiences remind me that when Blow extols "the masses" who are canceling people like me, the people he's praising are actually just a small coalition of activists such as Bird, working in effective concert with the risk-averse, upper-middle-class corporate bureaucrats who now have taken over decision-making on many college and university campuses.

Guilt by association is a hallmark of all social panics. And in early March, I received a text message from a close friend and research collaborator who is now an assistant professor at a major research university, informing me that his colleagues had started questioning him about our affiliation. He told me that this sort of thing was happening frequently enough that he felt the need to publicly denounce my views to clear his name. And that's exactly what he did. Ask yourself what other ideological movements and historical periods we tend to associate with such performative acts.

Later that month, someone again posted "Colin Wright Is a Transphobe Who Supports Race Science" to the EcoEvoJobs board. I contacted the board operator – again – expressing my concerns. This time, I received no response.

Meanwhile, an anonymous Twitter account informed me that "preemptive emails" had been sent to academic search committees about me. While it is impossible to verify these claims, I note that the same tactic is known to have been used against former psychology professor Bo Winegard, who was recently fired from Marietta College after a persistent effort by similar (perhaps the same) activists to smear him as a racist and "race scientist." In fact, these anonymous "masses," as Blow calls them, may just be one person.

In April, I chose to leave academia. To give credit

to Penn State, I was not fired. In fact, I had the opportunity to extend my fellowship contract for another year. However, I no longer believed that any amount of hard work or talent on my part would lead to a tenure-track academic job in the current climate. Nor did I want to spend my time constantly responding to false accusations of transphobia and racism. I had embarked on this journey because I love science, and wanted to help beat back the forces of pseudoscience in the public sphere. But that project is impossible when scientists themselves have become intimidated by small clusters of activists who demand that the scientific method be subordinated to magical thinking, and who seek to ruin the lives of those who dissent. If you follow in my footsteps, you can expect to receive similar treatment.

None of the views I have ever espoused are extreme. Indeed, all or most are taken as common sense by pretty much anyone who isn't an activist or professional academic. And I will repeat them here. Male and female are not social constructs, but are real biological categories that do not fall on a spectrum. Humans are sexually dimorphic, and this matters in certain contexts, such as sports. Ignoring the reality of sexual dimorphism can harm women and members of the gay community, whose experience of discrimination is rooted in the real differences between male and female bodies. Esoteric theories of gender that purport to deny the reality of biology, or that conflate biological sex with secondary sexual characteristics or sex-based stereotypes, can confuse children; and are likely partly responsible for the massive uptick in self-reported gender dysphoria among adolescents, especially teenage girls.

In the closing lines of *The New Evolution Deniers*, I wrote that academia was "no longer a refuge for outspoken, free-thinking intellectuals," and that "one must now choose between living a zipper-lipped life as an academic scientist, or living a life as a fulfilled intellectual." My own experience, reinforced by the steady flow of emails I receive from concerned academics, would suggest that the situation is only getting worse.

What you have read here is the story of just one ex-academic. But it should concern everyone that the entire academy is now being held hostage to a vocal minority that insists we should inhabit a fantasy intellectual milieu. Make no mistake: Cancel culture is very real. And its manifestations are not confined to the rich and powerful. As with many cultural processes, the fight to roll it back will be a long, hard struggle. I don't pretend to know how it will end. But I do know that it begins by opening our eyes to the problem. To do otherwise would represent — if I may borrow a phrase from the social justice lexicon — the literal erasure of my own lived experience.

AUTHOR'S POSTSCRIPT – SEPTEMBER 2020

I don't think I quite appreciated the amount of stress and anxiety I had been carrying around with me as a heretic in academia until I officially left and felt the enormous weight lifted off my shoulders. Much of this stress resulted from the fact that I was not in control of my own future; my future would have been in the hands of search, tenure, and diversity committees. Though choosing to leave the occupation for which I had been training for over a decade was scary and full of uncertainty, I was at least confident that my success in whatever I did next would be largely determined by my own efforts. That knowledge was incredibly freeing.

I wasn't entirely sure what I was going to do next. All I knew is that I needed a job I could do from anywhere, and that would be both cancel-proof and intellectually satisfying. I thought perhaps I'd make a living doing a combination of online fitness coaching and podcasting about science and culture. Maybe I'd even start a YouTube channel. Fortunately for me, however, an editorial position opened up at my favorite online magazine – *Quillette* – and founding editor-in-chief Claire Lehmann was kind enough to offer me the job. Given *Quillette*'s strong commitment to free speech, I think if I somehow manage to get myself cancelled working here then, in all likelihood, I'll probably deserve it.

Kicked Out of the Classics
By Mary Frances Williams

I am a Classics Ph.D. who recently attended the 2019 Annual Meeting of the Society for Classical Studies (SCS – formerly the American Philological Association), a yearly conference that provides papers on classical subjects and interviews for academic positions. I now regret doing so, since some remarks I made at the conference led to me being branded a "racist" and the loss of my editing job with the Association of Ancient Historians.

I don't usually attend because of the expense. I'm an independent scholar and cannot rely on universities for reimbursement. But it seemed like a good idea to go since the weather is always nice in San Diego. A bonus was the USS Midway, now a floating museum. This is a World War II-era aircraft carrier that served as the command center for the bombing of Bagdad during the Gulf War, and well worth visiting.

On January 5, I attended panel #45, a "Sesquicentennial Workshop" – it was the 150th anniversary of the SCS – titled "The Future of Classics." It was described in the meeting program as "an open and free-form large-room discussion of what we think the trajectories of our field, broadly defined, will and/or should be, not just in the immediate future but for the next 150 years." Based on the description (the word "discussion" appeared three times), the panel seemed like an opportunity to raise some questions and obtain answers about what was happening in the field.

Although I am a Classics Ph.D. and a former professor, it has been some time since I taught. But I have noticed a decline in the number of Classics courses being offered at universities, a shift in teaching focus, and, at least this past Fall, a concentration on archaeology positions in the academic job market rather than Classics generalists. I thought that I might contribute to the discussion, and that by asking questions, I might learn what was going on and what others thought about the direction of the field. I knew nothing about the people who'd been invited to speak.

A typical session at the SCS Annual Meeting involves six speakers giving papers, with a few minutes for one or two questions after each one, and usually lasts two-and-three-quarter hours. Papers are normally submitted through the Program Committee and classed by topic. However, this particular panel/workshop was atypical: The invited speakers, who only spoke for four or five minutes apiece, did not give true papers or have paper titles listed in the program, and therefore did not go through the Program Committee. Nor were they sponsored by any affiliated group as far as I know. Although Stephen Hinds (University of Washington) was listed as the organizer of the workshop, he did not chair the panel, keep order, call on members of the audience, or time the speakers. In short, it was an odd affair that seemed not to follow the (admittedly Byzantine) rules for SCS Meetings. The SCS Director, Helen Cullyer, was present in the audience and gave a few anodyne remarks of welcome, but sat quietly throughout the subsequent uproar.

The first speaker, Sarah Bond (University of Iowa), emphasized how she runs the Twitter feed, Facebook page and blog for the SCS. This work gave her occasion "to reflect often on whether in the field of Classics we can separate the art from the artist." Bond encouraged SCS members to consider the legacy of classicists like Basil Lanneau Gildersleeve (1831-1924), because he wrote "some of the most racist and abominable columns for the *Richmond Times-Dispatch* that we actually know of, defending slavery, defending the South; and yet we continue to celebrate Basil Gildersleeve within our society. What does that say to the future classicists that are coming into the field?...It does not tell people of color that it is welcoming to them."

From Gildersleeve, she went on to "other very influential scholars that oftentimes go silent at this meeting." This was puzzling, but then she immediately clarified that she was talking about people "we don't talk about, or we whisper about, because we know things, but we can't say them aloud." She recounted how she was "summarily cut off" in the question-and-answer period of a "digital pedagogy for mapping" conference panel by a "very prominent digital humanist" when she mentioned that she no longer cited the work of a former Classics professor "because of the rape allegations against him currently." An allegation against this scholar was made on Facebook in November 2017 of a sexual assault in 1985, but neither his university nor the police investigated the charge, and no formal proceeding has ever been opened against him.

From there, Bond seemed to accuse all classicists (or maybe just the SCS) of taking part in a conspiracy of silence:

> We are still about cronyism and supporting a very small group of people in many ways this can oftentimes silence other people. I, too, have had problems with whether to call people out or whether to say things, whether we should be anonymous or whether we should have a name attached to all the allegations that we put against people, but we have to think about the past of Classics and the present in order to make it welcoming for the future.

The way to correct this was to create "an environment for diversity and inclusion" by "calling out" "mistakes that we're making currently and in the past."

Next, she started talking about what another panelist would call "citational justice." This is a process of "diversifying our footnotes, and trying to include more people, rather than following the same path that we have been led to our entire careers as classicists." She described this as a way of "lifting as we climb." The idea was that if you cite women [of color] in your scholarship, instead of Basil Gildersleeve or "various scholars who are part of the canon," then "that is how we are going to climb."

Bond bemoaned the fact that her blog posts did not count toward tenure (even though, puzzlingly, she *has* tenure, or so she told us). She claimed to have written over 170,000 words over the past two years on her own blog and various other blogs. This writing was the equivalent of "two books over the past two years that I got almost no tenure credit for." She wanted to encourage universities to look at "outreach" activities like blog posts when assessing candidates for tenure and promotion in order to "break away from the monograph as the model for who gets tenure." She objected to the fact that she was granted tenure only because of a single scholarly monograph.

Bond's final topic was "inclusion." She had been in charge of organizing Classics colloquia at her university, and claimed that "those panels represented what we believed Classics is and should be." Over the past 10 years, there had only been three scholars of color in any of these colloquia. She tried to make them inclusive by inviting even numbers of men and women, and bringing in as many people of color, dance professors, and other people "outside the traditional area of Classics" as she could. In Bond's eyes, inclusion "begins in the local university, telling people of color and women specifically that they can be a part of our field through simply presenting them with people who are not seen as the traditional classicists, i.e., white males, who are older."

She was particularly concerned about "manels" (all-male conference panels): "having [people in the SCS] refuse to be a part of manels is one reason why I started WOAH," she said. WOAH stands for "Women of Ancient History," a database of female ancient historians.

I was puzzled by Bond's discussion of Gildersleeve. Gildersleeve's 1885 *The Olympian and Pythian Odes* is still the best thing out there for anyone studying the Greek text of Pindar, an incredibly complex and difficult poet of the sixth century B.C., who wrote odes for Olympians and other athletic victors. Gildersleeve is unlikely to be supplanted by those who work on Pindar; in fact, it is impossible to read the poet in Greek without Gildersleeve's assistance with Greek grammar, myth, genealogy, and history. It struck me as odd to argue that his scholarship should be disregarded because of articles he wrote in a newspaper. There is nothing in his commentary (or his Latin grammar or work on Greek syntax) that comes even close to being racist. How can we not use him? Or is it fine to "use" anyone, even if they are racist, as long as they are not given any credit in the text?

The second speaker, Joy Connolly (former provost of the Graduate Center at The City University of New York), focused on what she called "the futureology of Classics." The big trend in education, she said, was the rising cost of higher education; meanwhile, Classics was "not in growth mode." Classicists needed to teach more students. "We have to decide what we want our field to be," she said. We had to put more of our energy into attracting students to justify hiring replacements for ourselves when we retire. The future of Classics was really ours to make.

Connolly's preferred vision of the future was, to my ears, rather alarming. "Let's imagine a field... where language study is not the core," she said. She hinted that she wanted "popular engagement" to determine research topics, and questioned the value of traditional notions of Classics, asking why so many students wrote their dissertations on great works of classical Greek and Latin literature, instead of topics like indigenous writing in the Americas and technical writing. She seemed generally hostile to the study of classical Greek and Latin, in fact, and said that the ancient languages should not be taught anymore by Classics departments, though she did not say why, besides cost.

But the abandonment of philology, the heart of our

discipline, means that there can be no true research in the field. We can have no new editions of texts, no new translations, no work on ancient history, no scholarly work on ancient authors, without knowledge of the languages. What Connolly seemed to be advocating is that classicists should discard the heart and soul of their discipline to make it more popular.

The final speaker, Dan-el Padilla Peralta (Princeton University), began by saying: "For the next few minutes I want to concentrate on the systemic marginalization of people of color in the credentialed and accredited knowledge production of the discipline."

Apparently, the organizers of the SCS annual meeting had contributed to this marginalisation by holding the conference at a hotel in San Diego:

Already by the historical process of convening this conference in locations that are not only ludicrously expensive to travel to but that are rife with micro- and macroaggressions that target people of color, the SCS does people of color no favors.

Padilla mentioned what he called "the revolting racial profiling" of two SCS members the day before, and discussed holding hotel and conference centre staff to "a racially equitable standard." (He was referring to a hotel security guard asking two non-white students for their credentials.) But Padilla's main subject was

Classics. He said he wanted to displace "the pre-eminence and priority of white privilege and white supremacy in the discipline's self-image." He then talked about the shortcomings of scholarly journals:

> I want to look at a blinding derangement: the responsibility of the major journals in the field for the replication of those asymmetries of power and authority that impoverish knowledge production in the field of Classics by perpetrating the epistemic and hermeneutic injustice of denying a space and a place for scholars of color.

Padilla had conducted what he called a "data-harvesting project," as part of his "emancipatory" project of "citational justice." He looked over his own course syllabi and reading lists for the purpose of "mapping the major landmarks of authorized knowledge production in this field," asking himself: "How many women scholars appear on these syllabi? How many people of color? How many women of color?"

He attacked Basil Gildersleeve for starting a scholarly journal:

> Although not normally acknowledged in the dossier of his most explicitly racist words and deeds, Gildersleeve's founding of [the *American Journal of Philology*] in 1880 helped to

shape American classical scholarship by spurring the development of a journal-centred disciplinary culture that has proven remarkably if unsurprisingly resistant to the pursuit of racial diversity and equity as a core objective.

Apparently, the entire discipline was riddled with this injustice:

> If one were intentionally to design a discipline whose institutional organs and gatekeeping protocols were explicitly aimed at disavowing the legitimate status of scholars of color as producers of knowledge, one could not do better than what Classics has done.

Padilla had compiled 20 years' worth of data related to the journals *Classical Antiquity*, the *American Journal of Philology* and *Transactions of the American Philological Association* to determine how much gender disparity there is in the field. He had also tried to find data on the racial and ethnic backgrounds of all the authors published by these journals.

Between 1997 and 2017, according to Padilla, none of these came close to achieving gender parity. To account for this, he claimed that "men receive more explicit encouragement" to contribute to journals, and suggested that the "extraordinary discretionary powers wielded by editors" be scrutinised, because

"discretionary power can and should be flexed to progressive consequence and outcome."

I wasn't persuaded. Surely, to determine whether bias and sexual discrimination is the cause of gender disparity among these journal contributors, you
would have to factor in the number of female classicists who had submitted articles in the same period?
Was the acceptance rate lower for women than for
men? Padilla said nothing about that.

Next, he looked at the "racial and ethnic makeup
of the publication rosters" of journals, "the bleakness
of which may not surprise some of you in attendance,
but which still deserves quantitative exposition."

As a rule, academic papers are submitted anonymously to journals, by email or through electronic
journal software, and are read anonymously through
peer review. There isn't any indication on the paper,
either before publication or after, that would tell an
editor, reviewer, or reader the race or ethnicity of an
author. How did Padilla arrive at his numbers? How
could anyone know what he was claiming to know?

Padilla said he had exhaustively searched the Internet to try to determine the racial and ethnic backgrounds of contributors. He concluded that "the
hegemony of whiteness is everywhere in evidence
across the three journals" — between 91-98 percent
of contributors turned out to be white Americans or
white Europeans: "These percentages remind me of
nothing so much as the figures for those intensely seg-

regated suburbs that define the childhoods [sic] and adolescence of my partner; publication in elite journals is a whites-only neighborhood."

Padilla's solution "for the wellbeing and the future of the discipline," was for Classics to "de-colonize" itself: "The most fundamental question for the future of knowledge production in Classics is this: how do we recognize, honor and repair the silencing of the knowledges that people of color carry?"

He called for "reparative epistemic justice," and asked for holders of "white privilege" to "surrender their privilege":

> In practical terms, this means that in an economy of academic prestige defined and governed by scarcity, white men will have to surrender the privilege they have of seeing their words printed and disseminated. They will have to take a back seat, so that people of color, and women, and gender-non-conforming scholars of color benefit from the privileges, career and otherwise, of seeing their words on the page.

Was he explicitly calling for Classics journals to stop publishing the scholarly work of white men? Apparently, he was:

> This is an economy of scarcity that, at the level of journal publication, will remain to a degree

zero-sum. Until and unless this system of publication is dismantled – which will be fine by
me – every person of color who is to be published will take the place of a white man whose
words could have or had already appeared in
the pages of that journal. And that would be a
future worth striving for.

Padilla said nothing about merit, the content of the articles in question, or how they were reasoned. He said
that articles by white men should be excluded from
consideration, regardless of their merit, if members
of other ethnic or racial groups submitted work for
publication at the same time.

Surely, this is just straightforward racism? Yet in
response to these remarks, the entire audience of classicists applauded. Since an unattended microphone
had been set up in the center of the room, attention
shifted to the "discussion," and someone encouraged
members of the audience to speak. Because the conference program indicated that everyone in the audience was invited to speak as part of a discussion about
"the future of classics," I decided to contribute a few
sentences on the stated topic.

I made a decision not to respond directly to what
I had heard from the invited speakers, since it would
have taken too much time. Also, I wanted to speak to
the SCS as a whole, to classicists in general, and to the
audience that was present, about Classics, not race.

I only wanted to make four very brief points, but I felt compelled to state at the beginning that we could not abandon the ancient languages because then we would have nothing left of our field. Of all the egregiously shocking things I had just heard, that seemed to be the one that most cried out to be challenged. I then attempted to say the following:

1   It is important to stand up for Classics as a discipline, and promote it as the political, literary, historical, philosophical, rhetorical, and artistic foundation of western civilization, and the basis of European history, tradition, culture, and religion. It gave us the concepts of liberty, equality, and democracy, which we should teach and promote. We should not apologize for our field;

2   It is important to go back to teaching undergraduates about the great classical authors – Cicero, the Athenian dramatists, Homer, Demosthenes, the Greek and Roman historians, Plato, and Aristotle – in English translation in introductory courses;

3   One way of promoting Classics is to offer more survey courses that cover many subject areas (epic, tragedy, comedy, rhetoric, philosophy, history, political theory, and art history), or to concentrate on one area such as in Freshmen seminars, or through western-civilization classes;

4   It should help with securing funding from ad-
    ministrators to argue that such survey courses
    are highly cost-effective: A student could learn
    a tremendous amount even if such a survey
    were the only Classics course taken. On the
    other hand, a seminar that concentrated on the
    close reading of a few texts would prove bene-
    ficial for all students.

Unfortunately, I was interrupted in the middle of my
first point by Sarah Bond, who forcefully insisted:
"We are not western civilization!"

What can one say to that? I didn't respond. But
as I then attempted to move on and make my second
point, I was interrupted by her and others, and not
permitted to finish what I had hoped would be four
very brief statements. A member of the audience with
no connection to the panel, Michael Gagarin (University of Texas Emeritus) rose, came over to me, and
told me I wasn't allowed to speak.

I had never been at an academic conference where
a member of an audience had the power to forbid another audience member from speaking. I continued:
"We don't teach Homer. We don't teach Cicero...
Why don't we teach Thucydides and Herodotus?...
So I'm saying: Cicero has value. Homer has value. Demosthenes has value, because it will teach you about
defending Democracy." (Sarah Bond then pointed
out that these writers were "all men" and seemed to

think she'd scored a devastating point at my expense.)

I went on to say that I believe the journals publish articles on the basis of merit, not because of the race or ethnicity of the authors. Padilla then challenged me, since I was clearly disagreeing with his argument.

In the hope of making my position clearer – that race should not be a determining factor when it comes to assessing the value of scholarship – I said to Padilla, "You may have got your job because you're black, but I'd prefer to think you got your job because of merit." Admittedly, I was under stress and did not express myself as clearly as I might have done, but what I was trying to convey is that the principle he was advocating clearly didn't apply to hiring decisions – and nor should it – because he *had* got his job on merit, not because he's black. Indeed, if I thought the opposite, and I imagined there was a chance of him saying, "You're right, I was only hired because I'm black," that would have contradicted the point I was trying to make, which is that it would have been wrong to hire him based only on his race, just as it would be wrong for an academic journal to publish an article based on the race of its author.

Padilla did not respond to my point directly. Instead, he let out a whoop of what sounded like triumph. He then made the following statement:

> I did not interrupt you once, so you are going
> to let me talk. You are going to let someone

who has been historically marginalized from the production of knowledge in the Classics talk. And here's what I have to say about the vision of classics that you've outlined: If that is in fact a vision that affirms you in your white supremacy, I want nothing to do with it. I hope the field dies...and that it dies as swiftly as possible!

* * *

The following day, Helen Cullyer, the SCS Director, sent me an email in which she forbade my attendance at the meeting on Sunday, the last day of the conference. Her email was sent at about 2:15 PM on Sunday, two hours before the end of the final meeting.

Her stated reason for expelling me was "harassment": The SCS executive had unilaterally introduced a new measure about two months previously, stating that people could have scholars kicked out of the annual general meeting for "stalking, queer/trans bullying, or hostility or abuse based on age, disability, religion, race or ethnicity."

Cullyer gave me no chance to explain or defend myself, and since she was present in the audience, she knew what had happened. In her view, I had violated SCS policy by disagreeing with Padilla. A grown man with a position at Princeton was apparently unable to endure the trauma caused by a woman asking rhetorically if he got his job based on his race. Yet it was fine with the SCS Director (a woman) for a man (Michael Gagarin) to try to prevent a woman from speaking – that's not harassment, apparently.

I received another email on January 11 from the president of the SCS. This was sent out to all SCS members. In it, she slammed the "independent scholar" who told a black professor that "he only got his job because he was black," and explained that the director had banned me from events and panels at the meeting. She bemoaned how terrible this incident was since she had worked so hard to prevent "microaggressions" at the SCS, adding:

> But these and other immediate responses, such as the Board statement the SCS passed on the meeting's last day, by themselves can do little to redress the real and deep-seated problems the incidents disclose about not only U.S. society but also about our field.

She flagrantly mischaracterized what I had said. She never bothered to ask me for my account of what had happened, or to ascertain what my views actually are, before sending out her email and characterizing me as a racist.

I received an email from the president of a different professional society, the Association of Ancient Historians (AAH). Serena Connolly (Rutgers University), yet another white woman, informed me that the little job I had with the AAH had ended. She stated that I was fired because of my comments at the SCS panel and because I was opposed to "diversity" (news to me):

> I am writing to let you know that, as of this date, 11 January 2019, the Association of Ancient Historians will no longer require your services as Assistant Editor with the AAH newsletter…The AAH is committed to diversity in all its forms — in our membership, the field, and in our scholarship. We expect that those who hold office in the Association or perform work for it share that commitment.

I do not believe that Serena Connolly was present at the SCS. Nor did she ever ask me what had happened. Since I had been hired by, and worked for, the AAH Secretary, she arguably had no authority to fire me. But she was quick to do so, although we had never had any disagreements or conflicts and there have never been any complaints about my work.

To the best of my recollection, no one on the SCS panel ever used the word "diversity." No one talked about mentoring, or encouraging all students. They did not talk about teaching or students, or classes or courses, or the challenges facing teachers, or helping scholars get published beyond Padilla's suggestion of giving preference to non-white males; nor did they discuss Classics as an academic discipline (beyond what I have stated). This isn't surprising because the panel wasn't really about any of that, or even ultimately about race, but rather about how to destroy Classics.

Of all the academic disciplines, Classics has managed until now to withstand most of the corrupting influences of modern critical theory and "social justice" activism. Ours is the last bastion of western civilization in the academy. I wrote an email on January 11 to officials of the SCS to request an apology for their treatment of me, and to complain formally about the actions of the SCS director and president. In it I stated:

> The ancient Greeks defined democracy as majority rule that must have equality before the law and freedom of speech. It is unfortunate that the classicists don't know the value of their wonderful discipline and no longer accept free speech or due process. Without true equality in law, without free speech, democracy is destroyed. More than just Classics is at stake here.

The SCS responded on February 11, saying that Cullyer was within her rights to kick me out of the SCS Meeting because I "disrespected" Padilla, and in doing so violated the SCS' harassment policy and caused him "emotional distress." They added that while my remarks on western civilization were "protected by academic freedom," the comments I addressed directly to Padilla were not. They informed me it was acceptable for Bond to "interrupt" me and for Gagarin to forbid me from speaking because he "calmly" took the microphone from my hand. In sum, "academic freedom" is selective, free speech does not exist at the SCS, and I am not protected under the SCS harassment policy even though I was harassed, bullied, and intimidated.

* * *

I came away from my visit to the USS Midway (in contrast to my visit to the SCS) profoundly encouraged. One of the docents, a Vietnam-era Navy fighter pilot, explained aspects of his profession to visitors and concluded by saying that we should remember that every single person on a U.S. aircraft carrier was equally important, whatever their age, race, background, ethnicity, or position, because every one of them had an important job to do, whatever it is, and that by doing that job, they collectively made it possible for the ship to sail and for the naval aviators to survive. Lives depended on it. And that ship, in turn, not only represents, but is, in fact, the true defender of the west, its civilization, and its values.

The ship of state (to borrow an archaic Greek metaphor) of the Society for Classical Studies, and the field of Classics in general, requires a similar commitment on the part of all classicists, whether they are tenured or assistant professors, officers and directors of the SCS, part-time and temporary professors, independent scholars, undergraduates, graduates, retired faculty, avocational supporters, journal editors, and all others, to all do their jobs as best they can without regard for age, sex, race, and ethnicity. Only in this way will we avoid the infighting, excesses, discrimination, spite, harassment, inequality, suppression of free speech, and despotism that will sink our ship. Equally importantly, we must stand up to those who have no interest in the discipline of Classics or its survival – who even seek its destruction. We must defend the Classics; this is a war that must be fought and won.

AUTHOR'S POSTSCRIPT – SEPTEMBER 2020

I still live in California and continue to write academic papers. In mid-2019, the Society for Classical Studies decided to adopt a new harassment policy, which requires that anyone who had been judged to be a harasser (either in a court or by other means) be banned from attending their annual meeting in Washington, D.C. in 2020. They also required that all who registered accept their harassment policy or their registration would not be processed. Because the SCS had accused and punished me for "harassment" at the SCS annual meeting in 2019, I could not register for the 2020 meeting. The National Association of Scholars objected to this policy.

When They Came for Flannery O'Connor

By Charlotte Allen

On June 15, 2020, Paul Elie – a senior fellow at Georgetown University's Berkley Center for Religion, Peace, and World Affairs, and a frequent contributor to upscale magazines – published a 3,800-word essay in *The New Yorker* bluntly accusing the acclaimed Southern Catholic writer Flannery O'Connor (1925–1964) of racism. The essay, which has since gone viral, is ostensibly a review of *Radical Ambivalence: Race in Flannery O'Connor*, a new book by Angela Alaimo O'Donnell, an O'Connor scholar at Fordham University. O'Donnell surveys O'Connor's two novels, numerous short stories and essays, and voluminous correspondence (most of which was published following her untimely death aged 39 of complications from lupus), and concludes that O'Connor was "a walking contradiction when it came to matters of race." O'Connor's dark and mordantly humorous fiction was written as the Civil Rights movement tore through the South, dismantling Jim Crow during the 1950s and 1960s, and it frequently mocks Southern whites for their condescension and rudeness toward blacks. However, O'Donnell also argues that "rac-

ism" is the correct description of O'Connor's privately expressed views about black people in equally sar-
donic letters to friends. In her correspondences, she
was especially critical of the black celebrities admired
by Northern white liberals. Nonetheless, O'Donnell
concludes that O'Connor, prompted by her better angels and devout Catholic faith, strove assiduously to
overcome that attitude in the stories and novels she
wrote for public consumption.

In his *New Yorker* essay, Elie has no patience for
the "ambivalence" and "complexity" O'Donnell identifies in her book. O'Connor, he flatly announces, was
a "bigot." His evidence – also discussed by O'Donnell – consists of previously unpublished letters that
O'Connor wrote to her mother when she first visited the North in 1943 aged 18, in which she expressed
shock that blacks and whites shared classrooms, re-
strooms, and bus seats. There is also a long-since-pub-
lished 1964 letter to her ultra-liberal playwright friend
Maryat Lee in which she declared that, although she
was an integrationist by principle, she was a segregationist by instinct; she didn't *like* blacks. O'Connor
also frequently used the "n-word" (although usually
in the mouths of her fictional characters or to satirize
Southern attitudes – her preferred term for serious
discourse was the then-polite "Negro"). "O'Con-
nor-lovers have been downplaying those remarks
ever since," Elie writes. "But they are not hot-mike
moments or loose talk. They were written at the same

desk where O'Connor wrote her fiction and are found in the same lode of correspondence that has brought about the rise in her stature. This has put her champions in a bind – upholding her letters as eloquently expressive of her character, but carving out exceptions for the nasty parts." The print version of Elie's *New Yorker* essay was titled "Everything That Rises," a riff on "Everything That Rises Must Converge," the title of a well-known 1961 short story by O'Connor about black-white encounters on a newly integrated bus that turn disastrous. But the online edition's title was a when-did-you-stop-beating-your-wife rhetorical question: "How Racist Was Flannery O'Connor?" To which Elie's answer is: Very, very racist. It is the latter title that has become permanently attached to Elie's essay, including on his own web page at the Georgetown site.

It is an odd performance from Elie. In 2003, he published a book entitled *The Life You Save May Be Your Own*, a study of four mid-century Catholic figures: O'Connor, Dorothy Day, Thomas Merton, and Walker Percy. His treatment of O'Connor in that book was reverential; indeed, he lifted its very title from one of O'Connor's stories (I reviewed that book for the *Washington Post*). But in his *New Yorker* essay, he seems to have changed his mind. He also seems to be irked at the appearance of a new, prize-winning biographical documentary, *Flannery*. Almost always sick, and toward the end unable to walk without crutches, the novelist passed most of her life on her mother's dairy farm near Milledgeville, Georgia, where she lived as a charming eccentric and den mother to a flock of peacocks and other barnyard fowl (a commemorative stamp issued in 2015 features peacock feathers surrounding her portrait). The filmmakers, Elie grouses, had taken "up the idea that the most vivid character in her work is Flannery O'Connor."

Elie's *j'accuse* generated a social media storm among young Americans, many of whom had been assigned O'Connor's exquisitely crafted stories in their college English classes, but who were now caught up in the frenzy of Black Lives Matter protests that followed the death of George Floyd on May 25. "Flannery O'Connor is dead to me" was a typical Twitter post, and there were indications that professors in English departments are already vowing to stop teaching O'Connor's works altogether.

Within a few days of Elie's article appearing, a student (apparently white) at the Jesuit-run Loyola University in the predominantly black city of Baltimore, circulated a Change.org petition demanding that Loyola change the name of Flannery O'Connor Hall, a student dormitory on campus. The dorm was only 13 years old and had obviously received its name in deference to feminism by honoring a female Catholic writer. But it appeared that feminism would now have to cede to new conceptions of anti-racism. According to an article written by O'Donnell for the liberal Catholic magazine *Commonweal* on August 3, the petition's author had contacted her to try – unsuccessfully – to enlist her in the campaign, citing the "hate" O'Connor had allegedly manifested towards African Americans (a word O'Connor never used in that context in her writings, even as an 18-year-old). The student's petition, which eventually garnered 1,102 signatures, said as much about the current state of teaching as it did about the charges against O'Connor: "Recent letters and postcards written by Flannery O'Connor express strong racist sentiments and hate speech. Her name and legacy should not be honored nor glorified on our Evergreen Campus." Recent – as in 1943? One signatory called O'Connor "disgusting"; another declared that if Loyola failed to rename the building, students would be forced to live "under the name of bigotry." Some signatories admitted that they had no idea who Flannery O'Connor was, but denounced her even so.

It didn't take long for Loyola to capitulate to the petitioners. On July 29, Loyola's Jesuit president, Fr. Brian Linnane, announced that the university had duly removed O'Connor's name from the dormitory, which would be renamed after Thea Bowman (1937–1990). Bowman was a black Catholic nun and musician who had promoted a church ministry to African Americans and is currently being considered for official canonization with the support of the U.S. Catholic bishops. While expressing hope that O'Connor's fiction would continue to be taught in Loyola classrooms, Linnane's statement noted that O'Connor had displayed a "racist" perspective in her letters. "A residence hall is supposed to be the students' home," he declared. "If some of the students who live in that building find it to be unwelcoming and unsettling, that has to be taken seriously."

Linnane's decision provoked an extraordinary backlash among O'Connor's admirers, not least of whom was O'Donnell herself. O'Donnell was outraged by what she perceived to be Elie's distortion of her book's conclusions, and by his character assassination of O'Connor, who she described as "among the finest writers America has produced." In her *Commonweal* article, she accused Elie of trying to "make the erroneous claim that he is the only critic ever to deal frankly with O'Connor's complex attitude toward race. Critics have been wrestling with this since the early 1970s. Readers of Elie's essay are never informed of this." O'Donnell gathered 177 signatures from writers, O'Connor scholars, and leading Catholic academics for a July 31 open letter to Linnane begging him to reconsider his decision. "As you are surely aware, cancelling Confederate generals and dismantling Civil War monuments is a very different matter from cancelling writers, thinkers, and artists, none of whom were ever presumed to be saints or paragons of conventional virtue," the letter said. "This is antithetical to university culture and intellectual life."

At the top of the list of signatories was the black

novelist and poet Alice Walker. Walker and O'Connor had a brief parallel-lives relationship. As a teenager, Walker had lived across the road from the O'Connor dairy farm in more humble quarters, and one of her brothers had worked for the O'Connors. In a 1975 essay, Walker had written that while she found O'Connor's jocular use of racial slurs offensive, she found the "perfection" of O'Connor's fiction "dazzling," and declared that "*essential* O'Connor is not about race at all." In a July 27 statement to Loyola protesting the dorm renaming, she wrote, "We must honor Flannery for growing." The numerous Catholic signatories to O'Donnell's open letter included novelists Mary Gordon and Ron Hansen, essayist Richard Rodriguez, former *New York Times* religion columnist Peter Steinfels, and an array of Catholic academics whose religious views ranged from liberal to ultra-traditionalist. The signatories knew there was no hope that Linnane would retract his decision to rename the dormitory after a saintly black nun, but they expressed hope that O'Connor's name restored could share joint honors with Thea Bowman's. To date, neither Linnane nor any spokesman for Loyola has responded to the letter.

What is interesting about the defenses of O'Connor that have accompanied the furor over the Loyola dorm is that even her most ardent champions have appeared to accept the premise of that second incendiary title of Elie's *New Yorker* article — Not: Was Flannery O'Connor racist? But: How racist was she? This has meant that none of these literary defenders, and certainly none of O'Connor's opponents, has felt the need to define exactly what "racist" means, so the vocabulary they use to mount their arguments, although earnest and passionate, is also banal and clichéd. In an excerpt from her book, published on May 12, in the University of Notre Dame's *Church Life Journal*, Angela Alaimo O'Donnell writes that O'Connor was among the "great writers whose whiteness prevented them from understanding and engaging blackness with the same authoritative vision with which they could see and present the white world." Another *Church Life Journal* contributor, self-described "radical" Catholic David Griffith (who had cribbed a bit from O'Connor's 1953 story "A Good Man Is Hard to Find" with a 2006 book titled *A Good War Is Hard to Find*) wrote these blunt words on June 29: "O'Connor was a racist, even if a reluctant and reflective one."

Even O'Connor's most religiously conservative defenders agreed. In *First Things,* Jennifer Frey, an associate professor of philosophy at the University of South Carolina, decreed that O'Connor had committed the "sin of racism." (I have written for *First Things* myself.) Another *First Things* contributor, Jessica Hooten Wilson, an O'Connor scholar at the University of Dallas, wrote on June 24 that although O'Connor had indulged in "inexcusable racial slurs," she had also "used her fiction to call for Southerners to repent of racist attitudes" by giving the racist characters in her stories a "comeuppance" that led to their conversion.

But without a stable definition of racism, it remains an open question whether or not O'Connor really was a racist in any serious sense. Her use of the "n-word" (always in correspondence, never to the face of or with reference to individual black people) was her gravest offense – but it was also the offense of such staunchly anti-slavery Southern writers as Mark Twain and William Faulkner, who also indulged in Southern diction that became taboo for white people in the North. In her 1964 letter to Maryat Lee, in which she was clearly trying to get a rise out of her liberal confidant, she claimed not to "like" black people; but O'Connor did in fact have black friends, as Wilson pointed out in her *First Things* essay.

She considered James Baldwin to be a second-rate writer – which was actually true. Baldwin wrote a fine first novel, his semi-autobiographical *Go Tell It on the Mountain*, and several perceptive early stories and essays, but much of what he wrote after that was forgettable. "Pontificating" – O'Connor's descriptive adjective for Baldwin in that 1964 letter to Lee – was *le mot juste*: "If Baldwin were white, nobody would stand him in a minute." She considered Martin Luther King not to be "the ages [sic] great saint" (also true, at least as far as King's sex life was concerned), but respected his civil-rights leadership: "He's at least doing what he can do & has to do." What O'Connor actually couldn't abide was the sanctimonious sentimentality – often accompanied by hypocrisy – of white liberals who made fetishes out of black people solely on the basis of their skin color and presumed victim status. She called Harper Lee's *To Kill a Mockingbird* "children's literature." Again, right on the money.

The fact that this debate is taking place at all, however – whether or not Flannery O'Connor was a racist, how racist or not she might have been, whether she redeemed herself from her racism via her writing, or grew past her racism morally – is exactly what has gone fearfully wrong. The primary evil of cancel culture isn't toppled statues or renamed buildings or even destroyed livelihoods. It is that, once cancel culture has come for an artist, it becomes impossible to take that artist's artistry seriously. In his *New Yorker* essay, Paul Elie complains that O'Connor's admirers pass over the issue of her racism in order to focus on her literary gifts: "It's about protecting an author who is now as beloved as her stories." Now, O'Connor's admirers will be obliged to pass over her literary gifts in order to focus on the issue of her racism. Flannery O'Connor will forever have an asterisk next to her name, and that asterisk will be the Racism Question. Henceforth, it will be impossible to give a public lecture about O'Connor, teach a college class, write a critical essay, or adapt her fiction to stage or screen without appending a dreary prologue rehearsing all the arguments about her attitudes toward black people. And in the midst of such arguments, all nuance, humor, characterization, and subtlety in the works themselves gets flattened or lost. This is what cancel culture does: It reduces literature to ideology.

We can already see this ideological oversimplification, even in the valiant efforts to rescue O'Connor from Paul Elie's verbal darts. In her *First Things* essay, Jessica Hooten Wilson is so eager to defend O'Connor from charges of racial "hate" that she reinterprets O'Connor's stories as moralizing fables in which O'Connor "pointed a finger at racial bigots" and devised climactic episodes for those fictional characters in which they were "knocked down" to their "rightful place," presumably by the operation of God's grace. This kind of interpretation is as alien to literature — which speaks for itself — as reducing it to conceptual abstractions of "whiteness" and "blackness," as Angela Alaimo O'Donnell does. In his essay on O'Connor, Paul Griffith writes: "Characters are not puppets deployed to stand in for or represent larger ideas or issues." There are many points with which to argue in Griffith's own polemical interpretation of O'Connor's writings, but this is not one of them.

Let's look at that integrated-bus story of O'Connor's, "Everything That Rises Must Converge." Its plot involves the conflict between a dim and overweight (white) Southern woman suffering from high blood pressure and her unlikable son, Julian, who fancies himself a writer but is actually living off his mother. He also fancies himself an enlightened liberal, entitled to rebuke her at every turn for her backward racial attitudes. On the bus, Julian tries to show up his mother by striking up a conversation with a well-dressed black man who is impervious to his overtures. Julian's mother thinks it's nice to hand out coins to cute black children, and when she tries to offer a penny to a little boy sitting next to her, the boy's mother becomes enraged, her dignity affronted. When they get off the bus, Julian begins berating his mother for her condescension – and then the mother has the stroke toward which her medical condition has inevitably pointed. As for Julian, O'Connor writes:

> "Help, help!" he shouted, but his voice was thin, scarcely a thread of sound. The lights drifted farther away the faster he ran and his feet moved numbly as if they carried him nowhere. The tide of darkness seemed to sweep him back to her, postponing from moment to moment his entry into the world of guilt and sorrow.

Is this a story about racism, illustrated by two different kinds of racial condescension? It seems, rather, to be a story about opacity, in which mother and son fail to comprehend each other's mental world in the same way that both fail to comprehend the mental world of the blacks with whom they share the bus ride. In the story, blacks and whites inhabit separate universes, divided by Jim Crow, but also by vastly different cultures despite Southern physical proximity (neither mother notices, for example, that the two are wearing identical hats). People are ultimately opaque even to those who share their lives most intimately. It may be a sin to "other" others – but othering is a feature of the human condition. In one of her essays, O'Connor wrote that the theme of her fiction was "the action of grace in territory largely held by the devil." But God's grace in this story – or any other stories of O'Connor's – isn't an easy matter of a "comeuppance" after which the sinner repents. It is, rather, a fearful clattering lightning bolt followed by... who knows what, given that the devil doesn't relinquish territory easily.

To quote the New Testament, as O'Connor did so often in her fiction, the letter killeth, but the spirit giveth life. And there is nothing so literal in its after-effects as cancel culture, mowing down everything in its path in the name of anti-racism or whatever the ideology *du jour* might be. What cancel culture has just mown down isn't simply Flannery O'Connor or her works, but our ability to view them through any other lens except that of doctrine.

AUTHOR'S POSTSCRIPT – SEPTEMBER 2020

In my essay, I predicted that the result of bringing cancel culture to O'Connor would be that henceforth she would no longer be taken seriously as an artist, and that her novels and short stories would henceforth be read as two-dimensional parables reflecting either her own supposed bigotry or her supposedly valiant efforts to overcome it and educate her readers about its evils. My prediction has already proved accurate. In a second essay, this one for the liberal Catholic magazine *Commonweal*, Elie eviscerated several of O'Connor's stories as "barbed" defenses of Southern segregationist attitudes (one character is a black woman described as "sullen-looking" – to Elie that's "very nearly a stereotype"). On the other side, essayist Joseph Pearce, writing for the conservative *National Catholic Register*, agreed that O'Connor was a "miserable sinner," but concluded that she had mostly "exorcised" her "demons" through her fiction. We are already seeing cancel culture's most depressing effect: the cancellation of any reading of an author's works that is other than moralistic and ideological.

A Mathematics Paper Goes Down the Memory Hole
By Theodore P. Hill

In the highly controversial area of human intelligence, the "Greater Male Variability Hypothesis" (GMVH) asserts that there are more idiots and more geniuses among men than among women. Darwin's research on evolution in the nineteenth century found that, although there are many exceptions for specific traits and species, there is generally more variability in males than in females of the same species throughout the animal kingdom.

Evidence for this hypothesis is fairly robust, and has been reported in species ranging from adders and sockeye salmon to wasps and orangutans, as well as humans. Multiple studies have found that boys and men are over-represented at both the high and low ends of the distributions in categories ranging from birth weight, brain structures, and 60-meter dash times to reading and mathematics test scores. There are significantly more men than women, for example, among Nobel laureates, music composers, and chess champions – and also among homeless people, suicide victims, and federal prison inmates.

Darwin had also raised the question of *why* males

in many species might have evolved to be more variable than females, and when I learned that the answer to his question remained elusive, I set out to look for a scientific explanation. My aim was not to prove or disprove that the hypothesis applies to human intelligence or to any other specific traits or species, but simply to discover a *logical* reason that could help explain how gender differences in variability might naturally arise in the same species.

I came up with a simple intuitive mathematical argument based on biological and evolutionary principles, and enlisted Sergei Tabachnikov, a Professor of Mathematics at Pennsylvania State University, to help me flesh out the model. When I posted a preprint on the open-access mathematics archives in May of last year, a variability researcher at Durham University in the UK got in touch by email. He described our joint paper as "an excellent summary of the research to date in this field," adding that "it certainly underpins my earlier work on impulsivity, aggression and general evolutionary theory and it is nice to see an actual theoretical model that can be drawn upon in discussion (which I think the literature, particularly in education, has lacked to date). I think this is a welcome addition to the field."

So far, so good.

Once we had written up our findings, Sergei and I decided to try for publication in the *Mathematical Intelligencer*, the "Viewpoint" section of which specifically welcomes articles on contentious topics. The *Intelligencer*'s editor-in-chief is Marjorie Wikler Senechal, Professor Emerita of Mathematics and the History of Science at Smith College. She liked our draft, and declared herself to be untroubled by the prospect of controversy. "In principle," she told Sergei in an email, "I am happy to stir up controversy, and few topics generate more than this one…We could make a real contribution here by insisting that all views be heard, and providing links to them."

Professor Senechal suggested that we might enliven our paper by mentioning Harvard President Larry Summers, who was swiftly defenestrated in 2005 for saying that the GMVH might be a contributing factor to the dearth of women in physics and mathematics departments at top universities. With her editorial guidance, our paper underwent several further revisions until, on April 3, 2017, our manuscript was officially accepted for publication. The paper was typeset in India, and proofread by an assistant editor who is also a mathematics professor in Kansas. It was scheduled to appear in the international journal's first issue of 2018, with an acknowledgement of funding support to my co-author from the National Science Foundation. All normal academic procedure.

* * *

Coincidentally, at about the same time, anxiety about gender parity erupted in Silicon Valley. The same anti-variability argument used to justify the sacking of President Summers resurfaced when Google engineer James Damore suggested that several innate biological factors, including gender differences in variability, might help explain gender disparities in Silicon Valley high-tech jobs. For sending out an internal memo to that effect, he was summarily fired.

No sooner had Sergei posted a preprint of our accepted article on his web site than we began to encounter problems. On August 16, a representative of the Women In Mathematics (WIM) chapter in his department at Penn State contacted him to warn that the paper might be damaging to the aspirations of impressionable young women. "As a matter of principle," she wrote, "I support people discussing controversial matters openly... At the same time, I think it's good to be aware of the effects." While *she* was obviously able to debate the merits of our paper, she worried that other, presumably less sophisticated, readers "will just see someone wielding the authority of mathematics to support a very controversial, and potentially sexist, set of ideas."

A few days later, she again contacted Sergei on behalf of WIM, and invited him to attend a lunch that had been organized for a "frank and open discussion" about our paper. He would be allowed 15 minutes to describe and explain our results, and this short presentation would be followed by readings of prepared statements by WIM members and then an open discussion. "We promise to be friendly," she announced, "but you should know in advance that many (most?) of us have strong disagreements with what you did."

On September 4, Sergei sent me a weary email. "The scandal at our department," he wrote, "shows no signs of receding." At a faculty meeting the week before, the Department Head had explained that sometimes values such as academic freedom and free speech come into conflict with other values to which Penn State was committed. A female colleague had then instructed Sergei that he needed to admit and fight bias, adding that the belief that "women have a lesser chance to succeed in mathematics at the very top end is bias." Sergei said he had spent "endless hours" talking to people who explained that the paper was "bad and harmful" and tried to convince him to "withdraw my name to restore peace at the department and to avoid losing whatever political capital I may still have." Ominously, "analogies with scientific racism were made by some; I am afraid, we are likely to hear more of it in the future."

The following day, I wrote to the three organizers of the WIM lunch, and offered to address any concrete concerns they might have with our logic or conclusions or any other content. I explained that, since I was the paper's lead author, it was not fair that my colleague should be expected to take all the heat for our findings. I added that it would still be possible to revise our article before publication. I never received a response.

Instead, on September 8, Sergei and I were ambushed by two unexpected developments.

First, the National Science Foundation wrote to Sergei requesting that acknowledgment of NSF funding be removed from our paper with immediate effect. I was astonished. I had never before heard of the NSF requesting removal of acknowledgement of funding for any reason. On the contrary, they are usually delighted to have public recognition of their support for science.

The ostensible reason for this request was that our paper was unrelated to Sergei's funded proposal. However, a Freedom of Information request subsequently revealed that Penn State WIM administrator Diane Henderson ("Professor and Chair of the Climate and Diversity Committee") and Nate Brown ("Professor and Associate Head for Diversity and Equity") had secretly co-signed a letter to the NSF that same morning. "Our concern," they explained, "is that [this] paper appears to promote pseudoscientific ideas that are detrimental to the advancement of women in science, and at odds with the values of the NSF." Unaware of this at the time, and eager to err on the side of compromise, Sergei and I agreed to remove the acknowledgement as requested. At least, we thought, the paper was still on track to be published.

But that same day, the *Mathematical Intelligencer*'s editor-in-chief, Marjorie Senechal, notified us that, with "deep regret," she was rescinding her previous acceptance of our paper. "Several colleagues," she wrote, had warned her that publication would provoke "extremely strong reactions," and there existed a "very real possibility that the right-wing media may pick this up and hype it internationally." For the second time in a single day, I was left flabbergasted. Working mathematicians are usually thrilled if even five people in the world read their latest article. Now some progressive faction was worried that a fairly straightforward logical argument about male variability might encourage the conservative press to actually read and cite a science paper?

In my 40 years of publishing research papers, I had never heard of the rejection of an already-accepted paper. And so I emailed Professor Senechal. She replied that she had received no criticisms on scientific grounds, and that her decision to rescind was entirely about the reaction she feared our paper would elicit. By way of further explanation, Senechal even compared our paper to the Confederate statues that had recently been removed from the courthouse lawn in Lexington, Kentucky. In the interests of setting our arguments in a more responsible context, she proposed instead that Sergei and I participate in a "round table" discussion of our hypothesis argument, the proceedings of which the *Intelligencer* would publish in lieu of our paper. Her decision, we learned, enjoyed the approval of Springer, one of the world's leading publishers of scientific books and journals, including the *Intelligencer*. An editorial director of Springer Mathematics later apologized to me twice, in person, but did nothing to reverse the decision or to support us at the time.

So what in the world had happened at the *Intelligencer*? Unbeknownst to us, Amie Wilkinson, a senior professor of mathematics at the University of Chicago, had become aware of our paper, and written to the journal to complain. A back-and-forth had ensued. Wilkinson then enlisted the support of her father – a psychometrician and statistician – who wrote to the *Intelligencer* at his daughter's request to express his own misgivings, including his belief that "this article oversimplifies the issues to the point of embarrassment." Invited by Professor Senechal to participate in the proposed round table discussion, he declined, admitting to Senechal that "others are more expert on this." We discovered all this after he gave Senechal permission to forward his letter, inadvertently revealing Wilkinson's involvement in the process (an indiscretion his daughter would later – incorrectly – blame on the *Intelligencer*).

I wrote polite emails directly to both Wilkinson and her father, explaining that I planned to revise the paper for resubmission elsewhere, and asking for their criticisms or suggestions. (I also sent a more strongly worded, point-by-point rebuttal to her father.) Neither replied. Instead, even long after the *Intelligencer* rescinded acceptance of the paper, Wilkinson continued to trash both the journal and its editor-in-chief on social media, inciting her Facebook friends with the erroneous allegation that an entirely different (and more contentious) article had been accepted.

At this point, faced with career-threatening reprisals from their own departmental colleagues and the diversity committee at Penn State, as well as displeasure from the NSF, Sergei, along with a colleague of his who'd done computer simulations for us, withdrew their names from the research. Fortunately for me, I am now retired and rather less easily intimidated — one of the benefits of being a Vietnam combat veteran and former U.S. Army Ranger, I guess. So, I continued to revise the paper, and finally posted it on the online mathematics archives.

* * *

On October 13, Igor Rivin, an editor at the widely respected online research journal, the *New York Journal of Mathematics* (NYJM), got in touch with me. He had learned about the article from my erstwhile co-author, read the archived version, and asked me if I'd like to submit a newly revised draft for publication. Rivin said that Mark Steinberger, the NYJM's editor-in-chief, was also very positive and that they were confident the paper could be refereed fairly quickly. I duly submitted a new draft (this time as the sole author), and, after a very positive referee's report and a handful of supervised revisions, Steinberger wrote to confirm publication on November 6, 2017. Relieved that the ordeal was finally over, I forwarded the link to interested colleagues.

Three days later, however, the paper had vanished. And a few days after that, a completely different paper by different authors appeared at *exactly the same page of the same volume* (NYJM Volume 23, pages 1641 and following) where mine had once been. As it turned out, Amie Wilkinson is married to Benson Farb, a member of the NYJM editorial board. Upon discovering that the journal had published my paper, Professor Farb had written a furious email to Steinberger demanding that it be deleted at once. "Rivin," he complained, "is well-known as a person with extremist views who likes to pick fights with people via inflammatory statements." Farb's "father-in law...a famous statistician," he went on, had "already poked many holes in the ridiculous paper." My paper was "politically charged" and "pseudoscience," and "a piece of crap," and, by encouraging the NYJM to accept it, Rivin had "violat[ed] a scientific duty for purely political ends."

Unaware of any of this, I wrote to Steinberger on November 14, to find out what had happened. I pointed out that if the deletion were permanent, it would leave me in an impossible position. I would not be able to republish anywhere else because I would be unable to sign a copyright form declaring that it had not already been published elsewhere. Steinberger replied later that day. Half his board, he explained unhappily, had told him that unless he pulled the article, they would all resign and "harass the journal" he had founded 25 years earlier "until it died." Faced with the loss of his own scientific legacy, he had capitulated. "A publication in a dead journal," he offered, "wouldn't help you." (Supporting documentation detailing these exchanges may be found linked at the online version of this article, on the *Quillette* website).

* * *

Colleagues I spoke to were appalled. None of them had ever heard of a paper in any field being disappeared after formal publication. Rejected prior to publication? Of course. Retracted? Yes, but only after an investigation, the results of which would then be made public by way of explanation. But simply *disappeared*? Never. If a formally refereed and published paper can later be erased from the scientific record and replaced by a completely different article, without any discussion with the author or any announcement in the journal, what will this mean for the future of electronic journals?

Meanwhile, Professor Wilkinson had now widened her existing social media campaign against the *Intelligencer* to include attacks on the NYJM and its editorial staff. As recently as April of 2018, she was threatening Facebook friends with "unfriending" unless they severed social-media ties with Rivin.

In early February, a friend and colleague suggested that I write directly to University of Chicago President Robert Zimmer to complain about the conduct of Farb and Wilkinson, both of whom are University of Chicago professors. The previous October, the conservative *New York Times* columnist Bret Stephens had called Zimmer "America's Best University President." The week after I wrote to Zimmer, the *Wall Street Journal* would describe Chicago as "the Free-Speech University" based upon its president's professed commitment to the principles of free inquiry and expression. Furthermore, Professor Zimmer is a mathematician from the same department, and even the same subfield, as Farb and Wilkinson, the husband-wife team that had successfully suppressed my variability-hypothesis research and trampled on principles of academic liberty. Surely, I would receive a sympathetic hearing there.

And so I wrote directly to Professor Zimmer, mathematician to mathematician, detailing five concrete allegations against his two colleagues. When I eventually received a formal response in late April, it was a somewhat terse official letter from the vice-provost informing me that an inquiry had found no evidence of "academic fraud," and that, consequently, "the charges have been dismissed." But I had made no allegation of academic fraud. I had alleged "unprofessional, uncollegial, and unethical conduct damaging to my professional reputation and to the reputation of the University of Chicago."

When I appealed the decision to the President, I received a second official letter from the vice-provost, in which he argued that Farb and Wilkinson had "exercised their academic freedom in advocating against the publication of the papers," and that their behavior had not been either "unethical or unprofessional." A reasonable inference is that I was the one interfering in their academic freedom and not vice versa. My quarrel, the vice-provost concluded, was with the editors-in-chief who had spiked my papers, decisions for which the University of Chicago bore no responsibility. At the Free Speech University, it turns out, talk is cheap.

* * *

Over the years, there has undoubtedly been significant bias and discrimination against women in mathematics and technical fields. Unfortunately, some of that still persists, even though many of us have tried hard to help turn the tide. My own efforts have included tutoring and mentoring female undergraduates, graduating female PhD students, and supporting hiring directives from deans and departmental chairs to seek out and give special consideration to female candidates. I have been invited to serve on two National Science Foundation gender and race diversity panels in Washington.

Which is to say that I understand the importance of the causes that equal-opportunity activists and progressive academics are ostensibly championing. But pursuit of greater fairness and equality cannot be allowed to interfere with dispassionate academic study. No matter how unwelcome the implications of a logical argument may be, it must be allowed to stand or fall on its merits, not its desirability or political utility. First Harvard, then Google, and now the editors-in-chief of two esteemed scientific journals, the National Science Foundation, and the international publisher Springer have all surrendered to demands from the radical academic Left to suppress a controversial idea. Who will be the next, and for what perceived transgression? If bullying and censorship are now to be re-described as "advocacy" and "academic freedom," as the Chicago administrators would have it, they will simply replace empiricism and rational discourse as the academic instruments of choice.

Educators must practice what we preach and lead by example. In this way, we can help to foster intellectual curiosity and the discovery of fresh reasoning so compelling that it causes even the most skeptical to change their minds. But this necessarily requires us to reject censorship and open ourselves to the civil discussion of sensitive topics such as gender differences, and the variability hypothesis in particular. In 2015, the University of Chicago's Committee on Freedom of Expression summarized the importance of this principle beautifully in a report commissioned by none other than Professor Robert Zimmer:

> In a word, the University's fundamental commitment is to the principle that debate or deliberation may not be suppressed because the ideas put forth are thought by some or even by most members of the University community to be offensive, unwise, immoral, or wrong-headed.

AUTHOR'S POSTSCRIPT – SEPTEMBER 2020

The extensive and ardent responses to this article came as a complete surprise to me. Within days, it had been translated into a half-dozen languages and triggered a tsunami of remarks from around the globe. The published *Quillette* comments, a vital part of the permanent record, document the intensity of the reactions to both the memory-holed science paper and the ensuing story of its cancellation. Under the cover of anonymity, a few critics repeatedly branded my article as fundamentally dishonest and accused *Quillette* editors of sloppy fact-checking. Those allegations all ended abruptly when Retraction Watch posted my supporting documents. The majority of comments, however, both scientific and political, were very supportive. As my modest research paper zoomed around the world on the coattails of the *Quillette* piece, its scientific ideas reached a far wider audience than it normally would have (thanks to the so-called "Barbra Streisand Effect"). This led to numerous constructive exchanges with other scientists, and, as a direct result, after two years it has now been rescued from the memory hole, peer-reviewed, and published once again, ready for open scientific debate.

A parallel theme in the *Quillette* comments was that of the vital importance of freedom of speech in academics. In urging us to "stand strong against these people [and] this kind of tantrum and bullying," one female graduate student in mathematics anticipated Princeton mathematician and *Quillette* author Sergiu Klainerman's recent admonition that our scientific society must "stop being frightened, intimidated, and afraid to fight back." I am grateful to *Quillette* editor-in-chief Claire Lehman and her superb editorial staff for providing such an effective platform to do exactly that.

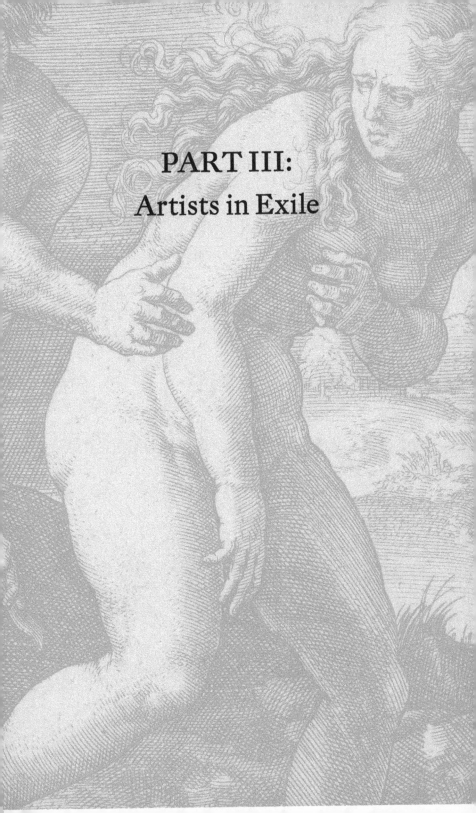

PART III:
Artists in Exile

Watching My Own Excommunication
By Sky Gilbert

I was officially excommunicated by the woke Left on November 19, 2018. There's a Facebook video of the event, which anyone can watch.

The social justice Left often is described as a manifestation of ideological, political, or cultural forces. I no longer believe that to be an accurate description. The behavior on display in that video didn't originate in a place of reason, but rather the realm of spiritual passions.

In a former article, I had already related to *Quillette* readers some parts of my story. In 1979, I founded Buddies in Bad Times Theatre, which for many years was Canada's preeminent professional gay and lesbian theatrical company. However, the queer Buddies that exists today was truly born in 1985, when my friend Dr. Johnny Golding (a female philosopher and queer activist) became its president. Dr. Golding spearheaded Buddies' 1994 move to its now permanent home on Alexander Street in Toronto, a 300-seat theatre (with a licensed cabaret) near the city's large queer village. I resigned from Buddies in 1997, and handed over the creative reins to Sarah Stanley, a lesbian director. The theatre saw two more artistic directors – David Oiye and Brendan Healey – before lesbian writer/director Evalyn Parry was appointed in 2015.

Given that I have not had an official position at Buddies for the last 22 years – a period during which I've made my living as an author, academic, and performer – why was it necessary for the theatre I founded to take a leading role in my excommunication? I got my first clue back at a queer-theatre symposium in Vancouver three years ago (one that Parry also attended), where I'd been scheduled to speak and perform. There was pushback against my presence – specifically, because of my identity as a proud drag queen. Various transgender attendees declared that the very idea of drag is anti-trans and misogynistic, and that drag-queen humor is inherently cruel.

Parry arranged for a "healing circle" – a ritual whereby a canceled event is replaced with a group meeting. Each participant would be given a moment or two to express themselves, focusing on the wounds that I'd allegedly caused by being a drag queen, and speaking openly about my identity. I didn't say much, as I'd been instructed to listen. People shared their feelings in a random fashion, giving full expression to their thoughts and feelings. (One straight woman, for instance, decided to tell the healing circle that she wanted to have sex with me.) And yet, somehow, the hoped-for "healing" proved elusive. I was simply removed from the speaking program without further ado.

Fast forward to 2018-19. Buddies' current theatre season coincides with the 40th anniversary of the company's founding in 1979. In celebration, Parry scheduled a reading of my 1980s hit play *Drag Queens in Outer Space*. I was flattered and excited, but also worried about some reprise of the 2016 debacle described above. In the mid-1980s, my play celebrating drag queens seemed risqué and transgressive. In the current climate, it's seen, by some, as reactionary.

The week before the *Drag Queens in Outer Space* reading, I happened to buy the book *I'm Afraid of Men* by Canadian writer Vivek Shraya, who had announced in 2016 that she was a trans woman. The book is presented as an extended attack on what is now called toxic masculinity.

I blogged my objections shortly before the scheduled event. "I'm sure that you have had the best of intentions, and like so many of us, you have had a lot of pain in your life," I wrote in a blog entry titled, *An Open Letter to Vivek Shraya*. "But that doesn't justify its title...What if someone titled their book, *I'm afraid of Jews*?" I also described how, as a young drag queen, I, too, had been afraid of straight men. But I got over that fear, wearing my high heels and mascara proudly when reading poems and plays at lecture halls, theatres, and bars filled with homophobic straights. I urged Vivek *not* to be afraid of men. Then I wrote a second blog post, entitled *I'm Afraid of Woke People*. And that's when things really got crazy.

Before she publicly identified herself as a trans woman in 2016, Vivek spent many years as a gay man. In her book, she recounts her many depressing and humiliating experiences, painting a picture of gay men and drag queens as shallow, superficial, selfish, petty, and mean. The view of gay men that pervades *I'm Afraid of Men* reflects the homophobic stereotypes that have dominated western culture since the days when Oscar Wilde mused that "I find it harder and harder every day to live up to my blue china." Don't get me wrong: I've met lots of shallow, superficial, selfish, petty, mean gay men. But gay men haven't cornered the market on these traits. And it angered me that Shraya — who identifies as queer — was so viciously attacking our still-vulnerable community.

I think that second blog entry might have been less controversial if it had been a simple, straightforward critique of Shraya's book. Instead, my post contained a satirical poem written in the spirit of Jonathan Swift's *A Modest Proposal.* I not only rose to the defense of drag queens, but also invoked camp irony to impersonate Shraya's wounded-victim voice. I also applied the same caustic tone to the poisonous reductionism of intersectionality more generally, and ended by apologizing for the fact of my very existence.

After some back and forth between me and Parry, I was informed that she was canceling the reading of *Drag Queens in Outer Space* due to the "problematic" nature of my poem. In place of the reading, she'd scheduled a "long table" in the tradition established by feminist playwright Lois Weaver (founder, along with Peggy Shaw, of New York's fabulous Split Britches theatre company). The long table was to be "a community discussion focused on intergenerational issues and allyship," a longer and more formal version of the "healing circle" I'd witnessed in 2016. She mentioned – parenthetically, I thought – that I was free to attend...as a spectator.

I was warned by friends not to attend the long table. They said it would be akin to a public lynching. And they were right. I didn't go. But I watched a livestream. And I was indeed "woken" by what I saw, though not in the intended manner.

I can see how the spectacle would bore anyone who is not personally affected by the underlying issues, or who doesn't share my (newfound) fascination with woke religious ritual.

From start to finish, the long table took almost three and a half hours. Surprisingly, my name was seldom spoken out loud, even by those who were clearly there to denounce me. There also were a few who defended me, describing me as a kind of King Lear-ish "foolish, fond, old man" – doddering, perhaps even demented, and deserving of more pity than scorn. When Parry tried to justify her decision to cancel my play by quoting from my blog posts, you can hear a voice ask faintly, "What exactly is so bad about Sky's *woke* poem?" This question wasn't answered, since it was incidental to the real subject of the Buddies long table: the spiritual and emotional lives of the congregants.

The structure of the meeting was explained upfront by a moderator: "One chair should always remain empty. If at any point someone comes up to join the table, and there is only one empty chair, someone else at the table must self-select themselves and leave the table." This structure allowed people to come and go. Some spoke at length about whether or not they had a *right* to speak. Early on, for instance, a person spoke about their mixed white and non-white roots: "And with this level of privilege" – they touched their face gently and made what really did seem like a prayer motion – "The fragility that comes...these feelings... of...of...of fear and pain...are also real."

There were tears and there was anger. There were hands literally raised, as if to god (or gods). Several people rambled about unrelated personal and career problems, using the long table as a sort of therapy session. Some read poems. There was little actual dialogue, but rather a succession of inward-focused monologues. Everyone seemed lost and lonely. The most common theme was that people felt unsafe, and it was vaguely asserted (or, in most cases, simply assumed) that my criticism of a book was connected to this feeling of despair and vulnerability. At what, in retrospect, seemed like the climax of the event, one especially dramatic person wailed, through tears: "Right now...sitting in this room, I do not feel safe. I...do... not...feel...safe. Home was not safe. Ceremony was not safe...I'm screwed. Where is a safe space?"

I do not mean to diminish the agony of these participants; as I believe everyone in that room did passionately believe in their own victimhood. In fact, most or all probably would benefit from *actual* therapy.

I am not a member of a religious faith, and my familiarity with religious ritual originates mostly from watching Sunday-morning television. However, I was born into a Protestant Congregationalist church family. And having been raised in New England, in an area settled by Puritans, I've learned of the Shakers — a religious group known for abjuring sex and participating in frenzied dances of worship (hence their name). In Quaker worship, people sit in silence until "the spirit finds them" — not unlike the attendees at the Buddies long table, who sat through the proceedings until moved to speak.

The very term "woke" is itself full of religious connotations, going back to the first Great Awakening that swept English-speaking countries in the eighteenth century. In its modern political sense, "woke" has African American origins, its first recorded usage being in 1938, when folk/blues singer Lead Belly sang, in *Scottsboro Boys*, that everybody should "be a little careful when they go along through there, stay woke, keep their eyes open." (The title of the song referred to a group of black Alabama teenagers who'd been falsely accused of raping a pair of white women in 1931.) In recent years, the term "woke" has been widely used to describe those who've attained doctrinal purity in regard to the social justice movement. While that movement is secular, it seems to fulfill many of the psycho-spiritual appetites once served by religion.

I am older than almost all of the people who attended that long-table ceremony. And so I have some perspective on shared aspects of their background and ideology that they might take for granted. One thing that pretty much everyone in that room had in common is that they were raised by social media. Facebook, Twitter, and Tumblr supply the only real community they know.

Yet while group denunciations can superficially supply a tribal spirit of bonding, social media is fundamentally a lonely place. We all crave actual, living, human contact. We all crave laughter, tears, and the human touch.

That same impulse is what inspires "kinksters" to dress up in leather and gather for a party at a hotel (even if they don't have sex), or comic geeks to meet up at a convention centre, or RuPaul fans to leave their computers and flat screens for a moment, run to a gay bar and watch the show with friends. In the past, people would go to church on Sunday, shop in public markets, and watch the same TV shows at the same time and talk about them over the office water cooler

the next day. This was community – in the days before we worked at home, shopped on Amazon, and
thereby curtailed our daily gatherings in the public
sphere.

* * *

In their classic 1997 historical analysis of the Salem
witch trials, *Salem Possessed: The Social Origins of
Witchcraft,* authors Paul Boyer and Stephen Nissen-
baum explained that the infamous trials weren't a
product of a sudden, random bout of social panic, but
rather occurred in the context of longstanding economic and political tensions between Salem Village
(populated mainly by struggling, poor Massachusetts
farmers) and Salem Town (populated in large part by
newly prosperous merchants). Salem Village's pastor
– a man by the name of Samuel Parris – would take a
leading role in the prosecution of local "witches." So
would a Salem Village family, the Putnams. While the
accusations of witchcraft were, of course, ludicrous,
the class-based grievances that stirred up the area and
created a sense of tribal enmity were very real. Impov-
erished villagers fighting for their own church began
by turning their accusations again a black servant, and
then quickly moved up the social ladder. "The witchcraft accusations against the powerless, the outcast or
the already victimized were not sufficiently powerful
for them," the authors wrote. "They were driven to

lash out at persons of real respectability – persons, in short who reminded them of the individuals responsible, so they believed, for their own reduced fortunes and prospects." As in many episodes of mass hysteria, a widespread sense of paralyzing fear and powerlessness had created a gateway to unhinged conspiracism.

Think about those young woke long-table attendees and their prospects. For many of them, the future must seem uncertain, even nightmarish – climate change, jobs replaced by machines, income inequality, racist populism. In their hopelessness, they lash out at those who are more rich and powerful, which, to them, seems like everyone. As they have no political power and see no hope of getting it, they seize the moral high ground wherever they can, and make accusations that they hope will hurt someone who has more than they do. "Unable to relive their frustrations politically, the members of the pro-Parris faction unconsciously fell back on a different and more archaic strategy," Boyer and Nussenbaum noted. "They traced those who threatened them not as political opposition but as an aggregate of morally defective individuals."

The term "morally defective individual" more or less describes how I am now seen in Canadian avant-garde LGBT theatre circles. I won't elaborate on the difficulties this has created for my life. However, I am genuinely saddened by the fact that I now have no contact with the theatre company I founded

40 years ago.

Vivek Shraya is an internationally fêted trans-gender author, performer and media star, praised in *Vanity Fair* and fawned over by the CBC. She is in her late 30s, while I am an old gay man whose heyday was rooted in a past age when I was fighting for gay and lesbian liberation. (We are both now university professors.) When I wrote about Shraya's homophobic book on my blog, I saw myself as speaking truth to power. But such is the creed of intersectionalism — whose tenets inform the woke faith's liturgy — that *I* am the one seen as having power.

It is but a short jump from this ordering or privilege to the idea that I — an effeminate gay man, drag queen, and veteran of the AIDS crisis — have personally oppressed the whole community. It is a frighteningly doctrinaire way of seeing the world. And I have every reason to fear woke people. So do many of us.

When I think of Salem, I identify with Susannah Martin, who didn't even live in Salem, but in nearby Amesbury. Martin, a mother of eight, was 48 years old when she was accused of witchcraft — an old lady by the standards of the era. Other, mostly younger people claimed that she had performed supernatural horrors, including bewitching a man's oxen so that they ran into a river and drowned. Before eventually being hanged, she was forced to submit to bizarre tests, such as a physical exam to determine whether she had a "witch's tit" that served to provide sustenance to the devil's minions.

Many of Martin's accusers hadn't even met Martin – or any of Massachusetts' so-called witches. Likewise, I knew few of the people I saw on that long-table video. I'm not sure if I can ever forgive them for lending their voices to this ugly attack on me. But at least I feel I have come to understand the sad religion to which they have pledged their loyalty.

AUTHOR'S POSTSCRIPT – SEPTEMBER 2020

This article was published a little over a year ago. Much has happened since; including the COVID-19 pandemic and the death of George Floyd. COVID-19 has been tragic – and thus deserving of widespread concern. And the Black Lives Matter movement is absolutely necessary. But the rhetoric over both has unfortunately contributed to the irrational, pseudo-religious atmosphere that now permeates public debate, making it nearly impossible to have a rational conversation about anything. Lately, it has become common to assume – at least in woke circles – that the term "free speech" applies only to those who lack privilege. In other words, if you are a marginalised person, then your speech is automatically assumed to have been curtailed due to your lack of privilege. Fair enough. But the corollary is that those who are considered "privileged" are not supposed to demand the right to freedom of speech, because – as the argument goes — entitled people have had freedom of speech for far too long — at the expense of others. Therefore, they must now be silent.

With regard to the theatre that excommunicated me (Buddies in Bad Times), it is interesting to note that the artistic director who worked so hard to publicly humiliate me, Evelyn Parry, was herself publicly disgraced and called a "racist" in a subsequent controversy. (She resigned her position in August 2020.) Ultimately, the overwhelmingly persuasive power of social media and digital technology has cast us all on either the "right" or the "wrong" side of any issue. As I am first of all a poet, playwright, and novelist, I have decided — at least for the moment — to abandon reason. In other words, I have abandoned carefully articulated journalistic articles for prose poems. I am now completely devoted to fiction. It is fiction that holds power in the public square, and the only way to fight fiction is with, well, *better* fiction. That's where I am, right now.

The Troll Who Terrorized Science Fiction
By Cathy Young

The blowup over *New York Times* editorial board hire Sarah Jeong and her racially charged Twitter trail turned into a brawl over a key question in today's cultural polemics: Whether derogatory speech about whites should be considered racist and, more generally, whether there is such a thing as anti-white racism. Most of Jeong's defenders on the Left not only argued that she shouldn't lose her job, but insisted that there was nothing particularly wrong with her white-bashing tweets, whether they were meant to mock racist trolls or criticize "white privilege." "To equate 'being mean to white people' with the actual systemic oppression and marginalization of minority groups is a false equivalency," wrote *Vox* reporter Aja Romano in a supposedly objective "explainer."

As the Jeong drama demonstrates, the view that "woke" white-bashing is a harmless, justified, and perhaps even commendable form of "punching up" is now mainstream in liberal/progressive culture in North America (and some other western countries). And yet another culture-war episode from four years ago – one that, as it happens, Romano also covered in detail – shows that this mindset can cause very real damage.

The defense of "punching up" is a fundamental part of the left-identitarian ideology (also known as "social justice" or "intersectionality") that became the quasi-official progressive creed in the 2010s. In this creed, all human interaction is seen primarily through the lens of "power dynamics" and the "oppression/privilege" hierarchy; thus, hostile or demeaning speech is judged by whether the speaker and the target are "privileged" or "marginalized."

There are many reasons, both moral and practical, to criticize this ideology. It inevitably undermines modern western society's hard-won taboo on racial insults and is likely to provoke a backlash. It relies on crude and often skewed definitions of power, privilege, and oppression – so that, for instance, Jeong, a Harvard Law School graduate and successful journalist from a minority group with higher income and lower incarceration rates than white Americans, can outscore an unemployed white high-school dropout in "oppression points" (or so that Jeong supporter Rani Molla, another journalist with an elite degree and from a thriving demographic, can deride "whiny" rural white workers at a chicken processing plant.)

However, the normalization of "punching up" can also do more immediate and tangible harm. In many cases, it can enable and excuse abusive behavior supposedly motivated by righteous anger or "anti-oppression" activism.

Jeong herself has been spotted minimizing the infamous Twitter-shaming of Justine Sacco in 2013. Sacco, a public-relations executive, lost her job and had to go into hiding after becoming the target of a social-media mob over a joke that was intended to mock "white privilege" but was perceived as racist.

But another incident the following year – which received fairly little notice outside the science fiction/ fantasy community, but was the subject of a long article by Romano in the digital culture magazine *The Daily Dot* – offers a far more dramatic example of wreckage left by a serial harasser cloaked in the mantle of "anti-racism" and "social justice."

In September 2014, the sci-fi/fantasy (SFF) world was rocked by revelations about the bizarre online past of a much-praised young author in the field, the Thaiborn, Hong Kong-based Benjanun Sriduangkaew, one of that year's finalists for the John W. Campbell Award for Best New Writer. Sriduangkaew was outed as a notorious social justice "rage-blogger" known by the fitting moniker "Requires Hate" (a shortened version of the title of her blog, "Requires Only That You Hate"), whose vitriol-soaked takedowns and callouts of "problematic" works and authors had sown fear in the SFF community since 2011. What's more, Requires Hate also doubled as a prolific troll and cyberbully who mainly went by "Winterfox," but sometimes used other handles.

After several weeks of heated debates, a lengthy, detailed, carefully researched report on Sriduang-kaew's activities under her various aliases was posted by sci-fi writer Laura Mixon on her LiveJournal blog.

It makes for a hair-raising read. Requires Hate's rants made Jeong's tweets sound like drawing-room pleasantries. She frequently resorted to graphic threats of murder, rape, mutilation, acid attacks, and other extreme violence. Of American sci-fi novelist Paolo Bacigalupi, whom she blasted as a "raging racist fuck" and an "appropriative bag of feces," she wrote, "If I see [him] being beaten in the street, I'll stop to cheer on the attackers and pour some gasoline on him," and "Let him be hurt, let him bleed, pound him into the fucking ground. No mercy." Irish-American author Caitlyn Kiernan was branded a "rape apologist" whose "hands should be cut off so she can never write another Asian character."

According to Mixon, Sriduangkaew, often aided by her followers, had at various times tried to "suppress the publication of fiction and reviews" and get speakers disinvited from panels and readings; cyber-stalked sci-fi fans who had crossed her; "chased down positive reviews" in order to "frighten reviewers and fans away" from promoting works she disliked; and "single-handedly destroyed several online SFF, fanfic, and videogaming communities with her negative, hostile comments and attacks." Moreover, "at least one of her targets was goaded into a suicide attempt."

Mixon's post prompted many of Requires Hate's victims – including some who were not named in the report, such as Canadian author J.M. Frey – to speak up in the comments. Their accounts were shocking, not only for what they revealed about Sriduangkaew's behavior, but for her targets' reactions. Frey, whose award-nominated, well-reviewed 2011 debut novel *Triptych* was repeatedly trashed on the Requires Hate blog, wrote:

> I nearly stopped writing when this happened. I shook every time I sat down to a keyboard. It took me 75 drafts to turn in a novel (with a [person of color] lead!) to my agent. I cried a lot...When I saw her site's links incoming in my web site metadata, I felt sick. I had to learn how to block them. Mostly, I've gotten over it, but every single time I sit down to write a new project, I have to give myself a pep talk about how I have to write what I want...I second guess everything I write now. I waffle, and bemoan, and I try to be good at representation and gender and sexuality in my books, but nobody is perfect and I feared, I genuinely feared putting more books out into the world because I was scared.

Frey also wrote that Requires Hate's tirades made her scared of more than social disapproval. She began to avoid conventions, fearing that she would run into her tormentor and that the latter "would escalate from words to something horrible, something physical," such as "come across a dance floor and hit me in the head with a beer bottle."

Several other commenters also wrote that being targeted by Requires Hate and her minions affected them profoundly. Charles Terhune, an American sci-fi author, said that as a new writer just getting his start in the field, the experience left him "scarred and skittish for a long time" — and wary of "writing anything other than white male characters." Colum Paget, a British writer who found himself on the receiving end of her invective, admitted that he "pretty much stopped writing because of it."

One commenter also provided striking details of how "Winterfox" was able to wreak havoc in a LiveJournal community (ironically, one dedicated to books by "people of color") and ultimately cause it to implode:

> Every time she viciously insulted an author or a fellow community member, she framed it as bravely speaking out against racism and other injustices. No matter what anyone said, Winterfox found a way to twist it into them being a racist pig and herself being the only one standing up for what's right. If she could not immediately find anything in a person's comments

to twist and misconstrue, she would simply accuse them of being white. If they responded that they were not white, she would accuse them of being mixed race or no longer living in the country of their ancestors. Only she was an authentic person of color, and only she could judge what was racist and what was not...The mods... were worried that by telling Winterfox she couldn't do this stuff anymore, they would be silencing a person of color who had a right to be angry about injustice. They eventually put up an "Insults Policy" post explaining that you couldn't insult community members for no reason, but that it was okay to "snarkily" call them out for being racist, sexist, etc.

Mixon herself was upfront about the fact that Sriduangkaew's reign of terror was made possible by the political culture in the SFF community: Since Requires Hate self-identified as an Asian lesbian, she had the backing of progressives "who appreciate[d] that – despite her sometimes over-the-top rhetoric – she unapologetically [spoke] up for people of color and queer/LGBTQI people, calling out racist, homophobic, misogynist content in many popular SFF novels and stories."

Interestingly, Mixon also pointed to evidence that Sriduangkaew's abusive online behavior had begun with nasty but nonpolitical forum trolling – until "at some point she discovered social justice-driven rage-speak and found it to be a particularly effective weapon."

Yet Mixon, herself a prominent member of the community's progressive elite (her husband, sci-fi writer Stephen Gould, was then president of the Science Fiction Writers' Association), took pains not to deviate too far from the party line. While she condemned Requires Hate's "social justice hackery," she emphasized that "discussions about colonialism, racism, sexism, and homophobia in our works" are difficult but "necessary," and that writers should welcome being sensitized to their "privilege."

Mixon also went out of her way to stress that Requires Hate's claims of "punching up" were belied by her tendency to go after "women, people of color, and other marginalized or vulnerable people." The post even featured pie charts showing that of the definitively identified victims of her cyberbullying, nearly three quarters were women, about 40 percent were "POCs," and a substantial proportion were "Queer/ LGBTQI." When one commenter expressed annoyance at the suggestion that white, straight, cisgender males were "Acceptable Targets," Mixon replied, "I do think a case can be made for marginalized people's right to punch up."

Meanwhile, Sriduangkaew — who had at first indignantly denied the rumors identifying her as Requires Hate/Winterfox, until they were confirmed by a prominent editor – posted an apology in which she admitted to being a "horrendous asshole" and doing terrible things while believing that she was "punching up and doing good." Her post promised "no excuses." Then, she followed up with another blogpost that amounted to a litany of excuses – from claims that she herself was a target of stalkers, to finger-pointing at white men who had supposedly gotten away with worse behavior. (Less than a year later, in a post on a protected Twitter account, she was comparing herself to a reputed victim of misogynist hate mobs and her opponents to various far-right bogeymen.)

As for Romano's *Daily Dot* article on the controversy, it was notable mainly for its almost comically doctrinaire identity-politics framing of the story:

> The question of whether to accept or repudiate Sriduangkaew after the discovery is complicated. On the one hand, Sriduangkaew, who has claimed to be a Thai-born Thai writer who is ethnically Chinese, is a much-needed example of an excellent, well-liked writer whose multicultural voice is an important addition to the sparse population of non-white writers in the world of speculative publishing. On the other hand, her troll voice has often worked to loudly silence other members of marginalized identities...Is the outing and subsequent repudiation of Sriduangkaew all just an act of tone

policing – an effort to silence a voice raised in anger?

Romano did briefly wonder if the tendency to circle the wagons around minority writers in the field could go too far (as with Samuel "Chip" Delany, a biracial gay author who openly supports a group championing sex between adult men and underage boys). But she also respectfully quoted the opinions of those who saw the rush to condemn Sriduangkaew's past trolling as "an example of white privilege attempting to silence writers of color." In the end, Romano concluded that "the condemnation is natural; but whether its work is to ultimately silence or empower the voices of women and minorities in speculative fiction remains to be seen."

Despite such misgivings, the anti-Sriduangkaew side mostly prevailed. Mixon's exposé was praised by notables such as George R. R. Martin. In August 2015, it even won the Hugo Award for Best Fan Writer, given to sci-fi-related non-fiction work for non-paying or low-paying magazines or web sites. The award could be seen as a repudiation of "social justice" extremism, in a year when the Hugos and the sci-fi/fantasy community faced a challenge from the Right (the so-called "Sad Puppies" slate created by mostly conservative authors who believed that the awards had become too politicized by the left). But it is worth noting that the "Requires Hate" debacle had specific elements that made it easier for progressives to rally against Sridu-angkaew. She had targeted not only people with bona fide "oppressed identities" – including sexual assault survivors – but prominent, highly regarded minority authors, such as N.K. Jemisin and Saladin Ahmed.

Even so, there were those who found the award for Mixon's piece troubling. "It just feels like a white woman elder putting the younger woman of color in her 'place,'" fretted one writer.

It's also noteworthy that mainstream media out-lets ignored the Benjanun Sriduangkaew/Requires Hate scandal (at the same time that they gave exten-sive coverage to claims of misogynist harassment in GamerGate, the anti-"political correctness" revolt in the videogame community). The lack of interest in a cyberbullying story that had a major impact in the sci-fi/fantasy world was especially remarkable given this story's fascinating twists – including the contin-uing mystery of the woman behind the masks. (It is open knowledge that "Benjanun Sriduangkaew" is a pseudonym; an unconfirmed, albeit persuasive, blog report identifies her as a California-born member of an extremely wealthy Thai family, now in her late twenties.)

Perhaps not surprisingly, Sriduangkaew was nev-er really ostracized by the sci-fi/fantasy establish-ment. A month after the Mixon report was recog-nized by the Hugos, one of Sriduangkaew's stories ran in Clarkesworld, a leading online sci-fi/fantasy magazine; last year, her novella *Winterglass* was published as a book by Apex, a major publisher in the field. (None of the generally mediocre reviews mentioned the author's notorious past; her cutesy official bio says that she "writes love letters to strange cities and the future.") Sriduangkaew has even started making a comeback as a "social justice warrior": Last February, Apex included her in an "intersectional roundtable" of authors, though the feature was eventually taken down after strong objections − and reports of more recent abusive behavior.

The Benjanun Sriduangkaew/Requires Hate saga is a striking cautionary tale in a number of ways. It shows how easily performative bashing of "the oppressors" or "the privileged" can turn into vicious bullying and harassment toward real people − and how easily a "marginalized" person can be reclassified as a "privileged" acceptable target. It shows what a devastating weapon anti-oppression outrage and social justice rhetoric can be in the hands of a malicious abuser, making it very difficult to curb the abuser's behavior and making the victims particularly susceptible: Witness the mind-boggling fact that an anonymous blogger's unhinged ranting could make published authors afraid to write. The Mixon report, Romano's *Daily Dot* article, and the comments on both pieces offer a rather scary glimpse into a toxic, cult-like social justice subculture.

Drama in the sci-fi/fantasy fandom may not be of great consequence for larger society (though the politicization of culture is a real and spreading problem). But when the ideology that enabled Requires Hate dominates academia, gains a strong presence in the mainstream media, and makes inroads into corporate culture, the cautionary tale should be a warning to us all.

Romance and Retribution
By Jamie Palmer

"This is a crisis of epic proportions," wrote an alarmed Romance Writers of America (RWA) board member on Christmas Eve as the scenery started to collapse.[1] Longstanding tensions within the trade organization had detonated the previous day when novelist Alyssa Cole revealed that RWA's board of directors had suspended her friend Courtney Milan. The decision provoked a hurricane of condemnation from the membership, mass resignations from the board, and a spectacularly vicious frenzy of internecine bloodletting online. Milan's suspension has been widely reported as the latest indignity suffered by a woman of color in an ongoing battle between RWA's old guard and minority authors struggling against marginalization. In this version of events, Milan had exposed and confronted the scourge of racism within RWA and been crucified for it.

For a few days, the 40-year-old organization looked like it might tear itself to pieces, until what remained of the board agreed to commission an independent review of the events that led to Milan's suspension. RWA retained multinational law firm Pillsbury Winthrop Shaw Pittman LLP to conduct the investigation, and on February 18, 2020, it published its findings. The 58-page report reveals an organization that had become procedurally inept, confused about its purpose, and internally weakened by political feuding. The first of these criticisms, in particular, was seized upon by Milan and her supporters as proof that she had been the casualty of a terrible injustice. But the report also explicitly rejects Milan's claim that she had been victimized for campaigning against racism: "The evidence Pillsbury reviewed does not suggest that the adverse finding against Ms. Milan was motivated by animus or bias against her."[2]

The controversy had been ignited when, on August 7, RWA's President-Elect Carolyn Jewel sent the following tweet:

> Well. I saw that someone who's been YEARS in the publishing (not writing) business liked a highly problematic tweet and when I checked if that was an accident, their timeline was full of likes of hateful, racist tweets. Sorry, but blocked.

Jewel did not identify the individual in question, but she informed those who contacted her by direct message that it was Sue Grimshaw.[3] The following day, romance novelist Ella Drake publicly identified Grimshaw by posting screenshots of tweets Grimshaw had liked. There was a Trump tweet in which the president thanked the people of El Paso and Dayton; three Charlie Kirk tweets, one of which praised the U.S. Immigration and Customs Enforcement agency; there was a Diamond and Silk tweet, which included a video of their appearance on Tucker Carlson's Fox News show; and there were a few tweets of prayers and Biblical verse from Christian accounts.

In June 2019, Grimshaw had joined romance author Suzan Tisdale's new indie venture Glenfinnan Publishing. And on August 12, it emerged that romance author Marie Force had hired Grimshaw as an editor at her Jack's House Publishing imprint. Both publishers now found themselves besieged by angry tweets and emails demanding to know why they were employing a notorious racist. Grimshaw began deleting her likes and unfollowing accounts in an attempt to escape harassment, before giving up and deleting her account. As far as Drake was concerned, this constituted an admission of guilt. The problem, she explained, was not just Grimshaw's "white supremacist leanings"; it was that someone with those leanings had previously worked as an acquisition editor at Random House and as a buyer for Borders Group. Grimshaw was one of the gatekeepers in an industry that had long marginalized authors of color. "If keeping romance white is what Jack's House is all about," Drake concluded, "then I guess she'll fit right in."

* * *

Romance Writers of America was established in 1980 to provide advocacy, networking opportunities, and support to writers of romantic fiction, a genre the organization's founders felt was then neglected by the publishing industry. In 1981, RWA held its first annual summer conference, followed the next year by its first awards ceremony. By the time 2019 drew to a close, it had amassed around 9,000 members and established over 100 local chapters nationwide. Its annual awards, known as the RITAs, had become the most prestigious in the genre.

By the 2000s, however, this flourishing community was suffering sporadic outbreaks of squabbling between its reformer and traditionalist tendencies. Reformers, who tended to be younger, wanted romantic fiction to be more socially aware. Parts of the romance canon had dated poorly, they argued, and the representations of blacks, Native Americans, LGBT characters, and other historically marginalized persons were frequently unacceptable by modern standards (when they appeared at all). Romance fiction was "becoming more inclusive," the founder of the *Smart Bitches, Trashy Books* web site, Sarah Wendell, told *Glamour*, "with more queer protagonists in different subgenres, more characters of color, from different ethnic and cultural backgrounds, and of different religions."

Risk-averse acquisition editors had often rejected non-traditional stories, believing that their readership wasn't interested in gay romance or minority couples. The advent of independent publishing revealed this to be poor business sense. Now that authors could bypass publishing houses, new sub-genres brought an explosion of innovative fiction and, with it, new fans to the romance genre. The industry's reluctance to feature people of color on the covers of novels by African American authors was also challenged and re-appraised, and it is fair to say that some anachronistic assumptions and practices were discarded during this time.

But whenever traditionalist objections interrupt-ed this progressive march, trouble resulted. In 2005, a furious row erupted after RWA's magazine, the *Ro-mance Writers Report*, included a poll asking members whether or not the romance genre ought to be defined as between "two people," or between "a man and a woman." Traditionalists at RWA were accused of at-tempting to narrow the genre's definition in order to exclude LGBT writing and depictions of group sex in explicit fiction known as "romantica." Then, in 2012, RWA's Oklahoma Chapter, Romance Writers Ink, decided they would not accept same-sex romance en-tries in their annual contest. Apparently, there wer-en't enough judges who felt comfortable reading, let alone evaluating, that kind of material.

But the most contentious flashpoint became the representation of people of color within RWA it-self, particularly among the nominees for its coveted RITA awards. In a long essay for the *Guardian* entitled "Fifty Shades of White: The Long Fight against Racism in Romance Novels," Lois Beckett reported: "The romance industry itself has remained overwhelmingly white, as have the industry's most prestigious awards ceremony, the RITAs... And just like the Oscars, the RITAs have become the center of controversy over unacknowledged racism and bias in the judging process."

In March 2018, Alyssa Cole's interracial-civil-war romance *An Extraordinary Union* was not nominated for that year's RITAs, even though it had already received multiple awards and been favorably reviewed. "The books that had beat Cole as finalists in the best short historical romance category were all by white women," wrote Beckett, "all but one set in nineteenth century Britain, featuring white women who fall in love with aristocrats. The heroes were, respectively, one 'rogue,' two dukes, two lords, and an earl." Beckett didn't venture an opinion on the *quality* of the finalists. Nor did she say which of the nominated books ought to have been replaced by Cole's, or on what grounds.

Under-representation of writers of color among RWA's membership (80 percent of which is white) and RITA finalists created the perception that the organization had a problem, and this perception rapidly became an accepted fact from which all further conversation was expected to follow. Nor was this simply a diversity problem, some of the more radical reformers began to insist — it was a *structural-racism* problem; a *white-supremacy* problem; and the only debate worth having was about how the battle against this menace ought to be prosecuted. When romance author Suzanne Brockmann collected her lifetime achievement award at the 2018 RITA awards, she had this to say to her hosts and anyone else who urged patience, civility, and forbearance in pursuit of social justice:

> RWA, I've been watching you grapple as you attempt to deal with the homophobic, racist white supremacy on which our nation and the publishing industry is based. It's long past time for that to change. But hear me, writers, when I say: It doesn't happen if we're *too fucking nice.*

Brockmann went on to call the 53 percent of white American women who had voted for Donald Trump racists, and challenged them to prove her wrong by voting the "hateful racist traitors" out of office. It was an inflammatory and divisive address marinated in bromides of love and tolerance, and it was rewarded with whoops, cheers, and a standing ovation. As 2018 drew to a close, sides were being chosen within RWA. Are you with us or are you with white supremacy?

For a white-supremacist organization, RWA responded to Brockmann's indictment with remarkable contrition. Following the RITAs, it released an unsigned statement acknowledging that "less than half of one percent of the total number of finalist books" between 2000 and 2017 were by black authors, and that "no black romance author has ever won a RITA." "It is impossible to deny," the statement continued, "that this is a serious issue and that it needs to be addressed. RWA Board is committed to serving all of its members. Educating everyone about these statistics is the first step in trying to fix this problem."

But when the slate of 2019 RITA finalists proved to be no more diverse than the 2018 cohort, the news was met with renewed resentment. "The list," tweeted romance author Bree Bridges, "is painfully, painfully white. And straight. And Christian. And cis. And just basically it is what it is." Nor did it pass unnoticed that Alyssa Cole's latest novel had been overlooked again. And so the board released yet another remorseful statement, in which President HelenKay Dimon promised various reforms to the selection process, judging and scoring, and anything else that might help to satisfy growing activist demands.

It was too late. An influential and growing component of the membership was by now disenchanted with such promises, and their rhetoric was becoming more strident. Whether or not Dimon's interventions would have produced the desired results is moot. The race row that was about to consume RWA would lead to the cancellation of the following year's RITA awards for the first time in the organization's 40-year history, and almost finish off the organization itself.

* * *

One of the most militant and powerful voices in RWA's reform movement belonged to a bestselling writer and former board member by the pen-name of Courtney Milan. Born Heidi Bond in 1976 to a Chinese mother and American father, Milan began writing in 2009 while she was teaching at Seattle's School of Law, and her first novel, *Proof by Seduction*, was published by Harlequin just a year later. Milan was so prolific and popular that only 18 months after she began self-publishing in 2011, she was able to quit her job to write full time. In 2014, she was elected to RWA's board of directors, and there she pursued diversity activism with a zeal that electrified her supporters and cowed her opponents. Both agreed that during the four years she served on the board — for good or ill, respectively — Milan played a central role in reshaping RWA policy.

In 2017, former RWA board member Linda Howard posted in a private RWA forum to register her unhappiness with the organization's new direction. "I just want to clear up a misconception," she began:

> RWA isn't a democracy, it's an organization, and that's a big difference. The board of direc-

tors aren't elected to represent the membership, they are elected to *run the organization* to
make it as strong and efficient as possible, because a strong organization can best represent
the interests of its members to the publishing
world...Unfortunately, the last four boards
have, with the best of intentions, drastically
weakened RWA.

RWA was hemorrhaging members, she warned,
"because an organization more focused on social issues than publishing ones doesn't meet their career
needs." Howard didn't mention Milan by name, but
it was to the influence of Milan's agenda that she was
plainly objecting. In a subsequent post, Howard was
even more direct:

> I've seen a drastic reduction in my local chapter.
> Members have just walked away, not because
> of where they are in their careers but because
> of the way some sensitive issues were handled.
> Diversity for the sake of diversity is discrim-
> ination. It just is. Discrimination against any
> group shouldn't be tolerated, it has no place in
> RWA, and there were already procedures in
> place to deal with it...Just make the rules clear,
> fair, and the playing field level. That's it.

Needless to say, when these remarks (reproduced on an author's web site, along with some deeply unsympathetic commentary) were leaked onto Twitter, they did not go down well at all. So brutal was the blowback that Howard left the organization of which she had been a member since the year it was established. "We collectively kicked her ass," Milan would later crow.

So by the time she joined the attacks on Sue Grimshaw in the summer of 2019, Courtney Milan had already established a reputation as a formidable personality and a ruthless activist able to command the attention of a loyal following. Just a few weeks previously, her moral authority within RWA had been reaffirmed with a Service Award, given in recognition of her contributions to diversity and inclusion. Her intervention on August 16, then, represented an escalation of hostilities: "Sue Grimshaw was the romance buyer for Borders, one of the biggest buyers for romance," Milan wrote. "She was capable of making a romance novelist's career by putting their work front and center around the country...And the corollary to being able to make someone's career with favorable placement? Is the ability to break it by not buying the book at all. We don't know. We don't KNOW. But for decades, Black romance authors heard there was no market for their work."

In fact, we do know. At Borders, all fiction by black authors – including romance – was handled by a dedicated buyer. Grimshaw was the romance buyer, so she was given no say in which black authors were or were not purchased. And no good evidence was ever produced, even by her most vehement critics, that Grimshaw had ever impeded the career of anyone, irrespective of their race or sexuality. But now that her Twitter history had been exposed, any aspersion or innuendo, no matter how thinly evidenced, could be tossed onto the charge sheet. Under the misapprehension that Grimshaw was an RWA member, Milan speculated that she might be in violation of the organization's non-discrimination clause. So, she solicited information from writers of color to help build a case. The next day, Marie Force announced that Grimshaw and Jack's House Publishing had "agreed to part company."

Attention now turned to Suzan Tisdale's new start-up. Glenfinnan Publishing, for which Grimshaw also worked as acquisition editor. Pressed by Milan and others to denounce and sack her colleague, Tisdale broadcast a 12-minute video defending her instead. She made a plea for greater tolerance, warned that negative partisanship was tearing the country apart, and affirmed that she didn't care about the race or sexual orientation of an author provided they could write a good story. Instead of calling for Sue Grimshaw's "head on a frickin' platter," she suggested, her critics ought to "try to get to know her better":

Sue is no more a racist or a bigot than I am. She is a conservative woman, but not the kind of conservative woman you might be conjuring up images of. Last I checked, this was still America, and we are all allowed our political opinions. Sue is a Christian, and she has conservative leanings, but that does not mean she is a skinhead or a member of the KKK or an anti-Semite or anything like that.

Milan was apoplectic, and responded with a new tweet thread, in which she moved with such rapidity and venom from suspicion to accusation to conviction, that it takes a moment to realize not a shred of evidence has been produced in support of anything:

Uhhh why is @SuzanTisdale gaslighting us?... Nobody is saying [Grimshaw]'s a skinhead or a member of the KKK. They're saying that she was a gatekeeper who may have kept marginalized people out of stores and publishing deals. And if your video says that Sue is no more a racist than you, you sound EXTREMELY racist. Nobody wants anyone to hate anyone, but like if someone used institutional power to discriminate on the basis of race, I don't think they should continue to have institutional power. And if your institution insists on giving that person institutional power, I hope your in-

≠

stitution fails. And like, if your line of accepta-
bility is "calling for the annihilation of a group
of people" but you don't have an issue with
systemically excluding a race of people from
bookstores and publishing contracts? Then
you are DEFINITELY a racist. And like, @
SuzanTisdale is entitled to be a racist and to
run her publishing house as a racist, but you
know, we're entitled to just not read or review
her books because I hate racist books.

The following evening, one of Milan's Twitter followers, Lisa Lin, sent her a message linking her to the
Amazon preview of a novel entitled *Somewhere Lies
the Moon*. It was, Lin pointed out, written by "Kathryn Lynn Davis, Suzan Tisdale's other editor at Glenfinnan."[4] Neither Milan nor Lin had actually read the
book, but Milan returned to Twitter armed with information gleaned from the previewed excerpts, and
denounced it as "a fucking racist mess." For another
18 tweets, she emptied ridicule and scorn over Davis
and her work, even though she admitted she hadn't
even bothered to read all of the free sample ("I don't
need to"). She was particularly bothered by Davis's
portrayal of the half-Chinese heroine with blue eyes:
"As a half-Chinese person with brown eyes, seriously
fuck this piece of shit. Thanks."

The following day, August 26, Sue Grimshaw
emailed Carol Ritter, RWA's Deputy Executive Di-

rector, asking for advice. A group of authors were targeting her on Twitter, she said, and the controversy had already cost her one job. Now she was worried she might lose her position at Glenfinnan, too. "The comments they are making are so far from the truth it's defaming, and now they are even becoming more vile...The author spearheading the hate toward myself and Suzan's company is Courtney Milan, along with a handful of her followers...Please share your thoughts and suggestions, I'm not sure what I can do at this point."[5]

Because Grimshaw was not an RWA member, there was nothing Ritter could do from an administrative standpoint, but she said she would forward Grimshaw's message to RWA's corporate counsel. The following afternoon, Suzan Tisdale and Kathryn Lynn Davis also called the RWA office in search of help and advice. Both were told that, as RWA members, they were entitled to file an ethics complaint if they thought RWA's code of ethics had been breached. The executive director would review the complaints and pass them to the ethics committee if she decided they merited further investigation.[6] Both Tisdale and Davis said they would do so.

This ought to have been the start of a routine bureaucratic procedure. But the crisis bearing down on RWA was not one the organization was equipped to handle.

* * *

The only person at RWA who seemed to grasp the danger the row posed to the organization was its executive director, Allison Kelley. Kelley had overseen the administration of RWA since 1995 and was due to retire at the end of the year. But the ethics procedures were in a muddle, and the situation was making her nervous. The last time the code of ethics had been redrafted on the advice of corporate counsel was in 2003. Since then, multiple amendments – many of them proposed by HelenKay Dimon after she and Courtney Milan joined the board in 2014 – had left its provisions confused and incoherent.

On June 14, Kelley wrote to Dimon, who was by now RWA board president, and President-Elect Carolyn Jewel, who would take over on September 1. "Complaints [between the members] are increasing," she warned, "and usually allege discrimination based on racism...In my opinion, we are on thin ice in many situations, and we need to tread carefully until all policies and related discipline are consistently written and applied."[7] In July, the board met and voted – again without consulting counsel – to incorporate RWA's anti-discrimination policy into the code of ethics and amend a provision that arbitrarily exempted member behavior on social media. On Friday, August 16, Dimon was still fretting about whether to remove the social media exemption entirely when Courtney Milan fired her opening salvo at Sue Grimshaw.[8]

The following Monday, Allison Kelley emailed senior board members to report that Milan was attacking Grimshaw on Twitter and that Grimshaw had just lost her job with Jack's House Publishing as a result. Milan, she added, was encouraging RWA members to file ethics complaints against Grimshaw for violating the recently adopted anti-discrimination provision. Neither Carolyn Jewel (who would become president on September 1) nor Damon Suede (who would take her place as president-elect the same day) were sympathetic. Jewel admitted that it was her tweet that had first brought attention to Grimshaw's Twitter history, and that she had passed Grimshaw's name to anyone who asked for it by direct message. She said she thought Milan "had pointed out the truth." Suede agreed, adding that if anyone deserved censure and stigmatization it was Grimshaw.[9]

But Kelley was still uneasy, and worried about the antitrust implications of punishing individuals for political views. "My concern is the implication that RWA can or should do something to Sue," she wrote. "...some members are now expecting RWA to take immediate action to discipline members and industry professionals without proof or due process. I don't think it should be RWA's job to do extensive research in order to determine motive, nor should RWA assume motive."[10] After Milan published her furious response to Suzan Tisdale's video and then tore into

Kathryn Lynn Davis and her novel, even HelenKay Dimon reluctantly acknowledged the problem. Allison Kelley had by now read Grimshaw's email asking for advice and had spoken to Tisdale and Davis. "FYI," she told her colleagues, "the complaints continue and authors are alleging defamation and injury to their careers."[11]

But when Tisdale filed her ethics complaint against Milan later that day, the board was faced with a new dilemma: The previous year, they had appointed Courtney Milan chair of the ethics committee. The ludicrous decision to give this job to one of the organization's most belligerent troublemakers had been Dimon's idea, and even Milan was uncertain that it was a smart move. "I am worried that because Courtney is Mean, someone will file an ethics complaint against me," she wrote when Dimon offered her the post, "and that will complicate things for a bit." Dimon's response to this rather prescient objection was deferential:

> Allison [Kelley] and I were talking today and [I] told her I asked you. She was greatly relieved and very excited. In my view, and Allison agrees with me, you profoundly changed the direction of RWA for the better by being on the Board. The general membership might not get how instrumental you were in making us look at RWA in a different way — seeing our

weaknesses, realizing we were leaving people behind and taking responsibility for our mistakes – but Allison and I know.[12]

By the time Suzan Tisdale's ethics complaint landed on her desk, Kelley's relief and excitement had evidently waned. Milan's zealotry had become an administrative headache, and now it was in danger of becoming a legal headache, too. She and her deputy Carol Ritter spoke to corporate counsel, who explained that RWA might be at risk because, as ethics committee chair, "Courtney has an official capacity at RWA." In a subsequent email, the lawyer added, "I don't think you are going to have any choice but to proceed with the ethics complaint."[13]

Dimon was not about to rethink her assessment of Milan, but it was now clear that Milan would have to be persuaded to resign her position as ethics committee chair. On August 29, Milan was notified that a complaint had been filed against her and she immediately agreed to step down. Two days later, having evidently reconsidered her response, she emailed HelenKay Dimon and Carolyn Jewel. It was Dimon's last day as president:

I hereby officially disagree with [Tisdale's] claims for the record. I don't want to unresign – my policy has always been that if you want my service, you have it, and if you don't, I will spare myself the workload – but I will remind HelenKay that I explicitly told her this could be an issue when she asked me to serve.

For Carolyn: Now that I have had a chance to review this complaint and think about it in depth, we are going to have to talk at some point about the fact that staff did not follow their usual procedure for Ethics complaints in this case – a thing that I am personally aware of, since I have had discussions with Allison about usual procedure, which I suspect very few other people have.

I can only guess at the reasons, and while I'm sure that the thinking was that this was in the institution's best interest and not anything personal to me, I am also not okay with the fact that I have not been given the same procedure as others.[14]

If Milan's complaint was handled differently, it was probably because the board had actually sought legal advice for a change, and because Allison Kelley was finally out of patience. The previous day, she had emailed Dimon asking permission to recuse herself from further involvement. "After defending Courtney's right to free speech to members for at least four years," Kelley wrote, "I have reached my limit. I honestly and sincerely appreciate that Courtney opened my eyes to problems I was blind to, but I simply cannot defend her tactics."[15]

* * *

On her first day as president, Carolyn Jewel, whose tweet about Grimshaw had been the proximate cause of the row in which her organization was now entangled, resolved to appoint an entirely separate ethics committee to handle the Tisdale and Davis complaints. This decision was later portrayed by Milan's supporters as sinister, but Jewel's reasoning was prudent under the circumstances. She worried that if the remaining committee members were asked to consider a complaint against their former chair, it risked the perception of a conflict of interest that might be used to discredit the process after the fact. The existence of the new panel was not revealed to the rest of the board or members of the existing committee.[16]

The newly impaneled ethics committee finally convened to consider Suzan Tisdale's and Kathryn Lynn Davis's complaints via conference call on November 19. Carolyn Jewel had recused herself, due to her involvement at the beginning of the controversy, so President-Elect Damon Suede, who until now had been unaware that a complaint was pending against Milan, became the board's liaison. Carol Ritter acted as staff liaison. Everyone involved signed confidentiality and conflict-of-interest agreements.

Before them, the committee had the formal complaints from Suzan Tisdale and Kathryn Lynn Davis, Courtney Milan's two responses, and supporting dossiers of screenshots submitted by Tisdale and Milan. No other information was provided, and none was requested by the committee. However, it soon became apparent that nobody really knew what they were doing. The committee members had no experience of, or training in, handling complaints. They had to ask Carol Ritter for a template report so they knew what kind of document they were expected to produce. And they were nonplussed by some of the language in RWA's various policy documents. The new provisions of the code of ethics incorporated early that summer prohibited "invidious discrimination" – but what did *that* mean? An idiosyncratic working definition was cobbled together after a Google search.[17]

The first half of Tisdale's complaint rehearsed the story of Milan's attacks on her publishing company and colleagues, which she described as "nothing short of libelous vitriol." She added that three authors had left Glenfinnan as a result of the controversy, and that Davis had lost a lucrative three-book contract with another publisher (she later clarified that the contract had not been signed but that negotiations had been derailed). The second half of Tisdale's complaint was a *cri de coeur*, beseeching the board to do something about Milan's behavior:

Ms. Milan has a history of similar vicious, false, and uncalled for confrontations. For reasons I cannot begin to comprehend, the RWA has ignored this unethical behavior for far too long. Is this truly what the RWA wants? Is your silence on these matters the board's way of saying you agree with Ms. Milan?[18]

Tisdale threatened RWA with legal action if they did not take steps to end Milan's attacks. "I will accept nothing less," she wrote, "than a full, public apology from Ms. Milan not only to myself, but to Ms. Grimshaw and Ms. Davis, as well as all the Glenfinnan authors."[19]

The Kathryn Lynn Davis complaint was longer because it included a defense of her book, which she said Milan had selectively quoted, misunderstood, and maliciously misrepresented. Her exasperation was palpable. "[Ms. Milan] speaks without authority, without thought, without actually *reading*, her only goal is to tear down those with whom she does not agree"[20]:

From her behavior on Twitter, she seems to believe diversity belongs only to her, to defend in the most divisive, vicious, and unprofessional way possible. Rather than fostering an environment of creative and professional growth, she inspires fear in her audience, who know how many writers she has already destroyed. She quashes creativity and growth through the use of terror tactics. She seems determined to stop the free exchange of ideas, knowledge, and diverse career experiences by aggressively and violently (through word choice) assaulting those who disagree with her. Or even those, like me, who have never had any interaction with her at all.[21]

To all this, Milan responded with haughty disdain. The Tisdale complaint, she wrote, "is simple to resolve for three reasons":

First, none of the conduct that Tisdale complains of is a violation of RWA's Code of Ethics. Second, Tisdale's complaint contains numerous assertions which are not supported by any evidence, refer to the speech of people other than myself, or are contradicted by her own screenshots. Finally, the primary conduct that Tisdale wants RWA to punish is that I, a half Chinese-American woman, spoke out against negative stereotypes of half Chinese-American women. Far from being dishonest or disingenuous, my expression here is that of deeply-held beliefs which I have discussed for years.[22]

Milan then proceeded through a detailed retelling of events from her perspective, followed by a scornful quasi-legal analysis of the ethics provisions she was

accused of violating. Since personal social-media accounts were not covered by RWA's code of ethics,
she pointed out, her behavior lay beyond the committee's jurisdiction. She concluded on a piteous note:

> I *am* emotional about these issues. Negative
> stereotypes of Chinese women have impact-
> ed my life, the life of my mother, my sisters,
> and my friends. They fuel violence and abuse
> against women like me. And they dishonor
> the memory of the strong women who I am
> descended from on my mother's side of the
> family. I have strong feeling about these ste-
> reotypes, and when I speak about them, I use
> strong language. It is hard not to be upset about
> something that has done me and my loved ones
> real harm.[23]

There would be, she vowed, no apology. In her response to Davis, she added:

> Even if I was entirely mistaken about
> everything I said about her book, RWA's Code
> of Ethics is very clearly meant to exclude hon-
> est discussions of books. Davis is mad about
> a negative book review. She has a right to be
> mad, but she does not have a right to drag RWA
> and the Ethics Committee into her anger.[24]

Between them, Tisdale and Davis had alleged seven violations of the RWA code of ethics, and on five counts the committee found that no violation of the code had occurred. But this was partly because Milan's conduct was protected by the clause exempting private social-media accounts. She had, the committee members pointedly noted, "served on the Board when this exception was approved, and very likely understood she would be able to act in the manner she did, without being in violation of the code." To their evident frustration, this precluded them from finding Milan guilty of "intimidating conduct that objectively threatens a member's career, reputation, safety or wellbeing."

Actually, this seems to have been the entire point of the exemption, which makes no sense otherwise. A code of ethics is intended to govern member conduct, so why provide for a public forum in which conduct expressly forbidden by the code could be engaged in with impunity? As one of the committee members pointed out at a preliminary meeting:

> It seems to me that considering the board did exclude social media – for whatever reason – in doing so they pretty much gutted that provision of the ethics policy that has to do with harming another member's business, career, etc. I'm not sure why we even have that clause now.[25]

However, the committee did find for Tisdale and Davis on one count each, and their verdict was unanimous. Milan's attacks on Glenfinnan, the committee decided, had violated the recently included provision prohibiting "invidious discrimination," and therefore a second clause in the code that forbids members from "repeatedly or intentionally engaging in conduct injurious to RWA or its purposes." Milan's actions, despite her protestations, reflected poorly on the RWA. The committee recommended that Milan be censured, suspended from RWA for a year, and banned from holding a leadership position in the RWA or any of its chapters. They added this recommendation, which makes clear their attitude to Milan's behavior and the rules that protected her:

> Inasmuch as the committee felt its hands were tied in the matter of adjudicating postings on social media not operated by RWA, no matter how egregious the author's intent, the committee recommends that the RWA Board revisit this matter in light of the circumstances of this complaint.[26]

The ethics committee completed its report on December 11, and sent it to RWA President Jewel. It now had to be ratified. On December 17, a board meeting was convened. At which point, the already groaning architecture of the RWA ethics procedure collapsed.

* * *

The terse five-page document the ethics committee submitted, following the template provided by Carol Ritter, was hopelessly inadequate. It mentioned only that Tisdale and Davis had been accused of racism by Milan, and that Milan felt that her accusations were justified and that her behavior was, in any case, permissible under the code. There was no discussion of the background to the case, the personalities involved, or the specifics of the claims and counterclaims at issue. Nor was there any clear explanation of the committee's reasoning – the report cites the code of ethics and the policy manual, but doesn't explain how the two documents or their relevant provisions relate to one another, or precisely how they had been violated. Board members were not provided with copies of the complaints, Milan's responses, or any of the supporting documentation.

President-Elect Damon Suede, who as board liaison had sat in on the committee's deliberations, suddenly found himself fielding a battery of questions. What was Milan supposed to have done, exactly? And why was she being punished for behavior on social media when that was explicitly excluded by a provision in the code? Was there additional evidence of misconduct outside of social media? Was the board expected to simply wave through whatever the committee recommended? Board members had every

reason to be anxious. Membership of the ethics committee was confidential, but membership of the board
was not. Once the board approved the committee's
report, they would be taking ownership of its findings
and might be called upon to defend them. How were
they expected to do that if they weren't permitted to
assess the grievances at issue and had no idea how or
why the committee had arrived at its conclusions?

When Sue Grimshaw was first attacked by Courtney Milan on Twitter, Suede had shrugged. But over
the intervening months, his view had changed. Now
he tried to assuage board members' misgivings and
encouraged them to approve the committee's findings. The problem was he incorrectly assumed that
the terms of the confidentiality agreement he had
signed prevented him from disclosing anything at all
about its deliberations. So instead, he spoke in general
terms of the fastidious care with which the committee
had considered the complaints, the "egregious" nature of Milan's behavior, and the "reams and reams"
of supporting evidence which unfortunately he could
not disclose, including information not already publicly available (there were, it would turn out, two DM
exchanges). Pressed to explain what was so terrible
about Milan's behavior, Suede compared her to a boss
who repeatedly exposes himself to his staff – a fantas-
tically unhelpful analogy.

Members of the board felt browbeaten and said so.
Perhaps aware he had gone too far, Suede told them

to vote according to conscience and reminded them that they could reject the report outright or request revisions. The report was approved by 10 votes to five with one abstention. The board declined to censure Milan, but voted to impose the one-year suspension and the lifetime ban on holding office in RWA. A number of board members remained unhappy about being asked to ratify a decision without the necessary background material, and urged a change in procedures so this situation was not repeated.[27]

The whole ugly episode seemed to be coming to an end. All that remained was for Carol Ritter to notify Milan, Tisdale, and Davis. She did not know that on August 30, the day after Suzan Tisdale filed her ethics complaint, Allison Kelley had told Milan that neither complainants nor accused were bound by confidentiality. So, on December 23, when Carol Ritter sent the three women copies of the ethics report, Milan passed it to her friend Alyssa Cole, who immediately published it on Twitter, along with the two complaints and Milan's responses:

> One of the reasons I believed in RWA was because I saw how hard my friend, Courtney Milan, worked to push the organization's inclusiveness. Today, the day before Christmas Eve, RWA notified her they'd agreed with ethics complaints filed against her for calling out racism.

Cole's tweet was shared over 1,600 times and received over 4,400 likes. At a stroke, it concretized a version of events in which Courtney Milan had been martyred by an institutionally racist organization. "If anyone wants to know why I'm posting this, and not her," Cole went on: "I've seen Courtney speak out on other people's behalf for years, without a second thought. There's no reason she should have to take this on by herself. Also: I'm furious."

Tisdale and Davis had submitted complaints on the understanding that they would be handled discreetly. Now those documents were splashed across social media and they were being vilified all over again. On Christmas Eve 2019, romance author Kathryn Lynn Davis posted a message on her Facebook page that read: "I wish all of my friends, followers and readers the Happiest of Holidays and a New Year filled with joy and promise." To which someone spat back: "Fuck you, you racist Nazi bitch."

The board watched aghast. RWA members were going berserk, and board members' Twitter mentions and email inboxes had become volcanoes of enraged invective. How on Earth did the public suddenly have access to material the board had been prevented from reviewing? A number of members accused Suede of misleading them, and improperly withholding evidence they needed to reach an informed judgement. At an emergency board meeting the next day, Suede attempted to defend the process, but it was a dead loss. A motion was hastily passed to rescind approval of Milan's punishment "pending an opinion from RWA's attorney,"[28] but two tweets announcing the decision only inflamed the situation:

> At a meeting today that identified a gap between policy and process, RWA's Board of Directors rescinded its vote accepting the findings of the Ethics Committee report and the consequent penalties against Courtney Milan pending a legal opinion. 1/2
>
> RWA reiterates its support for diversity, inclusivity and equity, and its commitment to provide an open environment for all members. 2/2

Over the Christmas period, each passing day was worse than the last for RWA. One of Milan's supporters, Claire Ryan, began to assemble a timeline of events as the crisis unfolded, which she updated as new information became available. The lengthy entries between Christmas Eve and the middle of January are just a rolling cascade of terrible news. RITA judges and committee members began an exodus; new allegations of bigotry and discrimination within RWA were posted and circulated; an unrelated controversy involving Damon Suede and DreamSpinner Press was revived; authors and agents announced their intention to boycott RWA events and return their RITA award statues.

On December 26, eight board members resigned and Carolyn Jewel stepped down as president. Ryan reported that hashtags #IStandWithCourtney and #IStandWithCourtneyMilan reached "23.7k tweets and 12.7k tweets respectively on Twitter." As the new president and board liaison who had overseen the deliberations of the ethics committee, Damon Suede now became the focus of members' incontinent rage as he tried to hold the disintegrating organization together. An RWA member posted an excerpt of one of Suede's novels on Twitter and accused him of racism. Allegations were made by numerous parties that he had falsified the number of books he had published to meet the eligibility requirement for president. A petition to force a recall election was circulated and delivered to RWA on New Year's Eve, signed by 1,092 members.

Meanwhile, publishers, partners, and sponsors announced their intention to boycott the RWA's annual conference, and were rewarded with thousands of likes and retweets for doing so. As confidence in RWA plummeted, individuals and organizations scrambled to disassociate themselves from the embattled organization. It was like watching a run on a bank. The legacy press was by now running stories on the crisis, almost all of which framed the story to Milan's advantage, implicitly – and sometimes explicitly – endorsing her claim to having been forced out of a racist organization. Milan and her supporters demanded an audit of the whole affair, and when that was duly commissioned, they demanded that the board of directors make the findings public. They were now dictating events, and they gloated as RWA reeled under their attacks.

On January 6, RWA announced that it would be cancelling the 2020 RITAs and refunding entry fees. Three days later, Damon Suede resigned. He'd only been in the job two weeks and it had become intolerable. Carol Ritter, who had briefly followed Allison Kelley as executive director, quit the same day. On January 12th, six days before publication of the Pillsbury audit, all remaining members of the board stepped down. Staff were busy processing member resignations. RWA was hanging by a thread.

* * *

On February 3, Milan gave an interview to Sarah Weddell's *Smart Bitches, Trashy Books* podcast. Invited by her ceaselessly ingratiating host to close out the discussion in her own words, Milan delivered a familiar rebuke to those she accused of "tone policing" women of color:

> It is not our job to make you comfortable, and it is, in fact, white supremacy that makes you

think it is our job to make you comfortable. The truth of the matter is we're in an uncomfortable situation, and your racism makes us uncomfortable, and when we make you uncomfortable by pointing it out, all we're doing is redistributing the load to where it belongs. So, stop telling people that you have to make people comfortable in order for them to address their racism. That is, in fact, itself an act of racism that reinforces white supremacy.

In other words: If you find my accusations of racism offensive, that's just confirmation of your racism. In 2010, the blogger Eric S. Raymond described this mode of argument as "so fallacious and manipulative that those subjected to it are entitled to reject it based entirely on the form of the argument, without reference to whatever particular sin or thoughtcrime is being alleged." He called it "kafkatrapping" because, like the protagonist of Franz Kafka's novel *The Trial*, the accused is offered no avenue of exoneration:

> Real crimes — actual transgressions against flesh-and-blood individuals — are generally not specified. The aim of the kafkatrap is to produce a kind of free-floating guilt in the subject, a conviction of sinfulness that can be manipulated by the operator to make the subject say and do things that are convenient to the oper-

ator's personal, political, or religious goals. Ideally, the subject will then internalize these demands, and then become complicit in the kafkatrapping of others.

Milan and her allies applied this technique with such pitiless efficiency that RWA was left unable to enforce the most basic standards of member conduct. The various provisions of the ethics code may have been a mess, and the committee may have misunderstood the legal meaning of "invidious discrimination," but the code's intention is made perfectly clear in its opening lines: "The RWA Member Code of Ethics... is designed to cause RWA members to exhibit integrity, honesty, and other good professional practices, thereby enhancing the romance writing profession." Milan's campaign against Glenfinnan Publishing exhibited none of these qualities, but in the fight against white supremacy, she felt entitled to use any means necessary.

RWA had welcomed Milan into its club; its members had voted her onto the board twice and appointed her chair of the ethics committee; its judges had nominated her for three RITAs and awarded her one; its board had embraced many of her diversity initiatives and recognized her dedication with an official service award; Carolyn Jewel and Damon Suede had even cravenly endorsed her unprovoked attacks on Sue Grimshaw. And yet, Milan and her supporters

managed to convince almost everyone of the preposterous idea that she had been punished for speaking
out about racism. "The kafkatrapper's objective is to
hook into chronic self-doubt in the subject and inflate
it," Raymond explained, "in much the same way an
emotional abuser convinces a victim that the abuse is
deserved — in fact, the mechanism is identical."

Milan claimed she had been denied due process,
but practiced reputational terrorism based on nothing
but hearsay and uninformed conjecture. She accused
Allison Kelley and Carol Ritter of suppressing complaints about racism, but as Kelley explained to the
auditor, "most members have declined to file formal
complaints after learning that the subject of the ethics
complaint would be informed of who had filed it."[29]
Milan even accused Ritter and Kelley of obstructing
her diversity demands with spurious legal objections,
apparently unaware that trying to get someone ex-
pelled for their politics was a violation of the organization's bylaws. "What we're dealing with," Milan
told Wendell, "is white supremacy."

The board was working in a poisonous environment that it had helped to create, and its members
certainly made their share of mistakes. But no one
behaved with the fanatical malice of Milan and her
supporters. Sue Grimshaw had no quarrel with anyone. She wasn't even an RWA member, and she was
attacked for being a conservative Republican and a
Christian. Suzan Tisdale was attacked for refusing to

sack Grimshaw. Kathryn Lynn Davis was attacked simply because she happened to work for Tisdale — the idea that Milan's spiteful attack on Davis's novel constituted "honest discussion" of a book she hadn't even bothered to read is absurd. And when Tisdale refused to surrender her colleagues to the mob, its retribution exacted a steep reputational price.

Protected from the effects of the kafkatrap by their anonymity, the ethics committee decided that, no, this was not okay. It is worth repeating that they reached this conclusion unanimously. The chair later told the authors of the audit that they would probably not have found Milan in breach of the ethics code, had she expressed her misgivings about Tisdale and Davis in a more temperate manner: "I think that probably would have cast it very differently, the language itself was so incendiary, it was so problematic, so horrible. It was considered a very horrific thing to go after another member of RWA's publishing house, and the reputation of RWA would suffer probably as much as anything else."

The idea that Milan's behavior was permitted by the code of ethics does violence to even the most basic sense of fairness. Nevertheless, the interim board elected on March 23 to complete the 2019–2020 term released a statement on April 2 announcing that its members had "voted by unanimous consent to expunge both of the ethics complaints against Courtney Milan, and their ensuing proceedings, from the record." They offered Milan "a heartfelt apology for how the proceedings were handled and for the impact of this terrible situation on her." With that declaration, the capitulation was complete. An organization founded to advance the shared interests of romance authors had allowed itself to be convinced that its diversity record was the true measure of its legitimacy.

Founding member Linda Howard had been right when she argued in 2017 that RWA was losing sight of its purpose. That she was drummed out for saying so was an early, unheeded warning of just how confused the organization had become. Its most serious mistake was to empower those within its ranks who most bitterly despised it – members like Courtney Milan and Suzanne Brockmann, who saw RWA as just another fortress of white supremacy to be conquered or destroyed. As institutions grow and evolve, they inevitably require reform, but that task can only be entrusted to those who love the institution – because only they will have its best interests at heart.

References

[1] *INDEPENDENT ETHICS AUDIT REPORT for Romance Writers of America*, by Julia E. Judish Jerald A. Jacobs for Pillsbury Winthrop Shaw Pittman LLP. February 19th, 2020, p. 41
[2] Ibid. p. 1
[3] Ibid. p. 16
[4] Courtney Milan Supporting Documents, Exhibit N, submitted September 4th, 2019

[5] *INDEPENDENT ETHICS AUDIT REPORT for Romance Writers of America*, by Julia E. Judish Jerald A. Jacobs for Pillsbury Winthrop Shaw Pittman LLP. February 19th, 2020. p. 19

[6] Ibid., p. 20

[7] Ibid., p. 7

[8] Ibid., pp. 14–15

[9] Ibid., pp. 15–18

[10] Ibid., pp. 17–18

[11] Ibid., pp. 20–21

[12] Ibid., pp. 13–14

[13] Ibid., p. 21

[14] Ibid., p. 23

[15] Ibid., pp. 22–23

[16] Ibid., p. 24–25

[17] Ibid., p. 31

[18] Suzan Tisdale Formal RWA complaint, submitted August 27th, 2019, p. 5

[19] Ibid., p. 6

[20] Kathryn Lynn Davis Formal RWA Complaint, submitted September 11th, 2019, p. 10

[21] Ibid., pp. 2–3

[22] Courtney Milan Formal Response to Suzan Tisdale Complaint, submitted September 4th, 2019, p. 1

[23] Ibid., p. 7

[24] Courtney Milan Formal Response to Kathryn Lynn Davis Complaint, submitted September 11th, 2019 p. 3

[25] *INDEPENDENT ETHICS AUDIT REPORT for Romance Writers of America*, by Julia E. Judish Jerald A. Jacobs for Pillsbury Winthrop Shaw Pittman LLP. February 19th, 2020, p. 21

[26] Report of the Ethics Committee, submitted December 11th, 2019, p. 5

[27] *INDEPENDENT ETHICS AUDIT REPORT for Romance Writers of America*, by Julia E. Judish Jerald A. Jacobs for Pillsbury Winthrop Shaw Pittman LLP. February 19th, 2020, pp. 35–40

[28] Ibid., p. 43

[29] Ibid., p. 10

Knitting's Infinity War on Instagram

By Kathrine Jebsen Moore

The Needles Come Out — February 17, 2019

"Knitting is just so white. Let's hope it gets better." I overheard this puzzling remark in my local yarn store in Edinburgh, Scotland, last week. The store is in the affluent area of Marchmont, just outside the city centre. Its Edwardian and Victorian tenement flats, adjacent to huge green spaces, are popular with students and families alike. Two customers were chatting to the store owner: "It's about time we had the conversation," one of them offered. Her companion nodded in solemn agreement.

Knitting, which helps lower the blood pressure and keep the mind busy, has enjoyed an upsurge in popularity in recent years. The Internet has allowed for the proliferation of new platforms from which to buy yarn and patterns, and has helped connect artisans and hobbyists worldwide. Usually, it's a calming and creative pastime focused on aesthetics rather than politics. However, a short browse through the knitting posts on Instagram steered me in the direction of the source of the exchange I had overhead and the "conversation" it had produced.

On January 7, 2019, Karen Templer, a knitting designer and owner of the online store Fringe Association, published an innocuous blog post on her web site entitled "2019: My Year of Color," in which she enthused about her forthcoming trip to India. To most observers, Templer's post will read like a guileless account of her hopes and aspirations for upcoming travels:

> I've wanted to go to India for as long as I can remember. I've a lifelong obsession with the literature and history of the continent. Photos of India fill me with longing like no other place. One of my closest friends [when I was 12] and her family had offered back then that if I ever wanted to go with them on one of their trips, I could. To a suburban midwestern teenager with a severe anxiety disorder, that was like being offered a seat on a flight to Mars...Then about six weeks ago, the opportunity presented itself − a chance to go with a friend who's been...I said yes. And I felt like the top of my head was going to fly off, I was so indescribably excited. Within 48 hours, three of those friends of mine who are so much better travelers than me − but who are all equally humbled at the idea of actually going to India − also said yes. There has hardly been a single day since

that I haven't said in disbelief, either in my head or out loud, *I'm going to India.*

And what on earth could be wrong with any of that? Rather a lot, it turns out. After a series of encouraging posts from well-wishers, the comment thread took an aggressively inquisitorial turn. Templer's previous posts had typically garnered between three and 30 comments, but "My Year of Color" has 197 at the time of writing.

One of the first people to attack Templer was a user named Alex J. Klein, who wrote:

> Karen, I'd ask you to re-read what you wrote and think about how your words feed into a colonial/imperialist mindset toward India and other non-Western countries. Multiple times you compare the idea of going to India to the idea of going to another planet – how do you think a person from India would feel to hear that?

Templer politely explained that Mars and India both felt unattainable to her as a child. This comparison did not strike her as imperialist, but she promised to give the matter some thought. "I have had responses from several Indian friends and readers today," she added, "who had nothing but positive and encouraging responses. I'll have to see if anything I said offended them." Evidently unimpressed, Klein retorted:

> Instead of asking your Indian friends to perform more emotional labor for you and assuage your white women's tears, maybe do some reflection on how your equation of India with an alien world reinforces an "other" mindset that is at the core of imperialism and colonialism.

"I want to say this gently," a comment from a user identified only as Sarah began, "because I can tell your intent is to share your personal evolution and celebrate facing your fear of the unknown, and that's great. I just need to point out that there's a lot of "othering" happening in this post." She went on to explain that, "Your post upset some of my friends who aren't white [and] who didn't grow up in America," and advised Templer to engage in "a little more reflection before you equate India with Mars."

In an ominous development, previously supportive commenters now began to turn against Templer. Marie Carter, who had originally written, "You are even more inspiring than I thought," seemed to have had a change of mind three days later, and returned to correct herself:

> I have read through the entire post again, and I am ashamed to say that I failed to consider the

impact of this post on all of us non-white people. I skipped over the offensive parts because
this space is so important to my wellbeing. But
my heart hurts and I won't be able to live with
myself unless I acknowledge the pain to me
and others like me of the words used. I am no
longer going to say nothing.

"Same here," replied "Liz n." (a "biracial POC") a
day later.

On and on it went. Templer patiently fielded these
criticisms as best she could, but her inquisitors were
not satisfied. "It is really disappointing," announced
Joey, "to see your defensive and dismissive responses
to the two thoughtful posts that point out some of the
problematic aspects of your writing. As white person
to another white person, we NEED to take feedback
with respect and integrity...Instead of your "year of
color" being about wearing brighter clothing, why
don't you make 2019 investing in contributing to people of color, buying their art, listening to their podcasts, following them, contributing money to them,
buying literature written by POC."

Comments like these set off a wave of critical voices across knitting communities on sites such as Ravel-
ry.com, the biggest source of online knitting patterns
by independent designers from around the world
and the home of many knitting chat forums. Most of
the criticism amounted to sharing words written by

knitting activists @su.krita and @thecolormustard, who posted "educational" content on their profiles for others to circulate. Instagram notes scorned Templer's "peak whiteness," and reminded her that "the world doesn't owe you a patient explanation and education," and that as a "coloniser" she ought to "stay in [her] lane." Su.krita also warned her white knitter friends that if they stayed silent and didn't speak up against racism then they would be considered "part of the problem."

For anyone unfamiliar with the jargon of contemporary anti-racism, the criticism of Templer reflects the movement's more general critique of western society. Overt racism, which anyone would agree is abhorrent, is not their main focus; rather, they are preoccupied with identifying subtle, implicit, and often *unconscious* manifestations of bias which, by their nature, are almost impossible to refute. In this fraught climate, writers may be shamed as racists, irrespective of their good intentions, which are held to be irrelevant. As Jonathan Haidt, the American social psychologist, observed during a recent conversation with Joe Rogan, "It doesn't matter what the intent was, all that matters is the impact – how the person felt." When confronted with accusations of bigotry, white people are expected to confess to their primordial sins, repent by acknowledging their racial privilege, and to resolve to "do better." Only then may they be granted absolution by the anti-racist clergy.

As outrage spread across Instagram's knitting community, Templer published a new post on her blog entitled "Words Matter," in which she prostrated herself before her critics and asked for their forgiveness:

> I have hurt, angered and disappointed a lot of people this week with my insensitive post about my upcoming trip to India and my handling of the response, and I am deeply sorry about it. I've spent the week listening hard, learning (in part about how much more I have to learn), and thinking about all of the things I can do to be more inclusive and supportive of people of color.

She reassured everyone that she was "shocked at herself" and was now reading *The Origin of Others* by Toni Morrison, as instructed.

* * *

Amid the conformist cacophony of affirming anti-racists, however, one knitter decided to object.

Maria Tusken of Tuskenknits.com posted a YouTube video in response to criticism she'd received in a (since deleted) Instagram post. She began by explaining that Instagram had been enormously helpful in growing her business, before announcing that, after nearly four years on the platform, she would be taking an indefinite break. Referring to the mobbing of Karen Templer, Tusken said:

> There was a very intense social justice issue that started infiltrating Instagram a few weeks ago. I would say it was very hostile, and people were being attacked and threatened and accused of things — small businesses, like mine, or slightly bigger with a few employees but still very small — all in the name of this social justice issue. And everyone was saying, "It's a conversation." But it is not a conversation. It's a one-sided...belief? And there was no room for discussion. It was just arguments; trolling; bullying.

Tusken dyes wool from her home in the countryside outside of Seattle, and uses wool from small farms in Peru and the UK. For her criticisms of those hounding Templer, Tusken found that she was now also the target of the mob. Having found the majority of her customers through Instagram, she was suddenly losing thousands of followers as she weathered a barrage of criticism, and was forced to make her account private.

"It will be easy to boycott this person," wrote an Instagram user with the handle @knitterotica. "No amount of reason will change a zealot like Tuskenknits' mind, but we can make sure they feel their hatred reflected in their bank accounts and their follower counts until they are crying into a void." Another Instagram user, @webloom, published a post in which she asked: "How does [Tuskenknits] still have 10,000 followers? Hope they keep dwindling. She doesn't deserve our support." Another user, @ melthengineerknits, offered Tuskenknits's customers the opportunity to offload their "unwanted yarn" in exchange for "yarn art."

It wasn't long before the knitting establishment weighed in, and not in favor of Tusken. Kate Heppell, the editor of British knitting magazine *Knit Now*, posted a short tweet-thread about her, part of which read:

> In my book, if you're against folks calling out racism, it's pretty clear whose side you're on. She's posted a video on her YouTube channel in which she points out that she is in the majority and all her friends agree with her. I honestly found it utterly chilling. Please don't be sucked in by her and people like her. Challenge them. Don't give them your money. Report hate speech.

To one of Heppell's tweets, Dave Fraser (@disco-dave75) replied: "I'd love to say I watched the whole video to make an informed decision about her, but I

was blinded by her (literally) gleaming white face."
This childish insult was liked by Heppell.

The "whiteness in knitting" debate seems to have
arisen from the demands of "BIPOC" (Black, Indigenous, and People Of Color) knitters and their allies
for greater representation in terms of knitting designers, models featured in patterns, and well-known
knitting artists. Rapidly, knitters on Instagram started using hashtags such as #pocknitters and #diversk-
nitty, and there were calls to support POC knitters by
buying from them (if they owned a business), to follow them on social media, and to "buy them a coffee"
by donating money to their Patreon accounts. "Train
your feed!" became the new mantra, as users accused
Instagram of not showing people of color in feeds.

At Ravelry, a heavily moderated discussion took
place, suggesting ways in which the site should use
positive discrimination to show more patterns by
non-white designers. Knitting has varied traditions
and origins from across the globe, but it is particularly
popular in Scandinavia, where even small towns typically have a well-stocked wool shop. Arne & Carlos,
the Norwegian/Swedish knitting design duo, who
have 55,000 followers on Instagram, dipped their toe
in the mud with a post in which they thanked "incredibly courageous women" such as @su.krita for drawing attention to the issues of diversity and alleged
racism. "We all have so much to learn and there is a
great deal more we can do, in order to make this world

a better and more inclusive one for everyone."

In an age in which freedom of speech seems to be under attack in many different spheres of society, heretics to the progressive creed find themselves persecuted *ad nauseam* by a choir of the self-righteous. This kind of vindictive activism has been described by Jordan Peterson as a hunt for people who dare to disagree. "What's happening on the radical end of the political spectrum is not good. But the conservatives are too afraid. They're afraid they will be targeted as individuals, mobbed by the social justice warriors, and taken out," he said in an interview. The writer and activist James Lindsay, meanwhile, told me that campaigns like these are simply "a power grab thinly clothed as a civil rights movement."

Karen Templer surrendered to her accusers. Although some of her critics remain adamant that she has not done enough for diversity, she seems to have been accepted back in the clique of "BIPOC knitter-friendly" knitting activists. "I think perhaps the original intent of this discussion has been hijacked in an effort to attack and accuse people who disagree with the methods of implementing change," Tusken told me in an email. "This debate has caused a lot of division, but the divide isn't between racists and non-racists. It is between those who agree and those who disagree with the bullying, harassment, and virtue-signalling tactics currently being used to solve the problem." She says she has received support from many well-known names in the knitting industry. Of her accusers, Tusken said: "I have known for a long time that the knitting community wasn't as supportive and loving as everyone claimed. In reality, there are strong cliques and it can be difficult to fit in. There have been many times I've had to keep my mouth shut due to fear of something like this happening. I have been called a 'hateful racist POS [piece of shit].' But this didn't hurt nearly as bad as being called a horrible person and publicly denounced by 'friends' who I have met in person and built relationships with." She was even accused of being a neo-Nazi because she enjoys drinking Guinness. But as incongruous as cruelty and knitting might seem, this is no laughing matter. People's livelihoods are being credibly threatened by this kind of behavior. "You can be bullied and destroyed," Tusken told me.

Knitting is the simple pleasure of turning a ball of yarn into something practical and beautiful. As Elizabeth Zimmermann, the British born hand-knitting teacher and designer once said, "Properly practiced, knitting soothes the troubled spirit, and it doesn't hurt the untroubled spirit either." Let's hope the world of knitting can return to a focus on designs, colors, and the value of something that's unique and handmade, rather than the nationality or race of whoever made it.

A Woolen Mob Comes for Kate Davies — June 7, 2019

In February, I wrote an essay for *Quillette* about the Durkheimian witch-hunting taking place on the picture-sharing platform Instagram, and how it was affecting the thousands of knitters, designers, and business owners who rely on social media for their custom. My article described how a blogger and online craft store owner was denounced for writing an innocuous blog about her forthcoming trip to India, and how the yarn dyer Maria Tusken was then harassed and accused of complicity in racism for objecting to the mobbing. Businesses were chastised for their failure to be "truly inclusive," or for apologising too late when they had put a foot wrong.

Since my article appeared, things have only gotten worse. Kate Davies became the next target for abuse. A well-known designer, yarn vendor, and knitwear brand owner, she set up Kate Davies Designs after suffering a stroke at the age of 36, which had ended her career as a literary academic. Davies is based in the Scottish Highlands, where she employs a small team of people and has won awards for sustainability. She is also a campaigner for disabled people, having had to cope with disability herself. One might assume that people committed to social justice would look elsewhere for enemies.

Her crime? In the aftermath of the "conversation," as the campaigns to root out supposed perpetrators of racism was called, the topic of "white silence" became widely discussed. Designers and others with large followings who'd hitherto failed to speak up about how they were confronting racism were now urged to do so, lest they contribute to the perpetuation of "oppression." In a post entitled "A Letter on My Not-So-'Cozy' Doocot Sweater: aka My First and Last Kate Davies Project," Helen Kim (@keinhelm4 on Instagram, where she describes herself as an advocate for anti-racism, and an astrophysicist), wrote:

> As more and more voices in the fiber community discussed their concerns about racism and lack of representation, I patiently waited for the designers I respected to do the same. Days went by, weeks, and yet I naively found myself wanting to give these makers the benefit of the doubt for withholding their views while they continued to advertise their products and snowy winters.

When Davies did offer a statement, it was denounced as "very harmful" by Kim. "Your words are demonstrations of entitlement to racial discomfort and racial arrogance (see Robin DiAngelo's work on white fragility)," Kim declared. "White privilege," she added, "is a white problem."

Davies deleted her Instagram account, which had 75,000 followers, and posted a since deleted statement on her blog on February 14. An archived copy of Davies's statement was retrieved and reposted by Kim, along with her own critical commentary. Davies had written that "real change and real action can be best implemented by me outside a particular social-media bubble – in promoting and amplifying the voices of BIPOC in our community by taking forward projects in writing, publishing, and design that are explicitly antiracist and inclusive." But she said she would not participate in finger-pointing or shaming on Instagram, and felt "deeply saddened" about being misrepresented and misunderstood.

> It is my own political decision to choose not to speak from the particular social media script that has repeatedly been presented to me (with various levels of demand); to carefully listen to marginalized voices rather than to shout; to not participate in acts of shaming and intimidation; and to refuse to engage with those who insist that the only way I can effectively demonstrate my antiracist solidarity is by continually displaying it in my Instagram stories.

Criticism mounted. Ysolda Teague, an Edinburgh-based knitting designer and owner of online knitting shop ysolda.com, weighed in, telling her followers that she would no longer stock Davies' books. Davies then withdrew as a speaker from the Edinburgh Yarn Festival, citing health reasons, following a campaign led by Kim to have her disinvited. Kim, who was probably Davies's most vocal critic, concluded a story entitled "Call Out" (which can be found at the top of her Instagram profile) with the following:

> To those who worry about [Kate Davies's] career and the impact her own reactions have caused her, perhaps you should consider that historically BIPOC have been the ones who have been wronged and oppressed. Ask yourselves: In what ways do you hold power? In what ways do you hold power over BIPOC? How have you been complicit in that structure of power? How do your actions, inactions, and privileges reflect systemic racism? How do you want to acknowledge the system and your complicity? ...KD actively SILENCED those who are different from her and tokenized them. That is called RACISM and DISCRIMINATION. As a white woman knitwear designer with over 75K followers and international renown, Kate Davies was NOT vulnerable. Rather, she was in a position of power.

In short, even though she is a disabled woman, Davies was a legitimate target because she is also white, straight, and middle class, and her business is thriving, which implies a degree of affluence.

Many of the influential activists on Instagram are

academics. They draw on the work of scholars such as DiAngelo, the author of *White Fragility*, and recommend *Me and White Supremacy* by Layla F. Saad to those needing a lesson in "how to dismantle the privilege within themselves so that they can stop (often unconsciously) inflicting damage on people of color, and in turn, help other white people do better, too." Only by adopting the correct political views, espoused in precisely the correct jargon, can an accused person demonstrate to the satisfaction of her persecutors that she is now a "true ally" who has "done the work." It's all about as inspiring as it sounds.

Each fresh campaign would last a few weeks before moving on. Inevitably, some other company or individual would make some trivial but apparently unforgivable error, such as giving their pattern or yarn an incorrect name.

Madelinetosh Co. is America's largest hand-dyed yarn producer, owned by Amy Hendrix. Her wool is sold in 800 independently owned yarn stores around the world. Their "Inclusivity" colorway was white, beige, brown, and black to reflect various skin tones, but it was pulled from sale after furious protests. In response, Hendrix posted the following note: "This yarn was developed by women of color in our office together. We heard your concern and removed this color from our site. All existing proceeds will be donated to the Martin Luther King Jr. Cultural Foundation." In a follow-up post, Hendrix offered a more fulsome apology and explained why the color had not been removed straight away:

> Hello. My name is Amy and I am the founder of Madelinetosh. I am sorry for the actions we have recently taken at our company. I have removed the colors Courage, Honor and Inclusive from our web site. I agree with the comments stating the color should not have been created for sale. I understand why people are upset, indeed it is not right to profit from a great man like MLK nor to profit on an idea related to racism and the struggle many deal with each and every day. Action was not taken sooner because I am indeed on a break working through a recent diagnosis of Multiple Sclerosis. I share this not for your empathy but only to explain why the colors were not removed and action taken sooner. To rectify the situation regarding the skeins sold we will be donating one hundred percent of the sales of these yarns to the Martin Luther King Jr.'s Cultural Foundation, a community-based organization. On my views towards racism and the lack of businesses owned by people of color in the knitting industry, I stand with diversity. I stand with people of color and any other struggle that limits a person's right to exist, most especially during these hard times. Yet,

actions speak louder than words. So we intend to show you how we will support groups like MLK's and others in the future. As an additional note, I would also like to apologize to the wonderful women within our office. I am proud of their hard work on this project, and they are in no way responsible for how this unfolded. I take full responsibility for any lack of communication, and I hope you will join with us in our future endeavors as we educate ourselves and work with others. Please note: We will continue to moderate and remove any comments using foul language, calling others names, using terms such as fascist, nazis, holocaust, lynching and any other word intended to incite others from any source. We do not condone or support statements declaring white supremacy. Please know if you are posting this language in personal DM's to others you do not speak on our behalf and never will.

Needless to say, this did not satisfy her critics. @ cdickdesigns, a knitting pattern designer with about 4,000 followers, said:

If a large company refuses to make a statement and refuses to moderate their own posts to protect people from vitriolic bigotry, and then make a colorway called "Inclusivity," it's a straight-up fucking slap in the face for people like me and other people who are currently suffering in their private lives due to the pains we have shared publicly and openly.

It means that this "Inclusivity" colorway was developed solely for profit. It wasn't created to help, educate or benefit anyone other than themselves. The colorway might as well have been called "All Lives Matter." Right now, Madelinetosh is profiting from my pain. Madelinetosh has 95K followers and a following of cishetero white women who go into LYS [Local Yarn Store] and say things like "Do you have Madelinetosh? The only hand-dyed yarn I like is my Tosh!"

Laine magazine describes itself as a "high-quality Nordic knit and lifestyle magazine for knit folks." A few months ago, it was criticized by Ysolda Teague, a stockist of *Laine*, for appearing to be

very white and that is extremely problematic. I appreciated how welcome lgbtq+ like me [were] in Laine, and I hoped they'd do better about representing POC. I made excuses to myself...but I didn't say anything because I didn't want to upset the editors. That wasn't good enough. I apologize for my silence. I'm taking my responsibility as a stockist, and as an advertiser and as someone who has been featured in *Laine* seriously...I'm expecting to see changes, and I'm committed to supporting that, and being accountable if we don't see it.

Then, a few weeks later, *Laine* magazine hired Ysolda's fiancé, photographer Kate O'Sullivan, who is also a writer and social justice activist. But O'Sullivan is white, and this did not go unnoticed. "Six weeks ago," wrote Kim,

> @ysolda posted in her stories heavy criticisms against *Laine* Magazine for not being inclusive of BIPOC. A couple of days ago, Ysolda's partner, Kate O'Sullivan, announced that she had gladly accepted Laine's offer to be their new regular photographer... In an ideal world, I would be able to ask: To what extent did Ysolda take advantage of her large platform, in voicing dissatisfaction, to allow someone close to her to personally gain from public criticism?...Who gets to call themselves an ally and to receive the protection, and compensation, for that label? In an ideal world, no one.

Teague and O'Sullivan both posted grateful and self-reproachful replies to Kim. "Hi Helen," O'Sullivan began, "thank you for once again holding this community to a high standard. You are right, my first commission for *Laine* was as a white woman. I pitched for somebody I knew I could interview nearby. This was back in Autumn, as *Laine* publish[es] biannually." She explained that it was up to *Laine* to decide who to hire, and that she would put forward BIPOC designers for the magazine. She ended her comment by announcing: "I also wanted to be clear I'm private for our daughter's safety as we had alt-right pseudo-journalists who live locally targeting us this weekend over another issue."

This sounds alarming. But it turned out that *I* was the "alt-right pseudo-journalist" in question. On February 19, I'd pointed out on Twitter that Teague and users on Ravelry.com were participating in the hounding of Kate Davies, which had just erupted. I was then blocked by Teague and O'Sullivan. End of story. Nevertheless, if O'Sullivan's tale was an attempt to solicit sympathy and alleviate the criticism she was facing, it met with some success. "I am sorry to hear that [the] local alt-right movement is threatening your safety," a concerned @burrobird replied. "Please be safe." Even Helen Kim thought it would be wise to step back in the light of this news. "I would like to reach out and apologize to @kateo_sullivan and @ysolda," she wrote. "No one – NO ONE – should have to face threats and violence from alt-right supremacists. This kind of violence is sadly the reality of racism and white supremacy today, here in our very own community."

It remains to be seen who will be the next object of the mob's attentions. Sophia Cai (@sophiatron) – a Melbourne-based writer, curator, and knitter; and a friend of O'Sullivan and Teague – has begun compiling a list of local yarn stores and other knitting businesses that fall short of the standards of anti-racism she expects from the community. She calls this list her "burn book":

> You might be surprised who is in this book. Many places with "inclusivity" statements or signs on doors or a token POC friend/employee/consultant. If there is one thing that unites yt [white] people it's white fragility. To all the LYS and yarn businesses I have spent so much time speaking to over the last few months who still don't get it. Who still think it's a matter up for debate or further "consideration." That's fine. Take the time you need. I just won't wait around for you. But maybe pay for the consultation and emotional labor.

Donations, she adds, can be directed to her Ko-fi account. A complete list of those included in her burn book can be obtained by messaging her. They apparently include "white feminists who don't care about intersectional feminism," "white feminists who are outraged by plastic straws but are quiet about white supremacy," and "people who don't see color or declare that 'everyone is welcome.'"

These campaigns are risible, but they are also ugly. They license pettiness, cruelty, and ruthlessness in the name of causes they do nothing to advance. They threaten the businesses and livelihoods and professional reputations of good people struggling to navigate a dense web of ideological trip-wires. Everyone has to watch what they say lest an innocuous remark is seized upon as a new excuse to denounce and shame. And yet, this intolerable situation persists because everyone involved is silently complicit in the pretense that this is noble behavior motivated by loving concern and righteous anger. It will only end when the revolution eats itself or when a critical mass of participants say, "Enough."

Showdown at Yarningham – July 28, 2019

This is my third report for *Quillette* on the shockingly vicious social-media wars that have erupted in the world of knitting. My first, written in February, described how knitters' blogs and Instagram accounts have become weaponized over the issue of racial representation after a knitting designer gushed publicly about her forthcoming trip to India. I concluded with the hope that "the world of knitting can return to a focus on designs, colors, and the value of something that's unique and handmade, rather than the nationality or race of whoever made it."

This proved to be extremely naïve.

In my second article on the subject, published last month, I described how this subcultural farce had descended into a full-blown tragicomedic soap opera, with knitters seeking to destroy one another's livelihoods because of arguments about whether certain yarn colors might be racist, or whether yarn-related publications profile enough black women.

I was surprised that such an esoteric subject would stir up so much reader interest. (My editors tell me that both articles went viral.) And I honestly never imagined that I'd be writing about this subject again. Surely, such fury within knitting circles could not sustain itself, right?

And yet, here I am. Over the last seven weeks, things have only become more insane.

Last month, for instance, Ravelry, the world's largest knitting web site, banned any expression of support for Donald Trump – arguing that "we cannot provide a space that is inclusive of all and also allow support for open white supremacy. Support of the Trump administration is unambiguously support for white supremacy."

The least that can be said in defense of the Ravelry policy is that Trump is a public figure, who probably will not be much put out by an editorial policy on a knitting site. What was far more unsettling was what happened two weeks later, when knitters who claim to be champions of social justice went after a gay man within the community because he'd written a satirical poem suggesting (correctly) that all the recent anti-racism mobbings might be having a toxic effect on the community.

On July 8, Nathan Taylor, known as the Sockmatician on social media – a full-time designer, knitting instructor, and web-shop operator (and the author of *Guys Knit*) – posted the following on his Instagram profile:

> With genuine SOLEM-KNITTY
> I beg you, stop the
> Enmity
> Don't use the word
> DIVERSKNITTY,
> To mask your
> ANIMOS-KNITTY.
> Stop bullying
> FEROC-KNITTY
> And insta-
> ANONYM-KNITTY
> And self-imposed
> IMPU-KNITTY
> Is breaking our COMMU-KNITTY

Taylor followed up his poem with a (since deleted) post:

One year on almost to the day, since I sent out the first ever post to use the #diversknitty hashtag – a word I made up – from Helsinki airport, I am, again, at Helsinki airport, and I feel compelled to speak up about this issue once again, but this time from a very different perspective. There are now over 17,000 posts using that hashtag. My word. And it is time to reboot it as a tool for good. Diversity is a beautiful and NECESSARY thing, and SHOULD be FOUGHT FOR...But there is poison out there, too. People who are self-proclaiming to be the arbiters of the whole diversity discussion, and deciding who is "enough" and whose reputation and livelihood they believe they have the right to destroy... Yes, ask people who do openly racist/homophobic/bigoted actions to re-evaluate their standpoint, but please, for the love of all that is good, do not go after people who are already doing what they feel they can to put this necessary situation right.

Predictably, the post brought out the worst of the knitting world's anti-racism mobs – since the last thing any mob likes to be told is that their mobbings (which they typically regard as necessary and virtuous) do more harm than good.

Social Justice Knitters, SJKs as I call them, weighed in *en masse* in the comments section. "What did I just read? Respectfully, your words are bigoted. You don't own the concept of diversity...How is this post doing anything other than protecting white fragility, tone policing, and white silence?" said Helen Kim, who has become a sort of self-appointed spokesperson and inquisitor-in-chief for the SJK community. "Interesting how your voicing of the need for 'positivity' in these discussions reminds me a lot of the rhetoric used by white supremacists."

Within a few hours, there were hundreds of comments, largely negative. A user who goes by Skeinanigans, for instance, wrote: "It is a product of privilege to be able to speak gently because you haven't had your personhood systematically degraded for your entire life" – to which Taylor replied: "Oh, but I have." And as a gay, HIV-positive man, Taylor would indeed be insulated from allegations of privilege in any normal discussion. But to the intersectionalists who act as SJK enforcers within this shrill subculture, that didn't matter. As an activist by the username of jessie-mae put it:

It is possible to be a member of a marginalized group and participate in oppressive behavior. Your marginalization does not absolve you, and you do not get to speak for those who are marginalized in ways that you are not. A gay white man claiming credit for movements that existed long before he used a cute word for them in an Instagram post one time doesn't get to dictate how bipoc+ [individuals] fight for their lives. This is basic shit, y'all. DO BET-TER!

Many of Taylor's 20,000 followers tried to offer words of encouragement and appreciation. Notably, Loop London, an iconic yarn shop in Camden, North London, stood by Taylor – which of course generated calls to boycott the shop. Some who originally had been supportive changed their tune as the criticism grew, apologized, thanked the people who called them out, and promised to educate themselves and "do better."

But the saga didn't end there. The next day, Taylor's husband Benjamin Till, a composer (who also happens to be Jewish) posted on Sockmatician's account: "This is Nathan's husband, Benjamin. At 3 pm today, Nathan was admitted to [the emergency room at] Barnet Hospital. Your messages of anger have been processed. Please now send love."

Till also wrote on his blog about what had happened:

The situation with the aggressive online trolls grew through the night, as the American knitters got involved and started to leap onto what they perceived as a ripe carcass. Nathan disabled comments when the sheer weight of them became too much, but the following morning, his other Instagram posts, and then his Twitter feed had been hijacked by the haters. The taunts continued. He was a white supremacist, a Nazi apologist...He started obsessively reading the posts but became increasingly worked up, then more and more erratic and then suddenly he snapped, screaming like a terrified animal, smashing boxes and thumping himself. I was forced to wrestle him to the ground and hold onto him for dear life as the waves of pain surged through his body. He made a run for the car keys. He said he wanted to drive at 100 miles per hour until he crashed. I called our doctor and they could hear him screaming in the background and said I was to immediately take him to [the hospital], where he was instantly assessed and put on suicide watch pending a decision about whether or not he needed to be, well, I suppose the word is sectioned.

Taylor was kept in the hospital for six hours, but was later released, although he was still frazzled, according to Till, and subsequently deleted his Instagram and Twitter accounts.

The accusations continued, however. Many said they didn't wish illness on anyone, but that his breakdown didn't excuse the "harm" he had caused. A user by the name of "Amy.might" replied to Taylor's now deleted post as follows: "Let's be clear here. Holding people accountable for the incredibly harmful words they *voluntarily* put out to the world is not cruel or bullying...I hope Nathan feels better soon so he can address the harm he caused regardless of what his intentions were. I believe that people are flawed, but redeemable."

Fast forward a few days to Yarningham, a knitting festival in Birmingham, where Taylor was scheduled to teach some classes. One of the vendors, Almas Khan, who goes by the name Witchcraftylady on Instagram, approached Taylor to tell him what she thought of his blog post. In her own words, Khan describes what happens next as follows:

> I watched him receiving hugs and people moving around the space uncomfortable with the fact he hadn't apologized for the harm he and his husband caused. I saw his stand was empty, so I went over. When he saw me standing there he switched on his smile and the minute I said I wasn't there for a book and wanted to talk about his posts he dropped the façade and actually started shouting at me. He had his fingers in my face, screaming at me to leave his sight, he had his clenched fists in my face...He was totally out of control.

Khan also broadcast a live video on her Instagram profile. While viewers provided words of support for Khan and mocked Taylor, Khan described how the sight of "people hugging him...was too much for me... I've never seen a grown man open his eyes so wide when I told him he was a fucking hypocrite. That's what's keeping me going – that look on his face." She also claimed to know that Taylor was going to hit her, and expressed hope that "more people call him out."

Taylor was approached by one of the organizers and taken outside, according to Khan. Another version of events, documented on Till's blog by an anonymous poster who said she had been present, went as follows:

A woman went rushing up to Sockmatician as he was doing a book signing today and screamed in his face. He asked her to stop, but she carried on. So he called for her to be removed, and then one of the organizers of Yarningham came over and started pushing Sockmatician out of the room whilst the first woman screamed at him "Why are you walking away? You're a hypocrite, stand here and face up to me like a man." Sockmatician was clearly very distressed. The woman went at him knowing fully well he'd been in hospital. Very unpleasant. Not too impressed by the

Yarningham organizer, either. She pushed the wrong person out of the room.

So far, no video footage has been released of the kerfuffle. Hence the jury is out on the exact nature of the scene. Taylor didn't return my request for comment. In a post titled *Fuck the Tone Police*, Helen Kim expressed support for such confrontations, saying it's time for people of color to express anger: "White people still need reminding: They are not, never were, and never will be the victims of white supremacy. Systemic racism is not positive, pleasant, pretty, feel-good, comfortable. Why should the experience of dismantling it be?"

Unlike some of the previous victims of these campaigns in the knitting world, however, Taylor hasn't bowed to the demands of his critics – not yet anyway. And so the mob is still hard at work trying to destroy his reputation and business. As a result, he has been removed from the lineup at the Woolness knitting festival in Newcastle in August, claims one Instagram user. And Taylor's events calendar, which once was displayed on his web site, has been deleted – perhaps to prevent more confrontations.

As for Khan, she's as active as ever on the web – selling her own "luxury yarns and hand made goods." On her Instagram profile, where she says her mission is to "spread joy" and sparkle, Khan boasts of having created the "Raiseyourhandinsolidarity" hashtag so that she might "share the beauty of all of our hands and unite everyone around the world."

Early days yet. But so far, it isn't working.

AUTHOR'S POSTSCRIPT – SEPTEMBER 2020

When the first of these essays was published in February, 2019, I was surprised by the attention it received. Among all the comments, there was one that kept appearing, summarized as, "What, knitting, of all things, is racist?"

Back then, of course, racism still meant racial prejudice or discrimination of people because of the color of their skin, and we, the general population, still didn't know what microaggressions or "white silence" meant. Looking back, what happened in knitting was a warning sign. It was sensational at the time, because these phenomena were still relatively rare: calling people out for a seemingly innocent misstep, the joining in of community members into what can best be described as witch hunts, and the endless apologies and repeated newspeak that would circulate in the aftermath. After a while, the cycle would repeat with a new victim.

After my third essay, describing the hounding and subsequent breakdown of the gay, male knitter Nathan Taylor, the activists were still looking for other targets. When the well-known knitting magazine *Laine* arranged a small retreat in the French countryside, it posted a photo of the knitters on Instagram. Three of the 12 participants can be described as non-white, based on the picture, which still features on their feed. This was widely condemned as a sign that *Laine*, a Finnish magazine known for its sparse Nordic style, was a purveyor of white supremacy. A lengthy, grovelling apology followed, as expected. The storm blew over. But the magazine announced that it would stop publishing. Gradually, the call outs seemed to occur less and less. The ringleaders still posted their grievances, but there seemed less willingness to join in.

Looking back, the world of knitting was ahead of its time, as it's only more recently that cancel culture has permeated larger swathes of the western world. I don't think you could say there is *one* knitting community anymore. Understandably, many knitters – those on the right, as well as those who are simply not interested in identity politics and are feeling repelled by what had been going on – instead made connections with each other, and decided not to give designers or yarn dyers who had participated in the witch hunts their money. Thousands left Ravelry, and some set up their own forums.

Knitting is a popular hobby, and most do it for their own, personal reasons – whether it's creating a garment for a child or themselves, to play with colors and textures, or to find an outlet for stress. For me, knitting will always be something that takes me away from the world around me. And although I find inspiration online, it is a distinctly individual, off-line experience. But this quote by avid knitter Stephanie Pearl-McPhee sums up the mentality of many-a-knitter, and might explain why you also find troublemakers enjoying this seemingly innocent activity: "The number-one reason knitters knit is because they are so smart that they need knitting to make boring things interesting. Knitters are so compellingly clever that they simply can't tolerate boredom. It takes more to engage and entertain this kind of human, and they need an outlet or they get into trouble."

A #MeToo Mob Tried to Destroy My Life as a Poet
By Joseph Massey

I'll begin by confessing: I fucked up. I fucked up as a friend, an acquaintance, a stranger, a neighbor, and as a partner. I said cruel things; I said provocative things; I said obscene things; I said manipulative things; I said psychotic things – to men and to women. My language crossed boundaries countless times, usually online. And my behavior, on a few occasions, crossed physical boundaries.

In 2009, I inappropriately touched a woman at a bar after a poetry reading. In 2005, I got into a fist fight with a man – again, after a poetry reading. As someone who attended the reading said, in a comment posted on the web site of the press that published the book I read from that night: "I remember the tension, angst, rage, and insecurity – all funneled through the 40 oz'er he was drinking while performing – and that my main impression of the work was a deep, devastating suffering... one that aroused concern." I was 26-years-old.

Throughout my 20s and early 30s, I rarely appeared in public unless alcohol was promised. I drank to protect myself from a constant state of anxiety, always verging on full-blown panic.

347

I'm now 40-years-old. For years, I've worked to reverse and dismantle my destructive patterns. I was in therapy for six years. At age 35, I joined Alcoholics Anonymous. A year later, I joined a group called Ananda, which taught me how to meditate. I also learned how to breathe and break through symptoms of trauma. For the first time in my adult life, I didn't fear anxiety and panic. I didn't fear *fear.* I wasn't depressed anymore, and the anger that was lodged in my chest – those knots dissolved. (I still meditate every day.) I made many apologies; I mended friendships; and I ended associations with people who preferred the person I was in the past.

Because of those changes, I acquired renewed vitality, which allowed me to write my best work. *Illocality,* a collection of poems published by Wave Books in the Fall of 2015 (reprinted by Hollyridge Press in 2018), was reviewed in *The New York Times* and other high-profile publications. I was invited to give readings at several universities. The University of Pennsylvania's Kelly Writers House invited me to give a reading, which eventually led to my participation in "ModPo," the school's online course in modern and contemporary poetry – a worldwide community serving thousands of students. I also ran my own course on my late mentor Cid Corman's poetry, which was virtually attended by hundreds of people. Had I still been the perpetually angry, boundary-crossing drunk I was in the past, I would not have experienced so much good fortune. After a decade of suicidal behavior, I realized that I could have a life – a decent, stable life – in poetry.

* * *

I discovered poetry while reading a biography of Jim Morrison. The Doors did nothing for me – I was 12 at the time and my favorite band was Fine Young Cannibals. I'm not sure what drew me to the book, but it was probably the urgency of the title, *No One Here Gets Out Alive*. The story of Morrison's adolescence appealed to me. He was weird; I was weird. We were both borderline delinquents. The book talked about the poets and philosophers he was obsessed with. I sought all of them out.

My discovery of poetry kept me company during a nearly year-long in-school suspension. I only lasted a few weeks in the 6th grade. Harlan Elementary in Wilmington, Delaware was a rough school. I fought with students who challenged me. After several suspensions, the principal told me to stop going to class and to go directly to the auditorium. I sat there, alone, every day for the rest of the year. I read Nietzsche's *Thus Spoke Zarathustra,* Arthur Rimbaud's *Collected Poems* (the Penguin Classics edition, with prose translations by Oliver Bernard), and Jack Kerouac's *On the Road*. I was far from alone. I was in fascinating company.

Those books were pure transgression and rebellion. This was alchemy. This was poetry, a world that I now knew I wanted to inhabit.

* * *

My parents conceived me while they were still in high school. They married shortly after they graduated, and my brother was born two years later. The following year, they split up. My mother and stepfather (she remarried shortly after the divorce) had primary custody. My brother and I spent every other weekend and most summers with my father, who lived with my grandmother and grandfather.

My uncle lived there as well. My dad wasn't around most of the time – he was busy working and hanging out in bars. So my grandmother was the dominant parental figure when we visited. She was nurturing in ways other adults in my life weren't: big meals, outings to Philadelphia to see museums and historical sites, activities that helped shape me and spark my interest in books, art, and history. My grandmother enhanced my world – a world of abuse and neglect. But she was also abusive herself, in ways I don't think I'll ever fully understand.

My stepfather was consumed by hair-trigger rage. My earliest memory is of him pinning me against a wall until I pissed and shit myself. I was no older than four. My grandmother's mode of abuse was stranger. She regaled my brother and I with stories about how she was abducted by aliens. They operated on her. We heard all of the gruesome, vivid details. Those traumatizing conversations, more like monologues, were frequent.

Sometimes the topic wasn't alien abduction, but Jesus Christ. She had a clear plastic cup that she would hold to her ear to communicate with Jesus. She took questions from me and my brother. "Is there a Show-biz Pizza in heaven?" "Does Jesus need to brush his teeth?" The sessions would last for hours.

I still feel chills when I see the classic image of Caucasian Jesus with his bleeding, beaming heart exposed, and his half-smile of boundless compassion. My grandmother wasn't Catholic, but her home was decorated with Catholic iconography: crucifixes, framed pictures of Jesus, palm fronds hanging from the frames. On Good Friday, my brother and I were forced to kneel on the floor as she wept and convulsed over Christ's crucifixion.

She insisted on bathing us when we were far too old to be bathed — bathed and then told to lie down on her bed with our legs in the air as she powdered our genitals. I remember her saying to me, "if you touch your dingle, it'll fall off." Until the age of 13, or thereabouts, whenever I used the bathroom to move my bowels, she insisted on cleaning me.

The first summer after I discovered poetry, I walked into the backyard and saw my grandmother standing over my notebook — it included the first poems I wrote. The thing was already in flames and dissolving into ash. She said something about "blasphemy" and "filth," and stomped out the fire. From then on, I had to hide my writing when visiting her home.

My uncle Jack lived in a room on the top floor of the house. He was deeply closeted and seemed miserable when he wasn't engaged in his hobby. He had one of the largest collections of *Gone With the Wind* memorabilia in the entire country. (This was confirmed after his death, when my grandmother sold the collection.) His life revolved around all things *Gone With the Wind*, a film I despised then and refuse to watch now.

He liked to sit with me in his room and drill me on trivia about the film. Sometimes, whether I got one of his questions right or wrong, it didn't matter, he would pin me down on his bed and stick his tongue in my mouth while groping me. I was 7, 8, 9 years old. One afternoon, he grabbed me and threw me into the trunk of his car and drove away, screaming about how he intended to drive off the Commodore Barry Bridge. As I write this, my entire body feels frozen from the inside out. It only struck me recently that maybe he really planned to do that, to kill us both. Instead, he drove around the block a few times. When the trunk popped open, I crawled out and fell flat on the asphalt, numb with terror.

By the time I was approaching adolescence, large enough to defend myself, he stopped touching me. He became verbally cruel instead. He'd walk by me as I played outside with friends and mumble insults: "fat boy," "asshole," "piece of shit."

After a trip to Rehoboth Beach with my grandmother and grandfather when I was 13, we pulled up to the house, and it looked as if the entire block were standing on the front lawn. An ambulance was there. One of the neighbors was drenched. Apparently, my uncle was found floating in the backyard pool, and the neighbor had jumped in to pull him out. He killed himself, but I was told at the time that he'd accidentally drowned. A month or two prior to that, he'd been hospitalized for overdosing on aspirin.

My grandmother always wore floral-patterned mumus with a low neckline. I remember a scar on the center of her chest, thick and pale, the size of a large fist. She mentioned that she had surgery there, but that was all she ever said about it.

She killed herself when I was 23-years-old by overdosing on pills. My brother, who lived with her at the time, found her half-dead on her bedroom floor. My father told me that day that she tried to kill herself in 1978, the year I was born. She laid down in the bathtub and shot herself in the chest with a gun. I don't know how she managed to survive it, nor did I ask.

* * *

When I was 15, I sent my work to poets I admired. I found their addresses in the reference section of the public library, in a large book titled *Contemporary Poets*. Allen Ginsberg was the first poet to respond:

> Dear Mr Massey..."Attack" is confusing, sounds like you cut your foot on an icicle? If so, describe the situation's details more clearly. "Crickets familiar chant from/ heavy dark grass beneath / trees silhouetted / where water choking...flows / Crisscross vehicle sounds / dawn hard solid rises / sudden lapse in blue" — all that has elements of good poem! Read W.C.Williams (old poet) & Gregory Corso (New Directions Publishing). Best take care of little details. See my "Mind-Writing Slogans."
> Yours,
> Allen Ginsberg

This confirmed things. I was a poet. The fact that my family had no idea (or just no interest) in what I was up to didn't bother me. I was content to follow through on my own.

I also heard back from Philip Whalen, Robert Bly, Jack Hirschman, and many others. I lived to check the mail every day, to make vital connections with practitioners of the art I loved — an art that still was a blessed mystery to me: a sacred pact with language, with silence, and other minds always alive, even if they were dead, on the page. I'm as committed now as I was then to the daily practice of poetry, despite being a fuck-up.

I dropped out of school in the 9th grade. I was hospitalized so many times for suicide attempts and suicidal ideation that I missed two years of school. By the time I made it to high school, I was as old as most of the juniors. My correspondence with poets, and the long hours I spent at the public library — that was my education.

At the age of 19, I wrote to Cid Corman, a key figure in what came to be known as "New American Poetry," whose first letter to me announced: "Your life is about to change!" He was right.

Cid Corman was my own private university degree. He saw the strengths and the weaknesses in my poetry, and in one letter after another, mailed from his home in Kyoto, Japan, he helped hone my work. He introduced me to poets in nearby Philadelphia, as well as poets all over the world. Cid Corman gave me a community.

When I was 23, I moved with my girlfriend from Dover, Delaware, where I'd been living alone in a roach-infested studio apartment, to Humboldt County, California. Up to that point, I'd never had much interest in drinking. But once I started, which was shortly after moving west, I found that it removed all my anxiety. I liked that feeling.

When my girlfriend and I broke up, I moved into a slanted shack — a woodshed barely converted into a livable space, which was my home for the next twelve years. The drinking increased.

During that time, this was the early to mid-aughts, I started a blog. I made contact with other poets with blogs. Facebook and Twitter weren't around then. The blogs were a way for us to communicate and to form community online. I often posted on my blog when I was drunk. I wrote manifestos; I agitated people. I was aggressive; I was an asshole. Not always, but most of the time.

Throughout this period, I was able to write poems that had no connection to my public persona: They were *still,* focused, image-based, and economical in their language. The online bravado and blathering masked the sensitivities, the need for silence, that was conveyed in the poetry.

I was desperately poor and unable to work due to what was eventually diagnosed as PTSD. I don't know how I survived those years.

* * *

In 2014, I became romantically involved with the poet Kate Colby, who is married. The affair lasted for two and a half years. I did not abuse her, as was later claimed, but the situation itself was destructive for both of us, and did not end well. I tried to exit the relationship, but the correspondence always started up again. I was weak, caught up in a toxic cycle of what felt like love, but in reality was a distortion of other emotions: namely lust and self-loathing. To put it plainly, the affair was an epic mind fuck.

Our relationship mostly took place through email. In-person visits were infrequent – once every three to four months. We rarely talked on the phone, and we rarely texted. For the first year of this, I was happy to be used. Rarely a week went by during those two and a half years when I wasn't sent a small portfolio of her poems to edit and comment on. When I failed to do so, she threatened to end the relationship. I shared my professional contacts with her. She often complained about her lack of fame – and told me that my own success made her jealous – despite the fact that she's widely published by reputable presses, regularly gives poetry readings, and has won awards.

In February of 2017, when I thought I was having, or close to having, some kind of nervous breakdown over the relationship, I wrote to her husband on Facebook, anonymously, and told him his wife was having an affair. That was a cowardly, pathetic move. Several days later, using my own name, I wrote to him again to apologize for the affair. I said it was over. Kate called me, angry that I'd told her husband the truth, and said she wouldn't speak to me again. I screamed on the phone. I don't know what I said, but I know I used vile, hurtful language.

We didn't speak again until a few months later. On April 15, she wrote to me: "I have been in hell and I don't know where you're at, but I think one way forward for me would be to try to clear the air. Let me know if you want that. If you don't, please just don't respond." We spoke on the phone the next day, and I apologized for the language I used when I screamed at her. She accepted my apology. We continued to email each other throughout the day. She said: "You don't have to keep apologizing. The whole 2.5 years was a shitty situation for you, and I was highly aware of that. I think it's my fault for letting it get out of hand, but we both knew there was no good way out."

Eleven days later, my manuscript *What Follows* was accepted for publication by Wesleyan University Press, a respected poetry publisher that had rejected Kate's work on two occasions. If you have followed similar personal dust-ups in the publishing world, you can see where this is going.

When I told Kate that Wesleyan wanted my book, she cut off all contact. I was blocked on all social media and she refused to respond to my messages. On July 6, she wrote to me with a list of grievances, ending with: "Then you decided to tell me that my personal dream press, over which I've worked so hard and suffered a lot of pain, is publishing your book."

In an article published in 2018, I was accused of being jealous and controlling — adjectives that, in my opinion, described Kate's own behavior. She thought I was sleeping with all of my female friends, in particular the ones who are younger than she is. There are thousands of messages of this variety in my Gmail archive.

* * *

On January 10, 2018 I received a call from a friend I hadn't heard from in a few years. "Someone named Kate Colby posted on Facebook that you're a 'serial abuser,'" she told me. "She tagged a bunch of people, and there's a link to a website."

That site, *The Poet Joseph Massey Is An Abuser*, contains an anonymously written letter. Its author (one of Kate's friends, it turns out) sent the letter to various publishers, including Wesleyan University Press, and my part-time employer, the University of Pennsylvania's Kelly Writers House. Kate tagged all of them in her Facebook post. As the anonymous letter put it, "I hope you end relations with him and make a public statement about it, especially in light of cultural shifts around believing victims." The MeToo movement was in full swing, and social media was a no-holds-barred outlet for accusations. The release of the letter was timed perfectly:

> This is in regards to Joseph Massey, a poet with whom you collaborate. Over the past several years, far too many people have told me about his verbal and psychological abuse. I no longer feel okay sitting silently with this

information. For many people in 'whisper networks,' it is now taken for granted that Massey is a predator.

The letter goes on to describe an alleged encounter the writer had with me at a poetry reading: "He was extremely drunk and told me several times, in front of a large crowd of published writers and my partner, that he thought I was hot."

There's no mention of a location or a date. I've given only a handful of poetry readings; I don't like reading in public and avoid it as much as possible. I lived in Northern California for 12 years and traveled outside of the area only three times to give poetry readings. To the best of my knowledge, the encounter described in the anonymous letter didn't happen. But that was beside the point: The letter was an invitation for others to pile on with additional allegations.

The link was shared hundreds of times over the course of the next several days and continued to occasionally reappear, and regain traction, months after Kate posted it on Facebook.

But in fact, I knew all this was coming. The previous October, I'd been contacted by the University of Georgia Press, which had invited me to serve as a preliminary judge for the university's Poetry Book Prize. I was told an employee received a letter from a friend that expressed "concern" over my involvement. This person, who was not named, said that I was verbally abusive. I knew this was connected to Kate Colby, and explained the situation in detail, on speaker phone, to a room full of University of Georgia Press employees — strangers to me.

In a panic, I posted about my feelings on Facebook, explaining to my friends that I was being smeared by an unnamed "married woman" with whom I'd had an affair. I also described my plan to drop out of the poetry world, having seen what happened to other poets who were "called out." Within minutes after that Facebook post went up, Kate emailed me and told me, "I forgive you." I asked her to stop smearing me and she agreed. That was four months before her Facebook post.

* * *

Kate spent months reaching out to my ex-girlfriends, friends, and anyone she thought I had anything to do with who happened to be female. I heard from several friends she contacted. Some of them sent me screen shots that showed Kate's overtures — such as "If you need to talk about Joe, I know how it goes and I'm here for you."

In the wake of her Facebook post, I was mobbed relentlessly on social media. When I attempted to apologize, my post instantly attracted hateful comments from strangers and people I barely knew. I deleted the post. I had to rely on close friends to maintain my stability. I was in shock.

Within 24 hours, *Barrelhouse* magazine told me they no longer wanted me to host one of their online workshops. Four poets who'd asked me to blurb their books wrote to me, telling me that I shouldn't bother. The pile-on allegations came thick and fast. "At a poetry reading, he looked at me like I was a meal, and it chilled me to the bone." "He invited me to his hotel room to have a drink with him." "He made a homophobic remark about a fellow poet." "He was rude to me on Facebook six years ago." "He messaged me once, trying to talk about poetry." "He was creepy toward me on Instagram." Some of these were from people I'd never met. Others were from people who'd been friendly toward me until that day. Some close friends cut off all contact. I was ghosted.

A week later, Al Filreis, the director of the Kelly Writers House, wrote to me to sever all ties, and to cancel several projects and events scheduled for later in the year. His letter was laden with legalese, and he said he would not even identify the allegations that had motivated his decision, let alone hear my side of things. I had no opportunity to face my accusers.

Only a few months before he sent that email, I gave a poetry reading at a fundraiser for the Kelly Writers House in a New York City art gallery. Al introduced me, calling me "a gift to the Kelly Writers House." At length, he lauded the work I'd done for them over the years.

He was one of the people Kate tagged on Facebook. Kate knew exactly who he was, and what he meant to my career, because I helped introduce them. I even proposed to Al that we record a podcast about Kate's work. I was also asked to call in to a ModPo webcast featuring Kate, whereupon Al asked about our relationship as poets. (You can view that discussion on YouTube.) Kate is now a regular fixture in ModPo, and is scheduled to read at the Kelly Writers House. She swept in to replace the ghost I'd become.

On May 16, an article about me appeared in *The Outline*, titled *The Poet Joseph Massey's Disturbing History of Abuse*, written by Rebekah Kirkman. When Kirkman contacted me in February to say she was "investigating" the allegations against me, she requested an interview. I was still in shock, and desperately wanted to be transparent. I never should've spoken to her. This is someone whose Twitter feed contained entries like "No matter how cool things seem in my life, I am always mad about men," "perennial hatred [of] men and their abuse of power," "fuck power fuck abusers [and] fuck men especially."

Kirkman made it clear during our interview that she was interested in how I used "power" over people. I'm still trying to figure out what that "power" was exactly, and how I would have used it. I'm poor. I don't leave the house often. I am not a professor, nor have I ever been a professor (unless you count my role as a teaching assistant at U Penn, where there was never a complaint from anyone about my work). I am not an editor. I am not a curator of a reading series or literary salon.

The article tells the story of "Emily," someone I met 13 years ago. She lived in Seattle. I lived in California. We spoke on the phone often and met in person a handful of times. I know I said all manner of inappropriate things during those conversations. I was a wreck and an asshole. But *The Outline* article goes way beyond that, claiming I held her ankles during an argument. I don't remember that — not in the way it's described. Kirkman's article is full of these kinds of vague, torqued, unverifiable accounts.

I remember arguments. I remember Emily once punching me hard in the chest. On two occasions, once while walking home from a bar in Arcata, and once while walking home from a bar in Seattle, in front of traffic and pedestrians, she put her hand down my pants and pulled my penis out. She thought it was hilarious. That relationship was mutually damaging, and I've had no contact with her since at least 2012. Nevertheless, I apologized to her for my behavior in 2014 when I was enrolled with Alcoholics Anonymous.

* * *

Throughout 2018, there were other disappointments,

betrayals, disconnections, more online mobbings, and efforts to erase my work completely. My publishers were hounded to the point where they buckled, or maybe they were happy to give in – I wouldn't know because Omnidawn Press and Wave Books refused to communicate with me – and they removed all mention of my books from their websites. In the case of Wave Books, my book was taken out of print. I voluntarily withdrew my manuscript from Wesleyan University Press after they decided to "indefinitely delay" publication of *What Follows*. The relationship was tainted, and, at that point, so was the book.

The Academy of American Poets deleted many years' worth of my work. I was featured often in their Poem-A-Day series, which transmits poems to subscribers' inboxes every morning. The poems are then archived on the website, along with a profile of the poet. All of my poems were deleted in June, 2018, along with an essay about my work by Pulitzer Prize winner Rae Armantrout and my entire profile. The director of the Academy, Jennifer Benka, claimed that the Academy was now abiding by "SaferLit" guidelines. I later found out that Benka is friends with a close friend of Kate Colby's, this friend being the founder of "SaferLit." What a coincidence.

More than a year has now passed, and I'm still the only poet The Academy has erased from its website. Benka still has not responded to any of my emails, other than to issue a form email to me and everyone who wrote to her on my behalf:

> Hi, Joseph. In response to your email regarding Poets.org, content on the website is curated by our staff in accordance with standards designed to meet the purposes and rules of the Academy of American Poets and changes are made to website content whenever deemed necessary or desirable.

I contacted several people who are chancellors of the Academy and they were clear in letting me know that they had no idea my work was going to be deleted. Supporters of the Academy might well ask: Who's next? Will Anne Sexton be deleted because she allegedly molested her daughter? What about Sherman Alexie, who was recently accused of misconduct? The list could stretch for dozens of pages.

* * *

I was hospitalized in June when I came close to making good on suicide. I had a plan and the means to execute it; I then had a panic attack and took a cab to the ER. I spent a week in a psychiatric ward, which was precisely what I needed. The staff were angelic. I was placed on medication and felt remarkably more stable after discharge.

Throughout the second half of 2018, I continued to write poetry. It was my lifeline, and I stayed in touch with close friends who'd stuck by my side. My forthcoming book, *A New Silence,* was composed during that period of time. I view it as evidence that my spirit was not extinguished. My life was not extinguished. The "cancellation" only went so far. I lost opportunities; I lost several dozen friends. I still feel like a pariah. I live in poverty. But poetry remains. Poetry was, and is, my survival skill. I wrote a poem to address all of this, "Poem Against Cancellation." I wanted to raise the vibration of the discourse, to transcend bile, and sing through the static.

Poetry is made of breath before any sound, any syllable, is uttered. The inhalation is the first word — and reclaiming my craft taught me how to breathe again. I believe it can teach others to breathe and remain open to their perceptions, too. It is a human art.

To those I've hurt, know that I'm not who I was, and that not all narratives are linear. I didn't give up on becoming a better person when it felt like my life was destroyed. I persisted on the path I've been on for a long time now. I'm a better, stronger, more compassionate person because of it all.

No human being is immutable. No one is irredeemable. To believe otherwise is to diminish our unlimited capacity for change.

AUTHOR'S POSTSCRIPT – SEPTEMBER 2020

Over the last year, in the wake of my essay appearing, I reestablished myself within a community of other people who've been publicly shamed and excommunicated from polite society, including many people who are sympathetic and opposed to cancel culture. I received several dozen messages, from both women and men, who expressed to me that they related to various aspects of my essay; and, in some ways, I helped counsel individuals who are enduring similar situations. I still receive several messages a month, at least, in response to the essay. My own healing process is helped considerably by those connections. I continue to write poetry, and I'm currently working on a full-length memoir. The mob didn't win.

How an Anonymous Accusation Derailed My Life

By Stephen Elliot

In early October 2017, following the public emergence of the allegations against Harvey Weinstein, a writer and activist living in Brooklyn named Moira Donegan created a Google Doc entitled "Shitty Media Men." She sent it to female friends working in media, and encouraged them to add to it and forward it on. The idea was to spread the word about predatory men in the business so that women would be forewarned. Anyone with access to the link could edit and add to the list. At the top of the spreadsheet were the following instructions: "Log out of gmail in order to edit anonymously, never name an accuser, never share the document with any men." In the first column was this disclaimer: "This document is only a collection of misconduct allegations and rumors. Take everything with a grain of salt." Nobody did.

The list had only been live for 12 hours when word reached Donegan that *BuzzFeed* reporters were preparing to publish a story about it. She immediately closed it down. By that time, there were already 74 entries. The *BuzzFeed* article ran the following day. Other media outlets soon followed up on the story and, shortly thereafter, the list was weaponized by right-wing blogger and conspiracy theorist Mike Cernovich. My entry reads: "Rape accusations, sexual harassment, coercion, unsolicited invitations to his apartment, a dude who snuck into Binders???"

I was shocked to find myself accused of rape. I don't like intercourse, I don't like penetrating people with objects, and I don't like receiving oral sex. My entire sexuality is wrapped up in BDSM. Cross-dressing, bondage, masochism. I'm always the bottom. I've been in long romantic relationships with women without ever seeing them naked. Almost every time I've had intercourse during the past 10 years, it has been in the context of dominance/submission, often without my consent, and usually while I'm tied up or in a straitjacket and hood. I've never had sex with anyone who works in media.

I am not seeking to come out about my sexuality as a means of creating a diversion, as Kevin Spacey appeared to do when he was accused of sexual misconduct. I've always been open about my sexuality, and I have even written entire books on the topic. I've never raped anybody. I would even go one step further: There is no one in the world who believes that I raped them. Whoever added me to Donegan's list, it was not someone with whom I've had sex.

Even though I was living in Los Angeles at the time, I found out that I was on the list immediately. It didn't take much effort to find a copy; although the list was closed, it had been downloaded and was circulating freely on Reddit and WordPress. It was mentioned in an opening monologue by Samantha Bee, it was the basis of an episode of *The Good Fight* on CBS, and stories were being published about it in *The New Yorker*, *Slate* and *The New York Times*. Even so, most people didn't bother to look at the list itself, and so didn't know who was actually named on it. At the same time, many people did.

A few months after the list became public, an editor friend called me. *The New Yorker* had fired Ryan Lizza, who had been named, so the list was in the news again and my friend had looked it up. Then my sister, who works in the medical industry in Chicago, contacted me. Her friend had brought it up casually at dinner and I had to tell my sister that I hadn't raped anyone. "I believe you," she said.

Graywolf Press published a collection of my essays in November 2017. The pre-publication reviews had been positive, but the book was greeted with silence. It's impossible to know how many publications would have covered the book had my name not been on that list. At least a few cancelled their planned coverage. The *Paris Review* decided not to run an interview they had already completed with me for their web site. I was disinvited from several events, including a panel at the Los Angeles Festival of Books. Someone even called a bookstore in New York where I was scheduled to do a reading and urged them to cancel their event.

Similar lists were started in the advertising industry, fashion world, Canadian literature, and, of course, academia. Every time a new list appeared, there was a new round of stories mentioning the original list. This month, almost a year later, the Shitty Media Men List is mentioned in dozens of articles written about Leslie Moonves as he leaves CBS under a cloud of accusations.

I wondered if it would be possible for me to work with someone who didn't know about the rape accusation. In Hollywood, the answer seemed to be yes. People there were only vaguely aware of the list and very few of them had seen it. Nevertheless, if I sold a pilot I'd written, or enjoyed any other kind of success, the company involved would almost certainly be made aware of the allegations quickly. If somebody was prepared to make the effort to call a bookstore to try to prevent me from reading to 25 people in Brooklyn, what chance did I have of flying under the radar after a post in *Deadline*?

Then my television agent stopped returning my calls. Was this just business as usual, or had she found out about the list? I didn't know. If she did know about the list, she certainly wouldn't be sending me to any meetings. Hollywood doesn't care if you're innocent or guilty; they just don't want to be anywhere near that kind of controversy. Friends who knew I had been named stopped inviting me out. I started to get depressed, because I was walking around with this awful secret. I'd look someone in the eye and I wouldn't know what they knew about me. I couldn't talk about what was happening without revealing that I had been accused of rape. For several months I didn't leave the house. I started taking drugs again, and tried to stop thinking about it as my savings dwindled. It seemed like an impossible riddle.

Being accused of sexual misconduct is extremely alienating. #MeToo was an expression of solidarity, but there is no solidarity for the accused. We don't talk to one another. We assume that if someone *else* has been accused, there must be a good reason. We're afraid of guilt by association. We don't want to be noticed so we lower our voices. Most of us stop posting on social media and stick to ever-dwindling circles of friends.

Someone I know tweeted that it was ironic that supposedly liberal guys keep saying they believe women, but they don't believe the women who accused them. I've wondered about the meaning of "believe women." I had assumed it was intended to encourage people to take accusations seriously. Certainly, sexual assault is enormously under-reported. But an anonymous accusation is problematic. What does "believe women" mean when it isn't even clear that an anonymous accuser is a woman? Anyone — male or female — with access to the list could have added my name while it was online.

* * *

Three or four months after the list was published, I wrote the first draft of this essay. I was trying to get sober and I was going to meetings. I wanted to build bridges and make amends, and I wanted to find a way to create space for my accuser to come forward. But I didn't want to pretend to believe that I was guilty of something if I didn't actually believe it. Fake apologies don't help anything: A fake apology is like sewing up a wound with garbage. Some of the apologies issued since the #MeToo movement began had been unconvincing. They read like statements made by a person trying to keep his job and salvage his reputation with an act of forced contrition. This has only made matters worse and further divided people.

In the first version of this essay, I tried to examine any possibly problematic erotic or romantic entanglements. I contacted ex-girlfriends, people I'd kissed, and people who had rejected me. I wrote about hanging out in the park with a volunteer from the web site I founded, *The Rumpus*, and laying my head in her lap. I wrote about a woman who thought I had cancelled an article about her book because she had rejected me (actually, it had been cancelled for violating rules about friends writing positive reviews of one another's work). But, in the end, I realized that it's simply impossible to respond to an anonymous accusation. You find yourself confessing to every sin you've ever committed, real or imagined. Meanwhile, your accuser doesn't even have a name.

The truth is, all of us have wronged someone at some point. At least I knew the rape accusation was false. But, about the other charges, I wasn't sure. My entry mentioned that I was "a dude who snuck into Binders." It turns out "Binders Full of Women" was a Facebook group for female and gender non-conforming writers. I'd never heard of it, and I still don't know who added me. My list entry also specified "unsolicited invitations to his apartment." Of course I had invited people to my apartment. And of course those invitations had been unsolicited: An invitation is, after all, an unsolicited offer. But they weren't my employees. I haven't employed many people in my lifetime. Nevertheless, maybe someone had felt that I had power over them and had exerted inappropriate pressure to get them to accept such an invitation. But who? And when? And under what circumstances? I had no idea. There's a conversation to be had about appropriate behavior, and I would always prefer to make amends. But I don't think it's a good reason to accuse someone of misconduct on an anonymous list.

When the Shitty Media Men List was first released, nobody knew who had created it. Then, in the early months of 2018, it was announced Katie Roiphe was writing an article about the list for *Harpers*, and speculation was rife that she would name its creator. And so Moira Donegan outed herself to beat Roiphe to the punch. "The value of the spreadsheet," she wrote, "was that it had no enforcement mechanisms: Without legal authority or professional power, it offered an impartial, rather than adversarial, tool to those who used it. It was intended specifically not to inflict consequences, not to be a weapon."

A number of commentators have pointed out that most of the men named on the list have not faced any consequences. Christina Cauterici, writing for *Slate*, drew her readers' attention to "the absence of definitive evidence that any wholly innocent men have as of yet been tarred or feathered." But Moira's statement is disingenuous, and Cauterici's article was intellectually dishonest. Just because you don't know of any consequences, that doesn't mean there haven't been any.

Of course, the list was a weapon. It was a way of saying: Do not associate with and do not hire these men. Freelancers named on the list could not have the benefit of a workplace investigation that might clear their name – they would just stop getting work. Their book sales would sink. They wouldn't be able to teach classes, and they would stop receiving offers for speaking engagements. They'd lose relationships and opportunities, and they'd have painful conversations with their families during which they'd have to tell their siblings, "I didn't rape anyone."

Someone told me I shouldn't deny the accusations. They asked if I wanted to be on the wrong side of the issue. Someone else asked me if I believed in the #MeToo movement enough to take a bullet. Over the course of this year, I've come to believe that if a movement embraces anonymous lists and a presumption of guilt, it is already poisoned and not worth supporting. I support reporting harassment and abuse in pursuit of safer workplace environments, and I believe we should be supportive of those with the courage to come forward. But I don't have common cause with people who believe innocent-until-proven-guilty is just a legal concept.

* * *

The original version of this essay was significantly more conciliatory. *New York* magazine agreed to run it. It would have been the perfect venue, since it was there that Moira Donegan's essay justifying her creation of the list had appeared in January. I worked with the editor for a few weeks, and then, just as I believed it was about to be published, they informed me that it wouldn't run after all. It was then accepted by two senior editors at the *Guardian*, but the essay was spiked again, apparently after other editors revolted. I've never had an essay accepted somewhere and then rejected. Now it's happened twice.

Through the editor at *New York*, I tried to contact Moira Donegan. I sent her a note asking if we could speak, at a place of her convenience, alone or in the presence of witnesses, either on or off the record — however she preferred. I wanted to ask her how I came to be on her list. Were there in fact two accusations that she had combined into "rape accusations"? Did she touch my entry as an editor, or even as a writer? Was she the one who highlighted my entry in red, one of 16 entries identified in this way to indicate supposed multiple accusations of rape or violent sexual assault? I did not receive a reply.

At which point, I decided not to publish the essay after all. I decided that I wouldn't be able to handle the blowback. As I struggled with depression, I was seriously contemplating suicide (every first-hand account I've read of public shaming — and I've read more than my share — includes thoughts of suicide). Maybe, I thought, I could find work in a writer's room for a television show and that would make things okay. But the chances that I could keep my inclusion on the list and the accusation of rape secret were, I decided, remote.

It wasn't until almost a year after the list became public that I realized I wasn't depressed anymore. I also realized that writing for television was not my life's goal. I packed my things and moved to a cheaper city where I could work in a less public discipline. I would pursue writing for its own sake, just as I had before I started publishing books.

When Donegan acknowledged creating the list, she wrote that she knew it was unreliable but that it was meant to protect women. She tweeted (or retweeted) the claim that many of the men on the list were being found guilty. She acknowledged that the document was indeed vulnerable to false accusations and sympathized with "the desire to be careful, even as all available information suggests that false allegations are rare." (U.S. numbers suggest that at least 5% of rape allegations are false or baseless, a higher rate than other major crimes, such as murder).

Of course, in some sense, Donegan didn't have to worry, because no one is truly innocent. Even if you're not guilty of the particular crime of which you stand accused, you're likely to be guilty of *something*. It's a Kafkaesque scenario. The accused can either refuse to engage, or try to maintain their specific innocence from a position of more general guilt. Either way, the trial is over before any defense can arrive.

AUTHOR'S POSTSCRIPT – SEPTEMBER 2020

Two weeks after publishing my essay in *Quillette*, I filed a defamation lawsuit against Moira Donegan. The case is still ongoing.

Policing the Creative Imagination
By Craig DeLancey

At a time when activist displeasure can sweep through social media and destabilize reputations and nascent careers overnight, publishers are taking unprecedented steps in an effort to mitigate the risks. Among these is the use of sensitivity readers – individuals tasked with reading a work of fiction prior to publication in an effort to determine whether or not offense is likely to be caused by an author's portrayal of characters from demographics considered marginalised or historically oppressed. Many readers, I suspect, will have become aware of this emerging trend following a series of nasty controversies in the world of Young Adult publishing.

In 2017, a fantasy novel by Kiera Drake entitled *The Continent* was attacked for its allegedly racist portrayal of Native Americans. The novel was hastily rewritten following guidance from sensitivity readers. In January of this year, Amelie Zhao's debut novel *Blood Heir*, set in a fantastical version of medieval Russia, was denounced online because its portrayal of chattel slavery was deemed insufficiently sensitive to America's own racist history. In response, Zhao thanked her persecutors profusely (a dismayingly common response) and explained that she would be withdrawing her novel from publication indefinitely. Like Drake, Zhao "sought feedback from scholars and sensitivity readers," made changes, and a new publication date for her novel has just been announced. Weeks after Zhao withdrew her book, *A Place for Wolves*, written by sensitivity reader Kosoko Jackson, was also withdrawn by its author following criticisms of his portrayal of an Albanian Muslim villain. It did not go unnoticed that Jackson had participated in the attacks on Zhao. "The schadenfreude," one Twitter user observed, "is delicious."

If the use of sensitivity readers is intended to prevent ignominious crises like these, it is almost certainly a futile exercise — many of those vandalizing Goodreads pages with vitriolic reviews make no secret of the fact that they have not read the book in question and do not intend to do so. Furthermore, a stamp of approval from two Muslim sensitivity readers was not enough to spare Laura Moriarty's *American Heart* accusations of bigotry. Nevertheless, publishers are increasingly relying on sensitivity readers, if only as an insurance policy. There are not, as far as I can tell, any qualifications required to become a sensitivity reader, other than membership in the relevant demographic. I asked a number of authors how they or their editors had selected such readers, and the answer invariably turned out to be that they searched for a representative of the group in question who hopefully had some additional interest in writing or reading.

This reveals a distressingly reductive essentialism – it suggests that African Americans, gays, women, transgender people, and so on possess some vaguely conceived but determinative essence which enables them to speak for their group, and to evaluate a text in its name. The logic of this essentialism, however, is at odds with the very idea of sensitivity readers, since it leads to a situation in which no one may write about anyone's experiences but their own. Nine months before his debut novel fell afoul of his own exacting sectarian standards, Kosoko Jackson issued this intemperate public announcement on Twitter:

> Stories about the civil-rights movement should be written by black people. Stories of suffrage should be written by women. Ergo, stories about boys during horrific and life changing times, like the AIDS EPIDEMIC, should be written by gay men. Why is this so hard to get?
>
> I'm tired of women profiting off of gay male stories. I'm tired of women profiting off of gay pain. I'm fucking sick of it.
>
> No, we (gay men) don't own gay stories. But some things are off limits. I don't understand why this is so god damn hard or fucking complex. There are millions of ideas. Leave us our pain and identities and don't fucking profit from them. Respect us enough to do that.

Jackson's reasoning may be valid, but it is not sound: If human experiences are socially constructed by membership in an identity group, and each group is opaque to anyone outside the group, then any attempt to write about people outside of one's group is certain to end in failure, and perhaps even ethical violation. As the novelist Lionel Shriver and others have pointed out, this doctrine convicts writers of the sin of empathy and throttles creativity and imagination. If an author wants to avoid trouble, they would do well to restrict the characters they create to people of their own sex, sexual orientation, religion, and ethnic group.

Theoretically, the sensitivity reader offers a way out of this collision between the demands of identity politics and the demands of creative writing. Supporters of the use of sensitivity readers tend to marshal three additional claims in defense of the practice: (1) The use of sensitivity readers is not censorship; (2) it is always voluntary and does not affect publishing decisions; and, most importantly, (3) it is merely a form of fact checking. The first of these claims is a red herring and the remaining two are false.

While it is true that employing a sensitivity reader does not amount to censorship in the strictest sense, this claim is also irrelevant. Writers understand that they are individuals entering into a contractual arrangement with a private business, and that publishers are not censoring when they make editorial decisions prior to publication. Nevertheless, writers are now routinely required to clear an extra hurdle if they wish to see their books in print, and doing so can directly impact their aesthetic choices, even though a sensitivity reader is unlikely to be a professional writer. Serious authors spend decades honing their craft, and can spend years on a book. They will be understandably nervous about an amateur evaluating their work with a red pen and recommending political changes that flatten nuance and character complexity, and have nothing to do with creative intention or coherence. For the same reason, screenwriters typically loathe "notes" from executives who are not writers.

Are sensitivity readings always voluntary? We do not have reliable information about how often, and under what circumstances, sensitivity readers are employed. In some cases, they are hired by writers who want to vet their book (or who want to be able to *say* they vetted their book) before self-publishing or submitting the manuscript to an agent or editor. Some of the authors I spoke to employ a sensitivity reader on their own initiative, believing that it might help them escape accusations of insensitivity. Some editors, and perhaps some agents, recommend using a sensitivity reader, especially in Young Adult, middle-grade, and genre fiction. If an editor makes such a request, agreement is voluntary only in the narrow sense that a person is not forced to obey their office boss because they have the freedom to quit. In such a situation, most writers feel compelled to follow the advice of an editor lest their publication deal disappear. For the same reason, writers will understand that they are expected to follow at least some of the advice offered by the sensitivity reader, whatever its merits.

But sometimes the use of sensitivity readers is explicitly mandatory. One writer I interviewed (who asked not to be identified) currently has a manuscript in the hands of a sensitivity reader tasked with checking that a secondary character – a heroic Native American scientist – has been portrayed in a sufficiently sympathetic light. The contract the author signed with the publisher stipulated that both publication and payment would be contingent upon approval by a sensitivity reader. In the event of a mob denunciation, the publisher explained, they could at least counter that the book had been vetted by a Native American. The reader has apparently been slow, which has delayed publication for months. The novel's author, meanwhile, is established, widely respected, and the recipient of multiple prestigious awards. If a sensitivity reading can be imposed on this writer, it can be imposed on anyone.

Should we care if the use of sensitivity readers becomes widespread and mandatory? Some art forms are, after all, created by committee – writing for television, for instance, is almost always a group effort. But the novel is a form better suited to the expression of a single creator's unique vision. Sensitivity readers are an affront to that autonomy. The novelist who understands that the representation of diverse characters could sabotage a book deal might reconsider whether it is worth writing about such people at all. The very existence of sensitivity readers may lead them to shy away from writing such characters, since so many in the industry believe they can't do it. If sensitivity readers become a publishing institution, they will only incentivize more cautious, conservative, and ideologically homogenous books, as authors seek to avoid controversy, costs, and loss of control that will arise from more daring and morally ambivalent fiction.

But it is the claim that sensitivity readers are merely fact checkers that is most troubling. Defenders of sensitivity readers often claim that hiring someone to evaluate the permissibility of a novel's character is analogous to hiring a scientist to check scientific claims or a historian to check historical events. But this is simply a category error, which disappears the vital distinction between fact and value – *what is* and *what ought to be.* There is a fundamental difference between telling an author that Miami is not the capital of Florida, and opining that the portrayal of this or that character is morally objectionable.

Presumably, sensitivity readers also perform some basic fact checks. But the goal of warding off moral offense requires ethical evaluation. Consider the following hypothetical: An author who is neither

African American nor female writes a novel in which an African American woman expressed regret for her multiple abortions. The sensitivity reader may be offended by abortion, and so will be sanguine about this narrative. Alternatively, the sensitivity reader may be offended by attempts to make abortion illegal, and so take great exception to this portrait of remorse. Is the book portraying women as flippant in their reproductive choices, or is it intended as a comment on African American attitudes to abortion and parenthood? Or is it neither? In any such case, the sensitivity reader will be invited to judge a complicated ethical issue in a work of fiction, and to render a judgment through a crude lens of bias detection.

Defenders of sensitivity readers may object that professionalism can prevent readers from projecting their own ethical values onto someone else's work, beyond specific matters relating to the representation of a particular group. As the hypothetical above is meant to illustrate, it is very difficult to draw such a clear line. But, even if it were theoretically possible to do so, sensitivity readers need have no training, so one cannot expect them to have well-defined professional standards. It is therefore hard to judge whether or not a sensitivity reader has performed their job competently. A copy editor may be evaluated by the number of typos that creep into a book. A fact checker may be evaluated by a subsequent verification of a novel's historical facts and claims. By what measure or standard are we to assess the work of the sensitivity reader if we cannot agree about challenging questions of ethics? Is a single objection by an aggrieved party disqualifying? Ten objections? Twenty?

There is a backhanded compliment lurking within these struggles for control over literature. People from diverse ideological perspectives appear to share the belief that fiction is important. But this belief has helped create a contradiction. The sensitivity reader is expected to evaluate norms that are often highly contentious – questions about the conflicting duties of the individual and society, about how different groups should live together, and about how individuals and groups should understand their own identities and histories. Questions like these have vexed us for centuries. For this reason, they are precisely the questions we expect literature to explore. Indeed, it is because literature explores these questions that it is so important. And literature cannot perform this vital task if it is first filtered through sensitivity readers who we believe already have all the answers – not because of what they know, but because of who they happen to be.

AUTHOR'S POSTSCRIPT – SEPTEMBER 2020
All indications are that sensitivity reads are becoming ever more embedded in the publishing process. Perhaps the most striking development to occur after this

article appeared in *Quillette* has been the call to extend sensitivity reads to journalism. The NewsGuild of New York, the union for *New York Times* employees, demanded on July 31 that sensitivity reads be added to the publishing process at the newspaper, and that the sensitivity readers be compensated for this role. Thus, not just fiction, but also reporting will be required to pass through a filter that screens for ideologically appropriate content and tone. The NewsGuild did not specify who could serve as a sensitivity reader, but it is safe to assume that the ideologically relevant minorities are expected to fill the role. This is the creeping institutionalization of the belief that "identities" are impenetrable essences, and each of us can speak for our identity but are incapable of understanding any other identity.

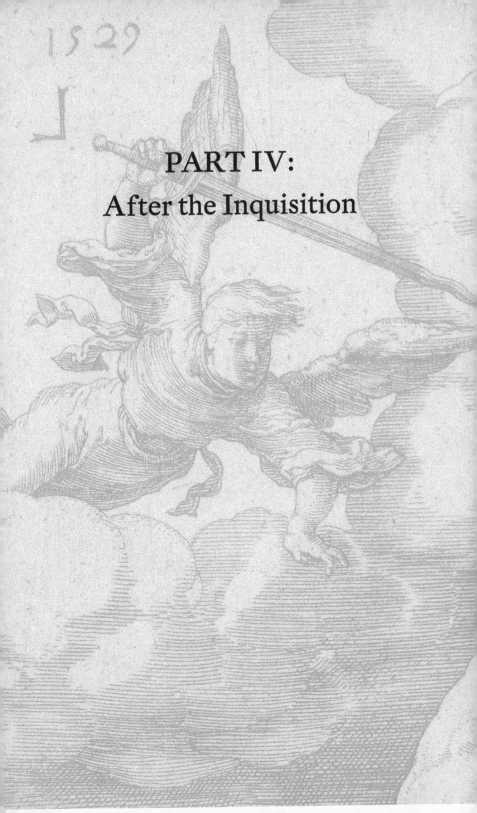

PART IV:
After the Inquisition

Sad Radicals
By Conor Barnes

When I became an anarchist, I was 18, depressed, anxious, and ready to save the world. I moved in with other anarchists and worked at a vegetarian co-op café. I protested against student tuition, prison privatization, and pipeline extensions. I had lawyer's numbers sharpied on my ankle and I assisted friends who were pepper-sprayed at demos. I tabled zines, lived with my "chosen family," and performed slam poems about the end of the world. While my radical community was deconstructing gender, monogamy, and mental health, we lived and breathed concepts and tools like call-outs, intersectionality, cultural appropriation, trigger warnings, safe spaces, privilege theory, and rape culture.

What is a radical community? For the purposes of this article, I will define it as a community that shares both an ideology of complete dissatisfaction with existing society due to its oppressive nature and a desire to radically alter or destroy that society because it cannot be redeemed by its own means. I eventually fell out with my own radical community. The ideology and the people within it had left me a burned and disillusioned wreck. As I deprogrammed, I watched a diluted version of my radical ideology explode out of academia and become fashionable: I watched the Left become woke.

Commentators have skewered social justice activists on the toxicity of the woke mindset. This is something that many radicals across North America are aware of and are trying to understand. Nicholas Montgomery and Carla Bergman's *Joyful Militancy*, published in 2017, is the most thorough look at radical toxicity from a radical perspective. Full disclosure: I very briefly met Montgomery years ago. My anarchist clique did not like his anarchist clique. As was noted in 2015, "there is a mild totalitarian undercurrent not just in call-out culture but also in how progressive communities police and define the bounds of who's in and who's out."

Montgomery and Bergman see radical toxicity as an exogenous issue. They do not wonder whether radicalism itself could be malignant. As a result, their proposed solutions are limp and abstract, like "increasing sensitivity and inhabiting situations more fully." Perhaps this is because the solutions all exist beyond the boundaries of radical thought. As Jonathan Haidt has pointed out, "morality binds and blinds."

Unfortunately, toxicity in radical communities is not a bug. It is a feature. The ideology and norms of radicalism have evolved to produce toxic, paranoid, depressed subjects. What follows is a picture of what happens in communities that are passionately, sincerely, radically woke, as seen from the perspective of an apostate.

Faith

Commentators have accurately noted how social justice seems to take the form of a religion. This captures the meaning and fulfilment I found in protests and occupations. It also captures how, outside of these harrowing festivals, everyday life in radical communities is mundane but pious. As a radical activist, much of my time was devoted to proselytizing. Non-anarchists were like pagans to be converted through zines and wheatpasted posters rather than by Bible and baptism. When non-radicals listened to my assertions that Nazis deserved death, that all life had devolved into spectacle, and that monogamy was a capitalist social construct, they were probably bewildered instead of enticed.

Instead of developing a relationship to God and a recognition of one's own imperfection, we wanted our non-anarchist families and friends to develop their "analysis" and recognize their complicity in the evil of capitalism. These non-anarchist friends grew increasingly sparse the longer I was an anarchist. They didn't see how terrible the world was, and they used problematic language that revealed hopelessly *bad politics*. Frustrated with them, I retreated further and further into the grey echo-chamber of my "chosen family."

Trent Eady says of his own radicalism in Montreal, "When I was part of groups like this, everyone was on exactly the same page about a suspiciously large range of issues." When my friends and I did have theoretical disagreements, they tended towards the purely strategic, or to philosophical minutiae. Are cops human? If we pay attention to the few white nationalists in town, will that stir them up? Is polyamory queer, or privileged?

Deep and sincere engagement with opposing points of view is out of the question. Radicalism is like a clan too suspicious of outsiders to abandon cousin marriage; and, like incestuous offspring, radicalism's intellectual offspring accumulate genetic load. Narrow theories must perform increasingly convoluted explanations of the world. For example, Montgomery and Bergman describe Michael Hardt and Antonio Negri's use of the term "Empire," in their book of the same name, as both a miasma that "*accumulates* and *spreads* sadness" and an anthropomorphized figure that "works to usher its subjects into flimsy relationships where nothing is at stake and to infuse intimacy with violence and domination."

No worldview maps reality perfectly. But when a worldview encounters discordant knowledge, it can either evolve to accommodate it, or it can treat it as a threat to the worldview's integrity. If a worldview treats *all* discordant knowledge as threat, then it is an ideology. Its adherents learn to see themselves as guardians rather than seekers of the truth. The practical consequences of such a worldview can be devastating.

Fear

When I became an anarchist, I was a depressed and anxious teenager in search of answers. Radicalism explained that these were not manageable issues with biological and lifestyle factors; they were the result of living in capitalist alienation. For, as Kelsey Cham C notes, "This whole world is based on fucking misery," and "In capitalist systems, we're not meant to feel joy." Radicalism not only finds that all oppressions intersect, but so does all suffering. The force that causes depression is the same that causes war, domestic abuse, and racism. By accepting this framework, I surrendered to an external locus of control. Personal agency in such a model is laughable. And then, when I became an even less happy and less strong person over the years as an anarchist, I had an explanation on hand.

There is an overdeveloped muscle in radicalism: the critical reflex. It is able to find oppression behind any mundanity. Where does this critical reflex come from? French philosopher Paul Ricœur famously coined the term "school of suspicion" to describe Marx, Nietzsche, and Freud's drive to uncover repressed meaning in text and society. Today's radicals have inherited this drive by way of Foucault and other

Marxo-Nietzscheans.

As radicals, we lived in what I call a *paradigm of suspicion*, one of the malignant ideas that emerge as a result of intellectual in-breeding. We inherited familial neuroses and saw insidious oppression and exploitation in all social relationships, stifling our ability to relate to others or ourselves without cynicism. Activists anxiously pore over interactions, looking for ways in which the mundane conceals domination. To see every interaction as containing hidden violence is to become a permanent victim, because if all you are is a nail, everything looks like a hammer.

The paradigm of suspicion leaves the radical exhausted and misanthropic, because any action or statement can be shown with sufficient effort to hide privilege, a microaggression, or unconscious bias. Quoted in *Joyful Militancy*, the anarchist professor Richard Day proposes "infinite responsibility": "We can never allow ourselves to think that we are 'done,' that we have identified all of the sites, structures, and processes of oppression 'out there' or 'in here,' inside our own individual and group identities." Infinite responsibility means infinite guilt, a kind of Christianity without salvation: To see power in every interaction is to see sin in every interaction. All that the activist can offer to absolve herself is Sisyphean effort until burnout. Eady's summarization is simpler: "Everything is problematic."

This effort is not only directed at the self, but

also outwards. Morality and politics are intertwined in this system, so that *good politics* become indicative of good morality. Montgomery and Bergman skewer this tendency mercilessly: "To remain pious, the priest must reveal new sins...The new Other is the not-radical-enough, the liberal, the perpetrator, the oppressor." Because one's good moral standing can never be guaranteed, the best way to maintain it is to attack the moral standing of others. As Montgomery and Bergman point out, this is also a thrilling and actionable alternative to the discouragement that haunts radicals after each loss in conflict with capitalism and the state. This is how cliques and status games emerge in communities that purport to be opposed to all hierarchy, turning people into what Freddie DeBoer once dubbed "offense archaeologists."

Bland friendships and events are the result. Conversations are awkward and tense, as radicals contort to avoid the risk of hurting each other. As an anarchist, I did not engage with individuals as individuals, but as porcelain, always thinking first and foremost of the group identities we inhabited.

Escape from the paradigm of suspicion is hindered by kafkatrapping: the idea that opposition to the radical viewpoint proves the radical viewpoint. Minorities who question it have internalized their oppression, and privileged individuals who question it prove their guilt. The only thing radicals are not suspicious of is the need for relentless suspicion. As Haidt and Greg Lukianoff write of similar norms on campuses, "If someone wanted to create an environment of perpetual anger and intergroup conflict, this would be an effective way to do it."

Failure Modes

Radical communities select for particular personality types. They attract deeply compassionate people, especially young people attuned to the suffering inherent to existence. They attract hurt people, looking for an explanation for the pain they've endured. And both of these derive *meaning* for that suffering by attributing it to the force that they now dedicate themselves to opposing. They are no longer purely a victim, but an underdog.

However, radical communities also attract people looking for an excuse to be violent illegalists. And the surplus of vulnerable and compassionate people attracts sadists and abusers ready to exploit them. The only gatekeeping that goes on in radical communities is that of language and passion – if you can rail against capitalism in woke language, you're in.

Every group of people has some mixture of stable, vulnerable, and predatory individuals. That radicals have a poor mix does not doom them. However, radicals also dismiss longstanding norms that would protect them, in favor of experimental norms. They are built with the best intentions and are aimed at solving real problems. But intentions do not matter if one does not consider incentives and human nature.

Abusers thrive in radical communities because radical norms are fragile and exploitable. A culture of freewheeling drug and alcohol use creates situations predators are waiting to exploit. A cultural fetishization of violence provides cover for violent and unstable people. The practice of public "call-outs" is used for power-plays far more often than for constructive feedback. Radicals value responding to claims of harm with compassion and belief. But abusers exploit this the way children exploit parents and teachers — crybullying becomes a way of punishing opponents or prey. While norms such as "believe claimed victims" are important in families and close friendships where trust and accountability are real, they become weapons in amorphous communities.

One particular practice illustrates this well. The *accountability process* is a subcultural institution whereby survivors can make demands of perpetrators, and the community must hold them accountable. Radicals are hesitant to report abusers and rapists to the police, for fear of subjecting comrades to the prison system. But turning victims into judge and jury and shared friends into executioners is a recipe for injustice that satisfies no one. And in light of the instant truth-value given to claims of abuse, accountability processes are an oddly perfect weapon for actual abusers. As one writer for the zine the *Broken Teapot* says: "The past few years I have watched with horror as the language of accountability became an easy front for a new generation of emotional manipulators. It's been used to perfect a new kind of predatory maverick — the one schooled in the language of sensitivity — using the illusion of accountability as community currency."

Entanglement with such an individual is what finally broke me from my own dogmatism. Having somebody yell at me that if I didn't admit to being a white supremacist her friends might beat me up and that I should pay her for her emotional labor, was too much for my ideology to spin. The internal crisis it induced led to gradual disillusion. In the end, however, this was the greatest gift I could ask for.

Flight

What is the alternative to radicalism, for the disillusioned radical? She could abandon the project and commit talent and energy elsewhere. Flee the cult. As Michael Huemer says, "fighting for a cause has significant costs. Typically, one expends a great deal of time and energy, while simultaneously imposing costs on others, particularly those who oppose one's own political position...In many cases, the effort is expended in bringing about a policy that turns out to be harmful or unjust. It would be better to spend one's time and energy on aims that one knows to be good." Slow, patient steps are a more reliable road to a better world than dramatic gestures that backfire as often as not. Conversation is less romantic than confrontation, small business ownership than Steal Something From Work Day, soup kitchens than vandalism. If an individual wants to end suffering, she should think hard about why she's joined communities that glamorize violence, vengeance, and anti-intellectualism. Having left that scene, I am amazed at how much effort we put into making the world a more painful and difficult place than it is, in service of a post-revolutionary utopia.

Radicals should take stock of the progress liberal democracies have made. As Steven Pinker points out in *The Better Angels of Our Nature*, nobody in the west has an argument for wife-beating or denying women the vote anymore. Infant mortality rates have cratered, and extreme-poverty rates are falling precipitously. With trends like these and more, liberal capitalism appears less like the arch-nemesis of humanity, and more like a miracle machine. It could even be improved by the compassion and devotion of former radicals. It is worth noting that this progress does not mean that exploitation and oppression have been solved; but it does mean that our current society is the only one to have made significant inroads against them.

Most of all, radicals should learn to abandon false truths. The only way to escape dogmatism is to resist the calcification and sanctification of values, and to learn from the wisdom of different perspectives. As Haidt argues, there are grains of truth in opposing political positions. Radicals do themselves a disservice by seeing the world outside the radical monoculture as tainted with reaction and evil. There is a rich diversity of thought awaiting them if they would only open their minds to it. One of the achievements of liberalism has been a norm of free speech wherein individuals can both share and consume that spectrum of thought. Every new and challenging school of thought I discovered after anarchism rocked my worldview, as somebody who formerly thought that wisdom could only be found through "the struggle" or in esoteric French theory. Even if opposing views are not assimilated, the ability to contend with them on the intellectual field instead of silencing them is a sign of a seeker of the truth, not a guardian.

Young adults often become radicals after they realize the immensity of the cruelty and malevolence in the world. They reject a society that tolerates such suffering. They sanctify justice as their telos. But without truth to orient justice, seekers of justice will crash and crash again into reality, and will craft increasingly nightmarish and paranoid ideological analyses, burning out activists, destroying lives through jail or abuse, and leaving the world an uglier, more painful place. To paraphrase Alice Dreger, there is no justice without wisdom, and no wisdom without surrender to uncertainty in the pursuit of truth.

AUTHOR'S POSTSCRIPT – SEPTEMBER 2020

I feel kind of like a fisherman watching the shoreline fall into the sea, inch by inch, year after year. In "Sad Radicals," I referred to deprogramming from radicalism while it became mainstream. Since then? More washes away. Every year, we become a little more woke, a little more vicious, a little less forgiving, a little less beautiful.

I like to think that I was able to illustrate what being in that mindset is like, but I don't think any of us have been quite able to pin down where the mindset comes from, or why it spreads so effectively. Does it give purpose to a generation without meaning? Is it intra-class competition among overproduced elites? Is it some byproduct of economic precarity? Or is it social media ruining our brains? Who knows. While we keep on debating where it comes from and pointing out its inconsistencies, it keeps on winning. Those of us waiting for a backlash to woke culture should probably remember Gilles Deleuze's quotation about capitalism: "No one has ever died from contradictions." And anyway, if a backlash does occur, it will probably be reactionary and much worse.

What comes next? It's simple: more of the same. I wish I could end this with a rousing call, but I've heard lots of rousing calls and much applause, and yet nobody stands up. The only call I can make is a personal one: Do not think that you have to be woke to be kind. And do not think that because you aren't woke you don't have to be kind. If we remember these things, maybe everything else in this crazy world will be less confusing.

I Was the Mob Until the Mob Came for Me

By Barrett Wilson

I drive food delivery for an online app to make rent and support myself and my young family. This is my new life. I once had a well-paid job in what might be described as the social justice industry. Then I upset the wrong person, and within a short window of time, I was considered too toxic for my employer's taste. I was publicly shamed, mobbed, and reduced to a symbol of male privilege. I was cast out of my career and my professional community. Writing anything under my own byline now would invite a renewal of this mobbing — which is why, with my editor's permission, I am writing this under a pseudonym. He knows who I am.

In my previous life, I was a self-righteous social justice crusader. I would use my mid-sized Twitter and Facebook platforms to signal my wokeness on topics such as LGBT rights, rape culture, and racial injustice. Many of the opinions I held then are still opinions that I hold today. But I now realize that my social-media hyperactivity was, in reality, doing more harm than good.

Within the world created by the various apps I used, I got plenty of shares and retweets. But this masked how ineffective I had become outside, in the real world. The only causes I was actually contributing to were the causes of mobbing and public shaming. Real change does not stem from these tactics. They only cause division, alienation, and bitterness.

How did I become that person? It happened because it was exhilarating. Every time I would call someone racist or sexist, I would get a rush. That rush would then be reaffirmed and sustained by the stars, hearts, and thumbs-up that constitute the nickels and dimes of social-media validation. The people giving me these stars, hearts, and thumbs-up were engaging in their own cynical game: A fear of being targeted by the mob induces us to signal publicly that we are part of it.

Just a few years ago, many of my friends and peers who self-identify as liberals or progressives were open fans of provocative standup comedians such as Sarah Silverman, and shows like *South Park*. Today, such material is seen as deeply "problematic," or even labeled as hate speech. I went from minding my own business when people told *risqué* jokes to practically fainting when they used the wrong pronoun or expressed a right-of-center view. I went from making fun of the guy who took edgy jokes too seriously, to becoming that guy.

When my callouts were met with approval and admiration, I was lavished with praise: "Thank you so much for speaking out!" "You're so brave!" "We need more men like you!"

Then one day, suddenly, I was accused of some of the very transgressions I'd called out in others. I was guilty, of course: There's no such thing as due process in this world. And once judgment has been rendered against you, the mob starts combing through your past, looking for similar transgressions that might have been missed at the time. I was now told that I'd been creating a toxic environment for *years* at my workplace; that I'd been making the space around me unsafe through microaggressions and macroaggressions alike.

Social justice is a surveillance culture, a snitch culture. The constant vigilance on the part of my colleagues and friends did me in. That's why I'm delivering sushi and pizza. Not that I'm complaining. It's honest work, and it's led me to rediscover how to interact with people in the real world. I am a kinder and more respectful person now that I'm not regularly on social media attacking people for not being "kind" and "respectful."

I mobbed and shamed people for incidents that became front-page news. But when they were vindicated or exonerated by some real-world investigation, it was treated as a footnote by my online community. If someone survives a social justice callout, it simply means that the mob has moved on to someone new. No one ever apologizes for a false accusation, and everyone has a selective memory regarding what they've done.

Upon reading Jon Ronson's 2015 book, *So You've Been Publicly Shamed*, I recently went back into my Twitter archives to study my own behavior. I was shocked to discover that I had actually participated quite enthusiastically in the public shaming of Justine Sacco, whose 2013 saga following a bad AIDS joke on Twitter forms one of Ronson's central case studies.

My memory had told me different. In my mind, I didn't really participate. It was *others* who took things too far. In reality, the evidence showed that I was among the most vicious of Sacco's mobbers. Ronson describes a central problem with Twitter shaming: There is a "disconnect between the severity of the crime and the gleeful savagery of the punishment." For years, I was blind to my own gleeful savagery.

I recently had a dream that played out in the cartoon universe of my food-delivery app, the dashboard software that guides my daily work life. The dream turned my workaday drive into a third-person video game, with my cartoon car standing in for me as protagonist. At some point, I started missing some of the streets, and the little line that marks my trail with blue pixels indicated where I'd gone off-road. My path got erratic, and the dream became other-worldly, as dreams eventually do. I drove over cartoon sidewalks, through cartoon buildings and cartoon parks.

It's a two-dimensional world in the app, so everything was flat. Through the unique logic of dreams, I survived all of this, all the while picking up and dropping off deliveries and making money. In my dream, I was making progress.

As my REM cycle intensified, my dream concluded. I was jolted from my two-dimensional app world and thrust back into the reality of the living world — where I could understand the suffering, carnage and death I would have caused by my in-app actions. There were bodies strewn along the streets, screaming bystanders, destroyed lives, chaos. My car, by contrast, was indestructible while I was living in the app.

The social justice vigilantism I was living on Twitter and Facebook was like the app in my dream. Aggressive online virtue signaling is a fundamentally two-dimensional act. It has no human depth. It's only when we snap out of it, see the world as it really is, and people as they really are, that we appreciate the destruction and human suffering we caused when we were trapped inside.

The Mission of *Quillette*
By Claire Lehmann

You probably have felt afraid to speak your mind freely at some point. Whether in a university class, a meeting at work, or among friends online, it's likely that
you have remained silent when you have had ideas or
opinions that haven't conformed to received wisdom.
This is not an unusual or maladaptive response. In
fact, knowing when to stay quiet and knowing how to
avoid conflict is a necessary and important part of being an adult. Most arguments are pointless, and there
is no reason to get into fights with people whom we
otherwise want to cooperate with and build mutually
beneficial relationships.

Nevertheless, as this collection of essays shows,
ideological self-policing today goes beyond social
pressure to be polite and avoid conflict. The current
cultural climate is draining creative people of their
courage to experiment, while arming the small-mind-
ed with a license to bully.

Since November 2015, essays written and published by *Quillette* have nucleated around the core
value that free thought must live. The idea is simple.
All one has to do is put pen to paper (or fingers to
keyboard) and construct a well-reasoned argument,

with consideration given to available evidence, and share it with others as widely as possible – and the intellectual legacy that was handed down to us by our forebears will be preserved and shepherded into the future for our descendants. *Quillette* is an old French word for a wicker tree off-cutting that, when planted in the ground, grows into a willow tree. In the same way, one original idea can grow from humble beginnings into something long-lasting and majestic. A quillette represents the potential for rebirth and new life emerging from old.

The unpleasant reality that we must face today is that there is a small subset of intolerant ideologues who oppose open discourse altogether. The fact that you may not feel comfortable speaking your mind openly, and may feel afraid of serious consequences, is viewed by these people as a good thing. The position of the censors is that debate "normalizes" unsavory people and unsavory ideas. This fanatical minority is tiny in size but has successfully cowed university administrators, corporate leaders, and large swathes of thoughtful people into silence. They have even created climates of fear in institutions that were established with the explicit purpose of defending free thought.

One might reasonably ask the question: What does it matter if writers in romance literature are bullied, or lecturers in computer science are demoted and placed on probation? Doesn't this happen all the time? Aren't these slings and arrows all part of having a career? What does it really matter if a few people lose their livelihoods if we can continue to live in nations that have free markets and scientific progress?

It matters because the nice things we often take for granted, such as technological invention and beautiful art, exist in the tailwind of cultural freedom. Mavericks and eccentrics provide the friction against conformity that allows the rest of us a path to follow. If we permit our best minds to be cowed into submission by cruel enforcers operating on petty pretexts, we will all experience a less advanced, vibrant and diverse world because of it.

It also matters because justice matters, and the people who are shutting down open discourse often are sadistic bullies. We must not let them win. But while many of them actually enjoy causing others distress – a frightening realization – we must also remember that they are few in number. While the rest of us may never match their foul tactics, we do have multitudes on our side. All people – whether they are apolitical, conservative, libertarian, centrist, moderate, or progressive – can join together to oppose the cultural stifling of free thought.

To do so, you can start by speaking and writing plainly, and with raw honesty and courage. Share your inner thoughts and support those around you who speak frankly. You should write well-reasoned arguments for your positions and spread them widely.

Don't be afraid of good-faith criticism, which helps us grow. Have the confidence to know that there is nothing more penetrating than the human imagination and our capacity for reason. All great ideas that transcend the ordinary first emerge from the interior world of an individual, however unknown, underprivileged or lacking in confidence he or she may be. Never forget that one day, that individual may be you.

9 781913 606725